Capitalism Before Corporations

OXFORD LEGAL HISTORY SERIES

General Editors: Paul Brand, Joshua Getzler, Daniel Hulsebosch, and Amalia Kessler

This series presents original work in legal history from all periods. Contributions to the series analyse diverse legal traditions, including common law; *ius* commune, civilian and canon law; colonial, imperial, and international law; and customary, religious, and non-Western cultures of law. The series embraces methods ranging from doctrinal and juristic analysis through to every variety of historical, social scientific, and philosophical enquiry. A leading purpose of the series is to investigate how legal ideas and practices operated in larger historical contexts. Our authors trace changes in legal thought and practice and the interactions of law with political and constitutional institutions and wider movements in social, economic, cultural, and intellectual life.

Capitalism Before Corporations

The Morality of Business Associations and the Roots of Commercial Equity and Law

ANDREAS TELEVANTOS

OXFORD
UNIVERSITY PRESS

OXFORD
UNIVERSITY PRESS

Great Clarendon Street, Oxford, OX2 6DP,
United Kingdom

Oxford University Press is a department of the University of Oxford.
It furthers the University's objective of excellence in research, scholarship,
and education by publishing worldwide. Oxford is a registered trade mark of
Oxford University Press in the UK and in certain other countries

First Edition published in 2020

Published in the United States of America by Oxford University Press
198 Madison Avenue, New York, NY 10016, United States of America

British Library Cataloguing in Publication Data

Data available

Library of Congress Control Number: 2020940073

ISBN 978–0–19–887034–0

DOI: 10.1093/oso/9780198870340.001.0001

Acknowledgements

This monograph began as a doctoral thesis completed at the University of Cambridge, and the research was made possible by a generous scholarship and travel expenses from the F.W. Maitland Fund and its managers. I'm also thankful to the Zilkha Fund for supporting a visit to Georgetown Law Library to examine the Lord Eldon Collection.

I am also very grateful to Dr David Foster, Professor David Fox, Dr Perry Gauci, Professor Joshua Getzler, Professor David Ibbetson, Dr Lorenzo Maniscalco, Professor Charles Mitchell, Professor Richard Nolan, Professor James Oldham, Mr Jeffrey Thomson, and Dr Peter Turner for exceedingly helpful criticism and encouragement. I am especially indebted to my doctoral supervisor, Dr Neil Jones, for all his help.

I owe a further debt of gratitude to Ms Hannah Miller, the Curator of the Lord Eldon Collection, for her kindness to me during my visit to Georgetown Law Library, as well as to Mr Astron Douglas for allowing me to inspect his collection of books from Lord Eldon's own library.

Contents

List of Figures

Table of Cases

Table of Statutes

List of Abbreviations

ABLJ	American Business Law Journal
Am Econ Rev	American Economic Review
BJIBFL	Butterworths Journal of International Banking and Financial Law
CLJ	Cambridge Law Journal
Colum L Rev	Columbia Law Review
Harv L Rev	Harvard Law Review
J Brit Stud	Journal of British Studies
J Corp L	Journal of Corporation Law
J L & Econ	Journal of Law and Economics
JLH	Journal of Legal History
JMCB	Journal of Money, Credit and Banking
J Pol Econ	Journal of Political Economy
L & Hist Rev	Law and History Review
LMCLQ	Lloyd's Maritime and Commercial Law Quarterly
LQR	Law Quarterly Review
LS	Legal Studies
MLR	Modern Law Review
OJLS	Oxford Journal of Legal Studies
Tex Int'l LJ	Texas International Law Journal
U Chi L Rev	University of Chicago Law Review
UCLA L Rev	UCLA Law Review
Yale LJ	Yale Law Journal

Introduction

Corporations are an integral part of modern life. We bank with corporations, we usually buy our groceries from them, and they provide us with most news and media. We take it for granted too that most large-scale business, and even much small-scale business, is carried out by corporations. When this author's undergraduates talk about wanting to become 'corporate lawyers', they mean that they want to join a law firm whose clients are all commercial corporations. Likewise, a barrister specialising in corporate law will typically advise his or her clients about how the law regulates such entities, when a corporation will be bound by employees acting fraudulently or without authority, and the duties and responsibilities of company directors to one and another and third parties. In the wake of the 2008 financial crash, stories of traders who had entered into enormous and risky deals without the authority of their corporate employers became a regular feature on the news.[1]

The role of English companies in commerce is not just an unavoidable feature of our own time, but Law and Finance scholars see it as historically significant. Such scholars argue that the commercial and industrial dominance of Britain in the nineteenth century, and the United States in the twentieth, can be explained in part by the willingness of the common law to allow traders to dedicate particular groups of assets to particular purposes through corporate law, securities law, and the law of trusts,[2] and to do so with greater freedom from state and judicial intervention than is possible in countries with civilian legal systems. In particular, some scholars have treated the law of trusts as allowing English traders a flexible way of creating large joint stock firms—that is to say businesses which raised capital by issuing shares and bonds.[3] As the economic historian Martin Daunton puts it:

[1] See for instance Fiona Walsh and David Gow, 'Société Générale Uncovers £3.7bn Fraud by Rogue Trader' *The Guardian* (January 2008) <https://www.theguardian.com/business/2008/jan/24/creditcrunch.banking> accessed 18 March 2020; David Teather, 'FSA Bans Morgan Stanley's Oiled Trader' *The Guardian* (20 May 2009) <https://www.theguardian.com/business/2009/may/20/fsa-ban-morgan-stanley-oiled-trader> accessed 18 March 2020.

[2] Rafael La Porta and others, 'Law and Finance' (1998) 106 J Pol Econ 1113 (creditor protection and size of debt and equity markets); Ross Levine, 'The Legal Environment, Banks, and Long-Run Economic Grow' (1998) 30 JMCB 596 (creditor protection and banking development); Guangdong Xu, *Does Law Matter for Economic Growth* (Intersentia 2014) (property law, securities law, corporate law). For an overview see Ron Harris, 'The Encounters of Economic and Legal History' (2003) 21 Law & Hist Rev 297; and William Cornish and others, *Law and Society 1750–1950* (Hart 2019) ch 3.

[3] Martin Daunton, *Progress and Poverty: An Economic and Social History of Britain 1700–1850* (OUP 1995) 238–40, 243–46, 486–88; John Morley, 'The Common Law Corporation: The Power of the Trust in Anglo-American Business History' (2016) 116 Colum L Rev 2145.

Capitalism Before Corporations. Andreas Televantos, Oxford University Press (2020). © Andreas Televantos.
DOI: 10.1093/oso/9780198870340.003.0001.

> The development of the law of trusts by the Court of Chancery meant that there were no serious legal institutional constraints upon investment, and the English legal system was arguably more flexible and responsive than in other European countries.[4]

Merchants in common law countries thus had a competitive advantage because they were governed by a legal system which was more sympathetic to their needs.[5] This belief that a legal system which recognises trusts is more commercially efficient has prompted many civilian jurisdictions to adopt them.[6]

This narrative still holds considerable sway in Law and Finance circles, but is problematic—empirical evidence can only point to the fact of England's early economic growth and the idiosyncratic features of its law. It cannot show the former was the product of the latter, especially whilst claiming also that the law was generated by forms of business practice and the interests of powerful groups, or that law and the economy had a reciprocal or dialectical relationship.[7] Further, the popularity of arbitration to avoid litigation;[8] compromises with creditors to involve formal bankruptcy procedures;[9] and popular local Courts of Record for resolving small debt claims (typically) without reference to established rules of law and equity,[10] point away from a legal system commercial parties found sympathetic to their needs.[11]

The narrative is also difficult from a legal historical perspective. After all, much of the modernisation of production in leading sectors had already happened by the middle of the nineteenth century when the first statutes allowing general incorporation[12] and limited liability were passed.[13] Even then, traders were slow to

[4] Daunton, *Progress and Poverty* (n 3) 290.

[5] Raphael La Porta and others, 'The Economic Consequences of Legal Origins' (2008) 46(2) J Economic Literature 285–332. See also Xu (n 2) 29–39.

[6] For a range of examples see Michele Graziadei, Ugo Mattei, and Lionel Smith (eds), *Commercial Trusts in European Private Law* (CUP 2009); Lionel Smith (ed), *Reimagining the Trust: Trusts in Civil Law* (CUP 2012).

[7] Cornish and others (n 2) ch 3; Paul Johnson, *Making the Market: The Victorian Origins of Corporate Capitalism* (CUP 2010) 108 (in the context of joint stock companies and corporate law); Ron Harris, 'Government and the Economy, 1688-1850' in Roderick Floud and Paul Johnson (eds), *Cambridge Economic History of Modern Britain* (CUP 2003).

[8] Patrick Polden, 'The Courts of Law' in William Cornish and others (eds), *The Oxford History of the Laws of England, Volume XI* (OUP 2010) 773–74. Arbitration clauses were common in the articles of association for large partnerships for instance, see Mark Freeman, Robin Pearson, and James Taylor, *Shareholder Democracies? Corporate Governance in Britain & Ireland before 1850* (University of Chicago Press 2012) 61–62.

[9] Julian Hoppit, *Risk and Failure in English Business 1700–1800* (CUP 1987) 29–30.

[10] WHD Winder, 'The Courts of Request' (1936) 52 LQR 369, 375, 388–91; Harry Arthurs, 'Without the Law: Courts of Local and Special Jurisdiction in Nineteenth Century England' (1984) 5 JLH 130; Michelle Slatter, 'The Norwich Court of Requests—A Tradition Continued' (1984) 5 JLH 97, 103; Polden (n 8) 851–857, 853–54.

[11] Polden (n 8) 773–74 (arbitration); Hoppit (n 9) 29–30 (bankruptcy).

[12] The Joint Stock Companies Act 1844 (7 & 8 Vict 1 c 110).

[13] Limited Liability Act 1855 (18 & 19 Vict c 133), swiftly replaced by the Joint Stock Companies Act 1856 (19 & 20 Vict c 47).

adopt the corporate form, suggesting that contemporary traders did not regard limited liability as crucial.[14] Until the mid-nineteenth century, corporate status was available only by Act of Parliament or Royal Charter, which were granted to quasi-public entities like canal companies and overseas trading companies: corporate status was generally seen as inappropriate for domestic private enterprise.[15] By contrast, from the mid-1820s non-managing partners in French firms could enjoy limited liability without grant of special privileges, but France nevertheless industrialised later.[16] Further, although it was not much enforced in the eighteenth century, the Bubble Act 1720 made it an offence for an entity to purport to act as a corporation through sale of freely transferable shares without Royal Charter or Act of Parliament.[17] There was also a general statutory prohibition on non-possessory security over personalty which would not be effective where the debtor was declared bankrupt,[18] and floating charges could only be granted by corporations expressly given that power by the state.[19] How then can English law's willingness to dedicate assets to particular purposes in any way explain England's exceptional economic success in the nineteenth century?

This book focuses on one core question. To what extent did English law facilitate trade before the advent of general incorporation and modern securities law? It concentrates on the period 1790 to 1827,[20] the period after Lord Mansfield's well-known contributions to commercial law,[21] and examines the extent to which legal institutions of that time were sympathetic to the needs of merchants and willing to accommodate their changing practices and demands within established legal doctrinal frameworks and contemporary political economic thought. It concentrates on cases of fraud and business failure, and the extent to which the English courts would shield society and third parties from the harmful effects of agreements reached by traders with one another. More technically, it deals with the organisational law of the period: the extent to which traders were able to create funds of assets for the purposes of trade and security, and to 'ringfence' those funds from their other dealings, and so to create 'workable organisational law' out of

14 Daunton, *Progress and Poverty* (n 3) 239; see also Ron Harris, 'The Private Origins of the Private Company: Britain 1862–1907' (2013) 33 OJLS 339.

15 Armand DuBois, *The English Business Company after the Bubble Act 1720–1800* (The Commonwealth Fund 1938) 12–41; Bishop Hunt, *Development of the Business Corporation in England, 1800–1867* (Harvard University Press 1936) 9–13, 22–29.

16 See Charles Freedeman, *Joint-Stock Enterprise in France, 1807–1867: From Privileged Company to Modern Corporation* (University of North Carolina Press 1979).

17 6 Geo I c 18, s 18 (1720). Repealed by 6 Geo IV c 91 (1825).

18 21 Jac c 19, s 10 (1623–24).

19 Richard Nolan, 'Property in a Fund' (2004) 120 LQR 108, 118.

20 The definition of the term 'Regency era' used in this book refers to a period in British history with distinctive culture and characteristics, but it will also be used as shorthand for the period 1790 to 1827.

21 See James Oldham, *The Mansfield Manuscripts and the Growth of English Law in the Eighteenth Century* (University of North Carolina Press 1992).

the 'basic concepts of contract, property and debt priorities'.[22] This book thereby seeks to combine the insights of the law and economics theorists Hansmann and Kraakman[23] that a key economic function of law is to split property into different pools which can be bonded to different creditors, with a close textured legal historical understanding of how lawyers and judges understood the law which played this function at a particularly crucial time in English commercial law's development.

The Regency era was such a time, for two main reasons. First, the unstable economic circumstances of the period, and the business failures this caused, brought commercial law issues into sharp focus. Enormous national debt in the 1780s skyrocketed further during the Napoleonic Wars between 1793 and 1815.[24] In response to national insolvency in 1797, the Bank of England suspended payment of bank notes to bullion, forcibly converting England into a paper economy for the first time.[25] On top of this credit crisis Napoleon's blockade of Britain created risk of famine and threatened British trade.[26] Perhaps unexpectedly, this printing of money, wartime demand, and the difficulty of obtaining imports did end up stimulating the British economy, encouraging investment in both domestic agriculture and industry, and showed Britain to the world as the first industrialised nation. However, this growth was unstable, characterised by short trade cycles with regular booms and busts, with low points in 1810–11 and 1825–26,[27] and increased rates of bankruptcy.[28] Regulating the economy in the face of such convulsions became a governmental preoccupation, and the Bubble Act was revived from dormancy in

[22] Joshua Getzler and Mike Macnair, 'The Firm as Entity before the Companies Acts' in Paul Brand, Kevin Costello, and WN Osborough (eds), *Adventures of the Law: Proceedings of the Sixteenth British Legal History Conference* (Four Courts 2005) 269.

[23] Henry Hansmann and Reinier Kraakman, 'The Essential Role of Organizational Law' (2000) 110 Yale LJ 387; Henry Hansmann, Reiner Kraakman, and Richard Squire, 'Law and the Rise of the Firm' (2006) 119 Harv L Rev 1333.

[24] The national debt was worth more than twice the national income, see Patrick O'Brien, 'The Political Economy of British Taxation, 1660–1815' (1988) 41 Economic History Rev 1.

[25] Bank Restriction Act 1797 (37 Geo III c 45). See Stephen Quinn, 'Money, Finance and Capital Markets' in Roderick Floud and Paul Johnson (eds), *Cambridge Economic History of Modern Britain* (CUP 2003) ch 6, 161–62; Boyd Hilton, *A Mad, Bad, & Dangerous People? England 1783–1846* (OUP 2006) 91–92.

[26] Hilton, *A Mad, Bad, & Dangerous People* (n 25) 211–12.

[27] Thomas Ashton, *The Industrial Revolution* (OUP 1964) 148–56; Arthur D Gayer and others, *The Growth and Fluctuation of the British Economy, 1790–1850: An Historical, Statistical, and Theoretical Study of Britain's Economic Development* (2nd edn, Harvester Press 1975); Barry Gordon, *Political Economy in Parliament 1819–1823* (Macmillan 1976) 155 (1820s growth) 176–84 (market fluctuations); Charles Knick Harley, 'Trade: Discovery, Mercantilism and Technology' in Roderick Floud and Paul Johnson (eds), *Cambridge Economic History of Modern Britain* (CUP 2004) ch 7, 190–203 (relationship between trade and growth); Stephen Broadberry and others, 'British Economic Growth and the Business Cycle, 1700–1870' <<https://warwick.ac.uk/fac/soc/economics/seminars/seminars/conferences/venice3/programme/british_economic_growth_and_the_business_cycle_1700-1850.pdf>> (growth in industrial output and GDP, especially from the late eighteenth century, and details of fluctuations, accessed 18 March 2020).

[28] Ian Duffy, *Bankruptcy and Insolvency in London during the Industrial Revolution* (Routledge 1985); MS Servian, *Eighteenth Century Bankruptcy Law: From Crime to Process* (University of Kent 1985); Hoppit (n 9); Markham Lester, *Victorian Insolvency* (Clarendon Press 1995) 73–76.

1807 in an attempt to curb the operation of joint stock businesses seeking to emulate the privileges of corporation without Act of Parliament.[29]

Likewise, after the end of the Napoleonic Wars in 1815, Lord Liverpool's ministry sought to put the economy on a more stable footing, and so to restore a sense of normalcy post war. According to contemporary ministerial thought—influenced by moderate evangelism—economic crises and bankruptcy were the natural response of the economic system to immoral 'overtrading' by merchants and banks: which were too willing to extend credit to those unlikely to be able to pay their debts.[30] Economic growth was not seen as per se desirable, what was key to a healthy economy was that trade should occur at its 'natural' level. If reckless traders exceeded this level then crisis and bankruptcies were the economy's—and indeed God's—way of restoring stability and the natural order. This was why, in the wake of the Napoleonic Wars, the government sought to rein in the wartime 'false credit' and stabilise the economy by restoring the gold standard to deliberately cause deflation,[31] restoring the convertibility of bank notes to bullion[32] and coins.[33] Depression between 1819 and 1822 was followed by a period of relative prosperity, and a cabinet reshuffle by Lord Liverpool in 1821 ushered in a series of measures designed to encourage British commerce. These measures were designed to encourage merchants internationally to warehouse their goods in Britain, turning it into 'the general depot, the great emporium of the commerce of the world': so that Britain would be well provisioned should war break out again.[34] As well as a reduction on charges and tariffs on those who used British warehouses,[35] reforms included an interest rate cut in 1822,[36] reform of the law concerning commercial agents,[37] bankruptcy,[38] banking,[39] and the repeal of the Bubble Act.[40] This last measure was prompted by a surge in company promotions and applications to Parliament for incorporation in 1824 and 1825, which was followed by a severe

[29] Discussed in Chapter 2, text from (n 62) to (n 70).

[30] Boyd Hilton, *Corn, Cash Commerce: The Economic Policies of Tory Government* (OUP 1978) 59–63, 303–14; Boyd Hilton, *Age of Atonement: The Influence of Evangelicalism on Social and Economic Thought, 1785–1865* (Clarendon Press 1997) chs 2 and 4; Hilton, *A Mad, Bad, & Dangerous People* (n 25) 326–28.

[31] William Huskisson, *The Question Concerning the Depreciation of Our Currency, Stated and Examined* (J Murray and J Hatchard 1810). See Also Hilton, *Corn, Cash, Commerce* (n 30) ch 2; Daunton, *Progress and Poverty* (n 3) 352–57.

[32] Resumption Act 1820, 59 Geo III c 49.

[33] Bank of England Act 1821, 1 & 2 Geo IV c 26.

[34] Thomas Wallace MP, HC Deb 25 June 1821, vol 1, col 129. See Hunt (n 15) 14–55; Hilton, *Corn, Cash, Commerce* (n 30) ch 6.

[35] Hilton, *Corn, Cash, Commerce* (n 30) 190–201.

[36] Ashton, *The Industrial Revolution* (n 27) 148–56.

[37] Factors Act 1823, 4 Geo IV c 83; Factors Act 1825, 6 Geo IV c 94.

[38] Bankruptcy Court Act 1821, 1 & 2 Geo IV, c 160; Bankrupts Act 1822, 3 Geo IV c 74; Bankrupt Laws (England) Act 1822, 3 Geo IV c 81; Bankrupts Act 1824, 5 Geo IV c 98; Bankrupts Act 1825, 6 Geo IV c 16.

[39] Country Bankers Act 1826, 7 Geo IV c 46.

[40] 6 Geo IV c 91 (1825).

financial crash. Lord Liverpool's ministry and the Bank of England saw this crash as a response to irresponsible market speculation and lending by country banks (private banks based outside of London), and responded to it by deliberately provoking deflation when the panic began to set in, and refusing to extend credit to large firms to help them weather the storm.[41] As Boyd Hilton has said of the period, 'the question to be asked is not why this country pioneered an economic revolution and a new form of social organization, but how it managed to pull through during a period of great economic strain'.[42]

Against this background of unstable growth, blamed by contemporaries on reckless trading, commercial law issues became contentious in the arena of public opinion, in Parliament, and also in the litigation generated by business failure. Regency era courts frequently had to decide whether a creditor had acted properly by buying or extending credit on the security of an asset which turned out to belong to a third party. Imagine A and B were in partnership, or B held assets on trust for A, or that B was A's agent. B then sells or mortgages assets he has been entrusted to manage to a third party, C. Should A or C bear the loss?[43] This scenario is at the heart of this book, and in such cases courts were forced directly to consider whether C was one of those immoral and reckless traders responsible for the country's economic instability. Further, the rise in bankruptcy rates meant that courts had to adjudicate disputes between different classes of creditor or disponee to particular asset pools. Such decisions forced courts to decide how to best balance their established doctrines, merchant expectations, and a responsibility to stem the perceived rising tide of commercial immorality and its associated crises.

The second reason the Regency era was particularly important in the development of commercial law relates to the availability of published legal materials. In the period, cases were continuously reported for the first time, and many new commercial law treatises were published.[44] Earlier in the eighteenth century, restrictive practices amongst legal publishers seeking to preserve the value of their rights to older works made it difficult to bring wholly new legal treatises to market. This meant that most available published treatises in the eighteenth century were revised editions of older works, the structure of which did not fully reflect legal thinking at the date of publication. It was only after late eighteenth century changes in the book trade that new treatises could find their way to market more easily. The increased availability of legal materials allowed counsel and judges to easily reference a wider range of material, while the treatises provided a public forum for

[41] Hunt (n 15) 30 to 55; Ashton, *The Industrial Revolution* (n 27) 155 to 156; Hilton, *Corn, Cash, Commerce* (n 30) ch 7.

[42] Hilton, *A Mad, Bad, & Dangerous People* (n 25) 7; also see Martin Daunton, 'Society and Economic Life' in Colin Matthew (ed), *The Nineteenth Century* (OUP 2000) 43–48.

[43] The terminology of A as original owner, B as errant partner, trustee, or agent, and C as third party, will be used throughout this book.

[44] Brian Simpson, 'Rise and Fall of the Treatise' (1981) 48 U Chi L Rev 632, 660–63.

views about contemporary law to be expressed. This allowed the development of a more sophisticated law from the late eighteenth century onwards.[45]

1. Dramatis Personae

This story of how the courts responded to the needs of commerce has four sets of main characters, the first being the traders and joint stock companies. In the absence of general incorporation for domestic private enterprise, traders were always personally liable for debts they contracted. Generally, such personal responsibility was seen as a way of incentivising responsible trading. However, traders were typically governed by a matrix of partnership, trust law, and agency law rules, which allowed trade credit and assets (in whole or in part) to be treated separately from the traders' other property. As we will see, these rules had the effect of determining the extent to which agreements between business partners, principals and mercantile agents, and even principal debtors and sureties, would affect third parties. It will be shown how traders might manipulate the legal mechanisms available to them in the Regency era to organise business.

The second set of main characters are the English courts, which had to determine the extent to which to give effect to merchant practices and expectations. Dealing with this issue is complicated by the fact that England in the Regency era did not have a unitary court system applying a unitary body of law, but was split (principally[46]) between courts of equity and courts of common law with different but overlapping jurisdictions over commercial cases. Matters concerning joint stock traders and security were usually, if not exclusively,[47] heard by: the Court of King's Bench, the premier common law court which heard matters relating to debt and the authority of partners and agents; the Court of Chancery, which administered equity, had inherent jurisdiction over trusts, and also heard cases where its accounting procedures were needed;[48] and the Bankruptcy Court.[49] This was

45 Tariq Baloch, 'Law Booksellers and Printers as Agents of Unchange' [2007] CLJ 389; Simpson (n 44).

46 There were courts administering other bodies of law, in particularly Admiralty Law and Ecclesiastical Law, see Polden (n 8) 692–796.

47 There are also instances of relevant cases heard by the Court of Exchequer (common law and equity); the Court of Common Pleas (common law); the Exchequer Chamber (common law and equity); and the House of Lords (common law and equity). Small commercial cases could be heard by local Courts of Request, Arthurs (n 10) 133–34, 144, though as the courts were often staffed with non-lawyers, typically decided cases without reference to established law or equity, and do not appear to have any reported decisions, they are less useful for examining the extent to which the law was sympathetic to commercial needs, see (n 10). For details of the different courts in the period see Polden (n 8).

48 John Mitford, *A Treatise on the Pleadings in Suits in the Court of Chancery by English Bill* (J and WT Clarke 1827) 119–120.

49 This is to be distinguished from the short-lived Court of Review established in 1831 to hear appeals from Bankruptcy Commissioners, replacing the Lord Chancellor's jurisdiction in such cases. As the court had only a slight workload, it was formally abolished and its jurisdiction was transferred to the

an institution formally separate from the Court of Chancery, in which Chancery judges exercised a mixed common law and equitable jurisdiction to hear appeals from the decisions of the commissioners who oversaw the administration of traders' bankrupt estates. Significant numbers of bankruptcy cases were heard by Lord Hardwicke LC, Lord Nottingham LC heard some, but the origin of the jurisdiction has been much discussed.[50] It seems to be rooted in the Lord Chancellor's statutory authority to appoint bankruptcy commissioners conferred by 13 Eliz c 7, s 2 (1571), and Sir Francis Bacon LK's standing order that 'No Commission of Bankrupts shall be Granted but upon petition first Exhibited to the Lord Chancellor'.[51]

It will be shown that the Regency era courts were willing to accommodate the demands of merchants, but that this willingness was tempered by the courts' commitment to their own established doctrines, as well as judges' views of what constituted responsible commercial practice. These views were not those of an out of touch judicial class but were shaped by contemporary political economic and religious ideas about commerce. Further, it will be shown that by and large the courts of common law and equity co-operated to create a unified body of commercial law based on the same values, and that in this area each was willing to apply and make use of the jurisprudence of the other. This *mutual* influence is significant in that it challenges the widespread assumption that borrowings between law and equity historically have been only one way: in the Regency era common law courts made as much use of equitable jurisprudence as courts of equity did of common law principles.[52] It shows closer relations between courts of equity and law in the period before Victorian reform than has been commonly supposed.[53]

The third main character is John Scott, better known to lawyers as Lord Eldon LC. Lord Eldon was the Lord Chancellor from 1801 to 1827, apart from a brief period in 1806–07, and the period covered by this book was chosen with reference to Lord Eldon's time on the woolsack. In this capacity, he was the chief judge in Chancery and Bankruptcy. Amongst historians, Lord Eldon is most famous as a High Tory who was 'baffled and frightened by political economy',[54] and resisted

Vice Chancellors in 1847. See Michael Lobban, 'Bankruptcy and Insolvency' in William Cornish and others (eds), *Oxford History of the Laws of England*, vol XII (OUP 2010) 795–96.

[50] See Edward Christian, *The Origin, Progress and Present Practise of Bankrupt Law, Both in England and Ireland.*, vol II (2nd edn, W Clarke & Sons 1818) 6–19; Basil Montagu, *Inquiries Respecting the Courts of Commissioners of Bankrupts and the Lord Chancellor's Court* (1825); DEC Yale, *Lord Nottingham's Chancery Cases*, vol I (73 Selden Soc) (Bernard Quaritch 1954) cxiv–xx.

[51] 16 Jac 1, 96 (5 June 1618); George Sanders (ed), *Orders of the High Court of Chancery, Vol 1, Part 1* (A Maxwell and Son 1845) 122.

[52] Polden (n 8) 757–60.

[53] See for instance *AIB Group* (UK) *plc v Mark Redler & Co Solicitors* [2014] UKSC 58, [2015] AC 1503 at [1], '140 years after the Judicature Act 1873 (36 & 37 Vict c 66), the *stitching* together of equity and the common law continues to cause problems at the seams', per Lord Toulson JSC (emphasis added).

[54] Hilton, *A Mad, Bad, & Dangerous People* (n 25) 287.

the dominant ideas of his age, a fierce opponent of liberalism, anti-Bullionism, Catholic emancipation, the immediate abolition of the slave trade, and the regularisation and moderation of criminal punishment.[55] Amongst contemporary and modern lawyers, however, Lord Eldon is famous for the quality of his jurisprudence, and he is seen as one of the fathers of modern equity and trusts.[56] However, his reputation as a commercial judge is more mixed, not least due to his reputed hostility towards joint stock companies seeking to emulate the privileges of incorporation without a Royal Charter or Act of Parliament.[57] Most famously, Sir William Holdsworth, despite acknowledging Eldon's contribution to partnership law, asserted that 'Eldon was not a commercial lawyer'.[58] This book will challenge that perception by showing the profound influence of Lord Eldon on the development of English commercial law, examining his decisions through law reports, the court record, as well as his own seldom-used judicial notebooks.[59] It will show why one commentator was able declare:

> Indeed, there is no branch of the law in which the exceeding merit of Lord Eldon is more strongly exhibited than this [partnership law], in which with the most painful and patient attention he laboured to obviate and overcome the difficulties of the subject, and by a particular examination and careful adoption of the customs of merchants, to established such principles as would eventually bring the law and practice of the courts of equity into conformity with the necessities of an extended commerce: and we find his repeatedly lamenting the strange rules so obviously at variance with mercantile customs with which he had to contend.[60]

The final set of main characters, if they can be called characters, are the doctrines of partnership law, trusts law, and agency themselves. Although other aspects

[55] Horace Twiss, *The Life of Lord Chancellor Eldon* (2nd edn, J Murray 1844); Rose Melikan, *Lord Eldon 1751–1838: The Duty of Loyalty* (CUP 1999); EA Smith, 'Scott, John' in Sir David Cannadine (ed), *The Oxford Dictionary of National Biography* <http://www.oxforddnb.com/view/article/24897?docPos=13> (accessed 18 March 2020); Hilton, *A Mad, Bad, & Dangerous People* (n 25) 318, 323.

[56] William Holdsworth, *A History of English Law*, vol xiii (Arthur Goodhart and Harold Hanbury eds, Methuen & Co 1952) 629–38; Gregory Alexander, 'Transformation of Trusts as a Legal Category, 1800-1914' (1987) 5 L & Hist Rev 303, 303–50; Stuart Anderson, 'Trusts and Trustees' in William Cornish and others (eds), *Oxford History of the Laws of England*, vol XII (OUP 2010) 238–68, esp 239; Mike Macnair, 'Arbitrary Lord Chancellors and the Problem of Predictability' in Egnert Koops and Willem Zwalve (eds), *Law & Equity: Approaches in Roman Law and Common Law* (Brill 2014) 79, 91; John McGhee (ed), *Snell's Equity* (34th edn, Sweet & Maxwell 2019) para 1-013; Dyson Heydon, Mark Leeming, and Peter Turner (eds), *Meagher, Gummow & Lehane's Equity: Doctrines & Remedies* (5th edn, Lexis Nexis Australia 2014) para 1-070; Smith (n 55).

[57] Discussed in Chapter 2 at text from (n 75) to (n 97).

[58] Holdsworth, *A History of English Law* (n 56) 631, 633, 635.

[59] Lord Eldon Judicial Notebooks (1801–1821), held by Georgetown Law Library within the Lord Eldon Collection at EM-033A to EM-033K, with the permission of Hannah Miller, Curator of Legal History Collections, Georgetown Law Library.

[60] Isaac Cory, *A Practical Treatise on Accounts* (2nd edn, W Pickering 1837) 70.

of commercial law in the Regency era have received scholarly attention,[61] these doctrines have been neglected despite their crucial importance. This book will examine the relationship between these areas in the Regency era, and the extent to which they formed a coherent law of businesses organisations. The combination of the rise of treatise writing, case reporting, and economic crises helped make the Regency era a formative period for the law in each of those areas, and many of the principles established then have enduring relevance. Although this book is a work of legal history, and we should not 'try to make history the handmaid of dogma',[62] much of this law is of relevance to modern legal debates. The cases examined reveal the apparent origins of modern law rules: including the rule in *Clayton's Case*,[63] which governs the default appropriation of payments within a running account and also (prima facie) the rights of innocent contributors to a wrongfully mixed fund to trace;[64] the rules concerning the treatment of trust creditors and trustees in the context of bankruptcy; the operation of trusts in the commercial sphere; *Quistclose* security devices, whereby a lender advances money to a borrower on trust to avoid taking the risk of the borrower's insolvency; the doctrine of ostensible authority; and the rules concerning hidden principals. Indeed, Richard Calnan traces the fundamental logic of modern insolvency distribution, and the rules governing what assets vest in an insolvent estate, to eighteenth-century cases considered later.[65] These are all areas which are the subject of controversy today. This book does not aim to directly address modern legal debates, but it will shed light on them by laying bare the policy considerations underlying these rules at their inception, thus obliquely allowing their desirability today better to be assessed.

Finally, it should be made clear what this book is not about. It is a work of doctrinal legal history setting out the Regency era history of the pre-corporate organisational law fashioned by the courts of equity and common law out of partnership, trusts, and agency. Much of this development can only be properly described in technical terms. This book does not purport to be an overall history of business in the era, and there is no original statistical analysis of litigation rates, bankruptcy rates, business structures, nor why businesses tended to fail.[66] Nor will there be

61 For illustrative examples see Su Jin Kim and James Oldham, 'Insuring Maritime Trade with the Enemy in the Napoleonic Era' (2012) 47 Tex Int'l LJ 561; James Oldham, 'Some Effects of War on the Law of Late-Eighteenth and Early-Nineteenth Century England' in Catherine MacMillan and Charlotte Smith (eds), *Challenges to Authority and Recognition of Rights* (CUP 2018).

62 Frederic William Maitland, 'Why the History of English Law Is Not Written' in Herbert Fisher (ed), *The collected papers of Frederick William Maitland*, vol 1 (CUP 1911) 480, 492.

63 *Clayton's Case; Devaynes v Noble* (1816) 1 Mer 529, 572; 35 ER 767, 781 (Ch).

64 See *Barlow Clowes International v Vaughan* [1992] 4 All ER 22.

65 Richard Calnan, *Proprietary Rights and Insolvency* (2nd edn, OUP 2016) paras 1.82–1.88; *Burdett v Willett* (1708) 2 Vern 638, 23 ER 1017 (Ch); *Ex p Dumas* (1754) 1 Atk 232, 26 ER 149; 2 Ves Sen 582, 28 ER 372 (BC); B 1/29, pp 199–203. Discussed in Chapter 6 at (n 51) to (n 54), (n 94) to (n 101).

66 For examples of works which deal with such issues see Hunt (n 15); DuBois (n 15); Thomas Ashton, *Economic Fluctuations in England, 1700–1800* (OUP 1969); Gayer and others (n 27); Duffy (n 28); Servian (n 28); Hoppit (n 9); Daunton, *Progress and Poverty* (n 3); Horwitz and Polden, 'Continuity or Change in the Court of Chancery in the Seventeenth and Eighteenth Centuries?' (1996) 35 J Brit Stud

extended discussions of who traders or lawyers were and how they lived. Such doctrinal legal history is sometimes regarded as rather old fashioned compared to so-called 'modern' legal history with a broader focus. This perception is unfair. Like any legal historical methodology, doctrinal legal history can only reveal aspects of historical development. However, those aspects that it illuminates—in this case the rules the courts applied to business organisations—are crucial to understanding why people in the past acted as they did. There is no better place than the nineteenth century literary canon to see how legal rules mould the course of people's lives: from the strictures of Chancery procedure in *Bleak House* (1852–53, set in 1827[67]), the corruption created by company promotion and general incorporation in *The Way We Live Now* (1875), and the authority doctrines which allow Paul Dombey's villainous agent James Carker to ruin his principal's business in *Dombey & Sons* (1846–48). It is only by understanding legal historical rules that we can understand how ostensibly niche points of law became matters of wider interest.

2. Structure

This book will be structured around the life cycle of a business, and be divided into three main parts, designed to mirror the concerns of traders establishing a business, running a business, and then dissolving it. Part I examines the extent to which legally stable business structures could be created in the Regency era in the absence of general incorporation. Chapter 1 shows how partnership was able to function as organisational law, in effectively allowing the assets dedicated to the concern to be used primarily for its purposes, but also highlight the fragility of this ringfencing effect. Chapter 2 will then examine the ways in which trusts could be used by joint stock traders to stabilise business structures and emulate some of the benefits of incorporation, and even limited liability in the testamentary context.

Part II deals with running a business and focuses on problems created by managers of funds acting without authority, including partners (Chapter 3), agents (Chapters 3 and 4), trustees and executors (Chapter 5). It shows how both courts of law and equity protected third parties who dealt with fund managers in what appeared to be the ordinary course of business.

Part III deals with business failure and insolvency. Chapter 6 looks at how commercial parties could use trusts law to avoid taking the risk of the insolvency of those with whom they dealt. Finally, Chapter 7 examines the rules governing the

25; Ron Harris, *Industrializing English Law: Entrepreneurship and Business Organization, 1720-1844* (CUP 2000).

[67] See William Holdsworth, *Charles Dickens as a Legal Historian* (Yale University Press 1928).

distribution of an insolvent partnership's assets, and shows how partnership's asset partitioning effects were justified by a blend of concerns relating to protecting creditors, doctrinal commitments, and a qualified willingness to give effect to merchant expectations.

Ultimately, it will be shown that the common law provided a range of forms for business persons to structure their relations, and was so willing to give effect to their associational rights through a range of doctrines which treated businesses as separate from individuals. However, judges echoed the wider political economic concerns that forcing traders to be personally liable for their business debts was crucial to stabilising the country's economy, in placing hard limits on the extent to which businesses were treated as separate from their owners.

PART I

REGENCY ERA BUSINESS STRUCTURES

1

Partnership as Organisational Law

It is trite modern law that a corporation has legal personality and owns property. Corporations are legal persons which can contract debts, and if they default on payment of those debts, their assets can be seized by creditors. Where the corporation has limited liability the personal assets of its owners (the shareholders), subject to a few exceptions,[1] are completely shielded from the creditors of the corporation. Likewise, although the personal creditors of shareholders may be able to execute judgment against the shares, they cannot directly claim the assets of the corporation. These are the 'asset partitioning' or 'ringfencing' features of corporate law, which is regarded as 'organisational law' because it partitions assets in these ways. The assets settled for the purpose of the business are treated as separate from the assets of the shareholders, and so 'bonded' to the business, its disponees, and its creditors.

'Organisational law' and 'asset petitioning' rules of this type are regarded by modern law and finance scholars as commercially efficient. In particular, Hansmann, Kraakman, and Squire have argued that those legal features which bond trade assets to trade creditors, and so insulate them from the personal creditors of the a firm's owners, are economically significant—to a greater degree than limited liability.[2] The focus of this chapter is on the extent to which Regency era legal rules allowed asset partitioning of this type, and so allowed what we would today regard as commercially efficient forms of trading. It also asks whether traders regarded the law of partnership as sufficient to meet their needs, in light of the limitations of its asset partitioning rules.

In the Regency era, commercial parties could not usually incorporate,[3] and a sole trader would simply be liable in the same way for any debts he contracted. Where he defaulted on repayment all his property would straightforwardly be available to his creditors. Crucially, no distinction was drawn between business creditors and personal creditors. This could create hazards for business creditors. Imagine a trader were running a visibly successful business and, seeing this, creditor X agreed

[1] Most notably where the shares are not fully paid up, the shareholder can be liable to pay the balance due, see for instance Insolvency Act 1986, s 74(1) and (2)(d).

[2] Henry Hansmann, Reiner Kraakman, and Richard Squire, 'Law and the Rise of the Firm' (2006) 119 Harv L Rev 1333; see also Hansmann and Kraakman, 'The Essential Role of Organizational Law' (2000) 110 Yale LJ 387.

[3] Again, corporate form lay in the gift of the Crown and Parliament and was regarded as inappropriate for domestic private enterprise without some public element, see Introduction, text to (n 15).

Capitalism Before Corporations. Andreas Televantos, Oxford University Press (2020).
DOI: 10.1093/oso/9780198870340.003.0002.

to lend him money to expand the business. That trader also owed a large amount of money to creditor Y in respect of gambling debts. Were the trader to default on his debts, both X and Y could levy judgment against his assets, and the first creditor to do so would claim them. Were the trader to be declared bankrupt, then his assets would be distributed pro rata to X and Y according to the bankruptcy statutes.[4] The difficulty here is that a creditor of a sole trader, to be sure of repayment, would have to make enquiries not just of the solvency of the business, but of the trader's personal affairs also.

The position of joint traders was not so straightforward and was generally governed by the law of partnership.[5] Joint traders were partners who typically raised the business capital jointly, and so any business which required more capital than one person could muster took this form, hence its importance. Going into partnership with someone did come with risk. The bankruptcy of a single partner could potentially sink an entire firm, and this explains why some precedents in partnership treatises included a term limiting or prohibiting the partners from gaming[6] or other acts which could result in extensive personal liability.[7] The personal reputation of a partner could also be an important part of the firm's ability to obtain credit or not. However the law of partnership, by automatically imposing a series of rights and duties on joint traders, would in part segregate the business assets (the 'joint stock' or 'joint estate') from the personal assets ('separate estates') of the partners, and did so without treating the business as having legal personality. This chapter will explain when and how partnership law would have this effect and assess how effectively it bonded joint stock to the partnership business.

1. When Did Partnership Rules Apply?

Whereas a corporation has to be deliberately created, a partnership would come into existence automatically whenever joint traders acted as 'partners'. The first English partnership law treatise, written by the barrister William Watson, described a partnership in civilian terms, as 'a voluntary contract, between two or

[4] 13 Eliz 7, s 2 (1571).

[5] The law did not apply straightforwardly to jointly run shipping and mining businesses, which were not treated as partnerships: Mark Freeman, Robin Pearson, and James Taylor, *Shareholder Democracies? Corporate Governance in Britain & Ireland before 1850* (University of Chicago Press 2012) 186–89.

[6] William Watson, *A Treatise of the Law of Partnership* (2nd edn, J Butterworth 1807) 471, 502.

[7] For an expansive example see Neil Gow, *A Practical Treatise on the Law of Partnership* (3rd edn, C Hunter and J Richards 1830) 385, ('none of the said partners shall, without the consent in writing of the others or other of them first obtained, enter into any bond, or become bound as bail, surety, or security, with or for any person or persons whomsoever, or subscribe any policy of insurance; or do, or knowingly suffer to be done, any act, matter or thing whatsoever, by means whereof the stock and effects, belonging or to belong to the said copartnership, shall or may be seized attached, extended or taken in execution'.)

more persons, for joining together their money, goods, labour, and skill, or either or all of them, upon an agreement that the gain or loss shall be divided proportionally between them, and having for its object the advancement and protection of fair and open trade'.[8] Similar definitions were used by other partnership treatise writers throughout the period,[9] and seem to be indebted to contemporary civil law formulations.[10] The description, however, was not quite accurate, and Lord Eldon in *Ex p Langdale* (1811)[11] made clear that an individual 'may also be a partner, when the contract is that he shall suffer no loss ... [T]he true criterion is, whether they are to participate in profit.'[12] The English definition was thus narrower than classical Roman *societas*, which did not require the division of profits.[13] If two people entered into a profit sharing agreement they would be partners, regardless of whether or not both partners had contributed capital to the firm[14] and written articles of partnership were used.[15]

It should be noted that many cases drew a distinction between a partnership as between the partners, and a partnership as between the partners and third parties. The latter did not involve running a business together and was not a true partnership, the principle was simply that if A and B appeared to be partners, then B had authority to bind A when acting in what appeared to be the partnership's business. A and B would not be treated as partners inter se.[16]

[8] Watson, *A Treatise of the Law of Partnership* (n 6) 1.

[9] Basil Montagu, *Digest of the Law of Partnership, with Cases* (1st edn, J Butterworth 1815) 3; Neil Gow, *A Practical Treatise on the Law of Partnership* (1st edn, C Hunter 1823) 1.

[10] For instant Robert Pothier wrote, 'Partnership is a contract, by which two or more persons put, or oblige themselves to put, something in common, in order to make therefrom in common a lawful profit, of which they reciprocally bind themselves to render each other account': Robert Pothier, *A Treatise on the Contract of Partnership (1765)* (Owen Tudor tr, Butterworths 1854) 1.

[11] 18 Ves Jun 300, 301; 34 ER 331 (Ch).

[12] Note Pothier's definition (n 10) makes no reference to loss either, and even in Roman law a partner could take a share of profit without contributing to loss. The classical position seems to have required proof that this partner had provided services commensurate with the loss incurred by the firm, see D.17.29.1 and G.3.148, whereas it is not clear that in Justinian's time the value of the contribution mattered, J.3.25.2,

[13] WW Buckland, *A Text-Book of Roman Law* (3rd edn, CUP 1963) 506–07.

[14] *Ex p Hamper* (1811) 17 Ves Jun 403, 34 ER 156 (Ch); see Partnership Select Committee, *Report on the Law of Partnership* (HC 1837, 530-XLIV) 2.

[15] Partnership Select Committee, ibid; *Stelly v Wilson* (1684) 1 Vern 297, 23 ER 480 (Ch); *Brown v Litton* (1711) 1 P Wms 140, 24 ER 329; 10 Mod 20, 88 ER 606 (Ch); *Gouthwaite v Duckworth* (1810) 12 East 421, 104 ER 164 (KB); *Ex p Gellar* (1812) 1 Rose 297 (BC); *Reid v Hollinshead* (1825) 4 B&C 867, 107 ER 1281 (KB).

[16] *Waugh v Carver* (1793) 2 H Black 235, 246; 126 ER 525, 532 (CP); *Hesketh v Blanchard* (1803) 4 East 144, 102 ER 785 (KB); *Parsons v Crosby* (1805) 5 Esp 199, 170 ER 785 (KB); *Ex p Hamper* (1811) 17 Ves Jun 404, 34 ER 156 (Ch); *Ex p Broome* (1811) 1 Rose 69 (BC); *Geddes v Wallace* (1820) 2 Bligh 270, 299–300; 3 ER 238, 338 (HL); *Smith v Watson* (1824) 2 B&C 401, 107 ER 43 (KB). See also Montagu (n 9) 2–7.

2. How Did Partnership Law Partition Assets?

As above a partnership was not a legal entity and so could not own property, but the partners would normally provide that property was to be used in the business. A partnership agreement, whether formal or informal, would provide that certain assets—the joint stock—were to be used for the benefit of the business. Articles of partnership would typically provide that partners would manage their trade and hold its stock for their 'mutual benefit',[17] and were entered into it 'in consideration of the mutual trust and confidence'[18] that the partners placed in one another. The income of the partnership, assets bought with partnership assets, and assets used for partnership purposes would be treated automatically as part of the joint stock. Partners would be presumed to be equally entitled to the joint stock and profits in the absence of agreement to the contrary.[19] Beyond this, no partner would be allowed payment or interest for their contributions to the firm's start-up capital, unless he were given that right expressly by the articles of partnership.[20]

The partners themselves were co-owners of the joint stock in equity.[21] Whether these equitable rights were a form of joint tenancy or tenancy in common was contested,[22] but the debate was academic.[23] It was accepted that survivorship did not apply as between partners and that partners had equal shares in the partnership assets, in the absence of contrary provisions in the articles of partnership.[24] It should be emphasised that, as partners were equitable co-owners of the firm's property, no partner could claim any particular asset of the firm as his own.

The partnership property would typically be vested in the partners at law, also, though as will be seen in Chapter 2 they could instead be vested in a body of trustees. Personal property would be treated by default as jointly belonging to the partners at law, and the legal title to real property would depend on the conveyance.[25]

The rights the partners had to the joint stock as co-owners were qualified by the terms of the articles of partnership. It was these qualifications which bonded the partnership assets to the business.

[17] Watson, *A Treatise of the Law of Partnership* (n 6) 461 (trade), 466 (joint capital and stock).

[18] Eg see ibid 465.

[19] Gow (n 9) 45–52.

[20] Isaac Cory, *A Practical Treatise on Accounts* (2nd edn, W Pickering 1837) 131–43.

[21] *Thornton v Proctor* (1794) 1 Anst 94, 145 ER 810 (Ex); *Burden v Burden* (1813) 1 V&B 172, 35 ER 67 (Ch) (per Lord Eldon).

[22] Sometimes it was described as joint tenancy without survivorship, *Devaynes v Noble* (1816) 1 Mer 529, 564; 35 ER 767, 778; Co Litt 182; sometimes as tenancy in common, eg see Watson, *A Treatise of the Law of Partnership* (n 6) 65–110; Gow (n 9) 46–47; Watson, *A Treatise of the Law of Partnership* (n 6) 65–110; and sometimes as sui generis, Joseph Story, *Commentaries on the Law of Partnership* (1st edn, Boston 1841) s 89–92; Andrew Bisset, *A Practical Treatise on the Law of Partnership* (London 1847) 45.

[23] It was so ultimately abandoned, see Nathaniel Lindley, *A Treatise on the Law of Partnership* (W Maxwell 1860) 560.

[24] Gow (n 9) 47.

[25] ibid 45–48.

2.1 Custodial Duties

The terms of the partnership made clear that partners could not freely use the co-owned assets. They determined, for instance, when and in what proportions profits were to be distributed to partners,[26] and when a partner could borrow money from the firm (if at all).[27] Further, the partnership agreement set out the nature of the business, and the terms of the authority of each partner to dispose of the assets in the joint stock.[28] Where a partner disposed of partnership property with authority under the partnership articles, this disposition would bind his co-partners, effectively overreaching their equitable shares of the business.[29] However, where a partner made dispositions of property without authority under the partnership articles, he would ultimately have to account to his co-partners for breach of his custodialduties.

2.2 Partners' Indemnity and Lien

A second significant effect of the partnership agreement was that no partner could freely withdraw assets from the joint stock while the firm had outstanding debts.[30] The reason was as follows.

Partners were treated as authorising one another to enter into debts within the scope of the partnership business, and so each were liable for the debts of the firm. Indeed, to protect partners from debts they had not agreed to, partners had to agree *unanimously* to change the scope of a firm's business.[31] However, each partner had personal rights to compel the others to contribute towards discharge of the debt, in this sense he had a right of indemnity good against the firm. Each partner's right of indemnity was secured by an equitable lien—effectively a charge—over the equitable shares of his co-partners in the partnership assets.[32] The effect of these rights

[26] For examples in precedents of deeds of partnership see Watson, *A Treatise of the Law of Partnership* (n 6) 472–73 ('Gains and Profits'), 487 ('Profits to be divided'), 503 ('Division of Profits'); Henry Cary, *A Practical Treatise on the Law of Partnership* (1st edn, J and WT Clarke 1827) 310–11 (9thly and 10thly); Gow (n 7) 378 (Clause 15), 382 (final paragraph).

[27] Watson, *A Treatise of the Law of Partnership* (n 6) 502 (example of a clause providing that no partner was to borrow from the firm without the consent in writing of all the partners).

[28] *Fox v Hanbury* (1776) 2 Cowp 445, 98 ER 1179; *Hope v Cust* (1774) 1 East 48, 53; 102 ER 19, 21 (per Lord Mansfield CJKB); *Sandilands v Marsh* (1819) 2 B&A 673, 106 ER 511.

[29] As a single partner would seldom have sole legal title to the partnership assets (as above), the transfer of legal title to those assets was effected by the co-partners' consent. Such title could also pass through the doctrine of ostensible authority also, see Chapter 3, Section 4.2.

[30] (n 28).

[31] *Const v Harris* (1824) T&R 496, 523–26; 37 ER 1191, 1201–02 (Ch); *Natusch v Irving* (1824) 2 CTC 358, 47 ER 1196; Gow (n 7) 404–06.

[32] *West v Skipp* (1749) 1 Ves Sen 239, 27 ER 1006 (Ch); *Doddington v Hallett* (1750) 1 Ves Sen 497, 499; 27 ER 1165, 1166 (Ch); *Fox v Habury* (1776) 2 Cowp 445, 98 ER 1179 (KB); *Smith v De Silva* (1776) 2 Cowp 469, 98 ER 1191 (KB); *Taylor v Fields* (1799) 4 Ves Jun 396, 31 ER 201 (Ex); *Ex p Ruffin* (1801) 6 Ves Jun 119, 31 ER 970 (Ch); *Ex p Williams* (1805) 11 Ves Jun 3, 4–5; 32 ER 988–89. See John Collyer, *A Practical Treatise on the Law of Partnership* (London 1832) 65.

of indemnity and lien were that each partner could compel his co-partners to use the joint property to discharge the debts of the firm. These rights would be treated as implied terms of any partnership agreement but would typically be provided for expressly in partnership articles.[33] Their effect was that a partner, at least without the consent of all the other partners, could not claim any asset of the firm personally until the creditors of the firm had been paid off, and an account had been taken for the purpose of determining his share. Where debts were outstanding on dissolution, partnership assets had to be sold for this purpose.

It should be noted that this differed from the classical Roman position, which despite superficial similarities had little influence here. Under Roman law, partners could get a court order to split up the firm's assets between themselves *even* where debts were outstanding, provided that each contracted with the others (through the formal unilateral contract, the *stipulatio*) that they would bear their share of any outstanding partnership debts.[34] This could be done either using a claim for partition, the *actio communi dividundo*, or through an action on the partnership contract, the *actio pro socio*.[35] English law, since the eighteenth century at least, fundamentally differed from this system: partners praying an account and dissolution of partnership assets in court could only claim their share of those assets once the creditors of the concern had been paid. Roman partnership law dealt almost entirely with the relations of the partners inter se,[36] whereas English partnership law preserved partnership assets for the benefit of creditors.

2.3 The Doctrine of Conversion

This duty to sell partnership assets to pay joint debts did not just prevent partners from personally taking the firm's assets before its creditors were paid off, but prevented their heirs from doing so too. In the Regency era, land and personal property descended on death differently, and a testator's land would pass to his heir automatically, unencumbered with any debts unless his will specifically provided otherwise.[37] Absent such a provision, the testator's debts would thus be paid out of the personal property only. Where a testator was a partner in a firm this could have created problems, in that the default rules could have put land (or shares in land) held by a partnership beyond the reach of the firm's creditors.

[33] See Watson, *A Treatise of the Law of Partnership* (n 6) 468; Gow (n 7) 382; Cory (n 20) 138–44.

[34] D.17.2.27 (Paul) ('Any debt contracted during the existence of a partnership is to be met out of the common property, even if the payment is to be made after the partnership has been dissolved ... Thus, if in the meantime the partnership is liquidated, *cautiones* must be provided'), Alan Watson (ed), *The Digest of Justinian*, vol 2 (University of Pennsylvania Press 1985) 42–43.

[35] D.17.2.38.1 (Paul, citing Proculus); D.17.2.43 (Ulpian).

[36] Buckland (n 13) 507.

[37] TE Tomlins, *A Familiar Explanation of The Law of Wills* (R Baldwin, BC Collins 1801) 78–80.

Lord Eldon dealt with the point in *Ripley v Waterworth* (1802).[38] In the language of his notebooks, he held that:

> I was of the opinion in this Case that the real property [held by the partnership] was to be considered as personal & was converted into personal by fact of the contracts, which the parties had entered into with each other.... [The freehold estate] was real property, embarked with Utensils &tc in a Trade, where all the different parties ... contracted with each other, on the Ground that it would be for the benefit of all & each, that the property should be converted.[39]

The point is best understood as follows. As above, each partner had a right to force his other co-partners to use the partnership assets to pay the joint debts. Correlative to this right, at least where the partnership did not have liquid assets sufficient for the purpose, each partner owed a duty to the others to sell the joint assets to pay the joint debts. This was seen by Lord Eldon as engaging the doctrine of conversion: which provided that land held on trust would be treated as personal property, where the terms of the trust imposed a duty on the trustees to sell the land. Accordingly, Lord Eldon ruled that even land held by a partnership should be treated as personal property. A firm's property was regarded as a fungible item of circulating stock due to the expectation that it would ultimately be sold. Lord Eldon repeated the decision a number of times.[40]

Lord Eldon's view here was not entirely uncontroversial. It directly contradicted Lord Thurlow LC's earlier ruling in *Thornton v Dixon* (1791)[41] that the doctrine of conversion would not apply automatically to land held for partnership purposes, which was itself upheld by Sir William Grant MR in *Bell v Phyn* (1802)[42] and *Balmain v Shore* (1804).[43] In Lord Eldon's own time his view was usually treated as the correct one,[44] though the debate about whether the doctrine applied automatically to partnerships would continue throughout the nineteenth century.[45]

[38] 7 Ves Jun 425, 32 ER 172; Eldon Notebook 1802 pp 144–48, 176–77 (Ch).

[39] Eldon Notebook 1802 p 176.

[40] Eg see *Townsend v Devaynes* (1808) 1 Montagu on Partnerships, Note 2A, 96–100; *Selkrig v Davies* (1814) 2 Dow 230, 242; 3 ER 848, 852, ('My own individual opinion is, that all property involved in a partnership concern ought to be considered as personal'); *Crawshay v Maule* (1818) 1 Swanst 495, 508, 521; 36 ER 479, 484, 485, ('It has been repeatedly decided, that interests in lands purchased for the purpose of carrying on trade, are no more than stock in trade').

[41] 3 Brown Ch Cas 199, 29 ER 488 (Ch).

[42] 7 Ves Jun 453, 32 ER 183 (Ch).

[43] 9 Ves Jun 500, 32 ER 696 (Ch).

[44] Montagu (n 9) 164; Gow (n 9) 50–52; Cary (n 26) 27. Note that Watson, *A Treatise of the Law of Partnership* (n 6) 81 takes the opposite view.

[45] In support of Eldon, *Philips v Philips* (1844) 1 Myl & Kn 649, 663–64 (per Sir John Leach MR, who had 'for some years, notwithstanding older authorities, considered it to be settled'); *Broom v Broom* (1834) 3 My & K 443, 40 ER 169 (Sir John Leach MR, applying *Philips*); *Morris v Kearsley* (1837) 2 Y & C Ex 139, 160 ER 344 (Ex); *Darby v Darby* (1856) 3 Drew 495, 61 ER 992 (Sir R T Kindersley V-C); and *Attorney General v Hubbuck* (1883) 10 QBD 488. In support of Thurlow see *Randall v Randall* (1835) 7 Sim 271, 58 ER 541 (Sir Lawrence Shadwell V-C); *Cookson v Cookson* (1837) 8 Sim 529, 59 ER 210 (Sir Lawrence Shadwell V-C).

Ultimately, Lord Eldon's view prevailed,[46] preventing the death of a partner taking his share of any land owned by the concern out of the joint stock free from the joint debts. In this sense, Lord Eldon's rule was a capital maintenance doctrine: it helped keep land held by the partnership within the business, and so available to its creditors.

2.4 The Jingle Rule

The partners' rights of lien and indemnity also acted to preserve partnership assets for the benefit of partnership creditors. Just as each partner could force the others to use the partnership assets to pay the business debts, each could prevent his co-partners' separate creditors from claiming partnership assets where there were outstanding partnership debts.[47]

The lien and indemnity were perhaps most important in cases where the partners were declared bankrupt. Under the bankruptcy statutes, the basic rule of distribution was that all the assets of a bankrupt were sold and were distributed amongst all his creditors equally. If this rule had been straightforwardly applied, then the partnership assets should have been sold, and their proceeds split amongst the partners in proportion to their shares. The creditors of the business would be treated exactly like the personal creditors of the partners, entitled to a rateable share of each partner's total property. This would mean that the creditors of a business which was doing well might in fact get very few of the business assets in cases where the partners had extensive personal debts, much like the case of the gambling sole trader described above.

However, the courts did not apply the basic rule of distribution to cases where partners were declared bankrupt. In that case a joint commission of bankruptcy would generally take possession of the joint assets, that is to say the partnership assets.[48] The proceeds of the partnership assets would be distributed to the partnership creditors in priority to the personal creditors of each partner. The rule was explained in *Ex p Ruffin*,[49] where Lord Eldon held that partnership creditors were entitled to take the benefit of the rights of indemnity and liens that the partners could assert against one another: in modern technical terms, partnership creditors

[46] See Partnership Act 1890, s 22. It remains good law today.

[47] *Taylor v Fields* (1799) 4 Ves Jun 396, 31 ER 201 (Ex); Watson, *A Treatise of the Law of Partnership* (n 6) 100–02; Gow (n 7) 205–07.

[48] For a summary of the rules see William Cooke, *The Bankrupt Laws* (7th edn, W Reed, C Hunter 1817) 11–16. Where there were joint and separate creditors who had sued out two different commissions, to save costs, one could be superseded, and the other would take all the assets but keep the separate accounts. Petitions for this to be done were quite common, for representative examples see *Ex p Loundes* (1815) B 1/133, pp 68–69; *Ex p Larkin* (1815) B 1/135, pp 34–35; *Ex p Hall* (1825) B 1/171, pp 352–53. This practice was put on a statutory footing in the Bankruptcy Act 1825 (6 Geo IV c 16), s 17.

[49] *Ex p Ruffin* (1801) 6 Ves Jun 119, 127; 31 ER 970, 974 (Ch).

were subrogated to those rights. Simply put, although partnership creditors had no direct legal or equitable property rights in the partnership assets, they could *force* the partners' bankrupt estates to use the partnership assets to pay them, and so claim the partnership assets in priority to the separate creditors of each partner. Further, just as the partnership creditors could claim partnership assets with priority over each partner's separate creditors, a bankrupt partner's personal assets would first be distributed to their personal creditors, and only the residue of those assets (if any) would be distributed amongst the partnership creditors.

These incidents of distribution were the application of what has become known as the 'jingle rule',[50] and effectively meant that a partner's individual estate was only liable as a surety for his partnership's debts, and vice versa.[51] It was applied strictly by Lord Hardwicke LC[52] and Lord Eldon, though Lord Eldon had doubts about its desirability.[53] Lord Loughborough LC applied the rule less strictly,[54] and Lord Thurlow disregarded it.[55] It should be noted that where a partner died insolvent, but had never been declared bankrupt, the same rule would apply to the distribution of his estate by analogy with bankruptcy.[56] The economic significance of the rule was that it allowed partnership creditors to assess a firm's creditworthiness by looking at the solvency of the business, without needing to inquire into

50 The term is usually attributed to the American jurist James Barr Ames, who thought the rule's appeal was rooted in its superficial symmetry, rather than any deep rooted principle, see James MacLachlan, *Handbook of the Law of Bankruptcy* (West Publishing Corporation 1956) § 355, at 424, note 9; Frank Kennedy, 'Partnerships And Partners Under The Bankruptcy Code: Claims and Distribution' (1983) 40 Washington and Lee L Rev 55, 56.

51 The rule was confirmed a number of times, *Ex p Barnaby* (1746) Cooke (8th edn) 269 (BC); *Ex p Elton* (1796) 3 Ves Jun 238, 30 ER 988 (BC); *Ex p Abell* (1799) 4 Ves Jun 837, 31 ER 434 (Ch); *Everett v Backhouse* (1804) 10 Ves Jun 94, 32 ER 779 (Ch); *Ex p Kensington* (1808) 14 Ves Jun 447, 33 ER 592 (BC); Eldon Notebook 1807–1809 p 3; *Ex p Peake* (1814) 2 Rose 54 (BC); *Re Wait* (1820) 1 J&W 605, 37 ER 449 (BC); *Bollin v York* (1823) CP Cooper 500, 47 ER 619 (Ch). It was codified in the Bankruptcy Act 1825 (6 Geo IV c 16), s 62. The accounts could be collapsed into one another by the consent of all the creditors, eg see *Ex p Barker* (1825) B 1/171, pp 118–21. Edward Christian, *The Origin, Progress and Present Practise of Bankrupt Law, Both in England and Ireland.* (1st edn, W Clarke & Sons 1812–1814) vol 2, 242–83; Joshua Getzler and Mike Macnair, 'The Firm as Entity before the Companies Acts' in Paul Brand, Kevin Costello, and WN Osborough (eds), *Adventures of the Law: Proceedings of the Sixteenth British Legal History Conference* (Four Courts 2005) 267, 275–85.

52 *Barnaby* (n 51); *Elton* (n 51).

53 For Lord Eldon's doubts see *Wait* (n 51).

54 Lord Loughborough would dispense with the rule in circumstances where the accounts were complicated (*Ex p Montague* (1794) B 1/89, pp 315–16; *Ex p Harris* (1794) B 1/89, pp 321–23) or there was a clear surplus (*Ex p Quintin* (1796) 3 Ves Jun 248, 30 ER 994 (BC); B 1/103, pp 9–13).

55 *Ex p Cobham* (1784) 1 Brown Ch Cas 576, 577; 28 ER 1307; noted in *Notes of Cases in Chancery and Exchequer 1780–1788*, held by Georgetown Law Library within the Lord Eldon Collection, at 327 ('Thurlow C said he was aware that [not allowing joint creditors to prove against the separate estate] was the constant practice but it did not seem founded on any Principle—for it was clear a joint Creditor was a Creditor on all the Partners & on each'); and *Ex p Copland* (1787) 1 Cox 420, 29 ER 1230 (BC). See also Eldon's notes on *Ex p Kensington* (1808) (n 51): Eldon wrote that Lord Hardwicke had said that joint creditors could not prove against the separate estate, but that 'Lord Thurlow thought otherwise', Eldon Notebook 1807–1809 p 3.

56 *Grey v Chiswell* (1803) 9 Ves Jun 118, 32 ER 547 (Ch); Eldon Notebook 1801–1802 pp 127–30, 194–98.

the personal financial affairs of the individual partners. It thus facilitated trade by reducing the cost of partnerships obtaining credit.

3. The Instability of Partnerships

3.1 The Ease of Dissolving Partnerships

Aspects of partnership law clearly bonded partners' joint assets to their business. However, a partnership's lack of legal personality made partnership law's asset partitioning effects relatively fragile. It took very little to dissolve a partnership, and even a new partner joining the firm would, as a matter of law, dissolve the old partnership and joint estate, and create a new one. Although the point was unsuccessfully challenged in the 1810s and 1820s, the default position was that a partnership could be unilaterally dissolved by any partner at any time by his retiring from the firm, his death, his bankruptcy, or simply at will.[57] Partners could expressly agree that the business was to continue beyond such an event, but the courts would refuse to infer such an agreement from the contractual obligations of the firm, the purchase of stock,[58] or the duration of leases belonging to the partnership.[59] The analogy is not explicitly drawn in the cases, but contemporaries recognised the parallel with the Roman rule that an agreement not to divide up partnership assets until a certain date would not be construed as an agreement to continue the partnership for that period.[60]

The English courts even took a restrictive view of express agreements to continue the business. For instance, Lord Eldon suggested that such a clause could never validly provide for the continuance of the partnership beyond the bankruptcy of one of the partners, on the basis that such a clause would be a fraud on the bankrupt laws.[61] Watson's treatise on partnership law states that the death of a partner would always dissolve a partnership,[62] as in Roman Law.[63] That being said,

[57] Eg see *Peacock v Peacock* (1808–09) 16 Ves Jun 49, 33 ER 902 (Ch). Also Watson, *A Treatise of the Law of Partnership* (n 6) 379–86; Gow (n 9) 268–85.

[58] *Featherstonaugh v Fenwick* (1810) 17 Ves Jun 298, 306–07; 34 ER 115, 118 (Ch); C 33/672, ff 362r–v, 368r.

[59] *Crawshay v Maule* (1818) 1 Swan 495, 504; 36 ER 479, 482–83 (Ch).

[60] D.17.2.14 (Ulpian).

[61] Eg see *Wilson v Greenwood* (1818) 1 Swan 471; 36 ER 469; 1 Wils Ch 233, 37 ER 97 (Ch). In the judgment Lord Eldon first says that he will express no opinion on the potential validity of such clauses, but nevertheless goes on to say that he doubts that they would be effective.

[62] Watson, *A Treatise of the Law of Partnership* (n 6) 358. Partners might covenant that upon the death of one of them, the others could effectively buy out the deceased partner's share, but such agreements would not necessarily be enforceable. For examples of such agreements in a precedent see ibid 489–94, 504–06.

[63] 'So completely is the partnership dissolved by the death of a partner, that partners when they form the partnership cannot even agree that they can at death be replaced as partners by an heir', D 17.2.59 (Pomponius), Alan Watson (ed), *The Digest of Justinian*, vol 4 (University of Pennsylvania Press 1985)

the precedents for partnership deeds in the appendix to the treatise do contain provisions governing what would happen on the dissolution of the firm following the death of a partner.[64] A more detailed treatment of the point is contained in Neil Gow's treatise on partnership.[65] Gow shows that a partnership would necessarily be dissolved by the death of a partner, but that an express stipulation in the partnership agreement could prevent the executor of a deceased partner seeking an account of the business, compelling its liquidation, and taking a share of the assets for the testamentary estate. For instance, it may provide that the continuing partners were to have an option to buy out the deceased partner's share. It was crucial that the clause specified exactly what was to happen upon the partner's death; a partnership agreement expressed to continue for a specific period, for instance, would not be enough.[66] The courts' strict approach in such cases appears to have been rooted in a desire to prevent the surviving partners being forced into trade with the executor or legatee of a deceased partner.[67] In turn, this would have exposed them to liability for debts contracted by the executor or legatee. This concern also explains why a partner, who purported to dispose of his share in the business without the power to do so under the articles of partnership, would be treated as declaring a trust over his share, rather than as forcing his co-partners into business with the disponee.[68]

Despite the strict rules governing when dissolution occurred, partnership law did allow partners a degree of control over the effects of dissolution. Where a partner wished to retire he would enter into an agreement usually involving a conveyance of the firm's goods to the continuing partner, an assignment (necessarily equitable[69]) of all the debts owing to the partnership to the continuing partner. In return, the continuing partner would typically covenant to pay off all the joint debts, and further pay the retiring partner the value of his share of the concern.[70] Partnership articles could also make provision for one partner to buy out the share

48. See also 'But if an agreement against dissolution is made, does it have validity? Pomponius, in a neat answer, says that such an agreement is null and void', D.17.2.14 (Ulpian).

64 Watson, *A Treatise of the Law of Partnership* (n 6) 489–96, 504–06.

65 Gow (n 9) 268–73.

66 *Gillespie v Hamilton* (1818) 3 Madd 251, 56 ER 501 (Ch). Where a partner bequeathed his share by will, and the executors or appointees refused to come into his place on the same terms on which he had been a partner, then his death would be deemed as dissolving the concern, *Kershaw v Matthews* (1826) 2 Russ 62, 38 ER 259 (Ch).

67 See for instance *Crawshay* (n 59).

68 *Pearson v Chamberlain* (1750) 2 Ves Sen 33, 28 ER 23 (Ch); *Crawford v Hamilton* (1818) 3 Madd 251, 56 ER 501; *Crawshay v Maule* (1818) 1 Swans 495, 36 ER 479; 1 Wil 181, 37 ER 79; *Bray v Fromont* (1821) 6 Madd 5, 56 ER 990; *Tatam v Williams* (1844) 3 Hare 347, 67 ER 415 (Ch). See Nathaniel Lindley, *A Treatise on the Law of Partnership* (5th edn, W Maxwell & Son 1888) 363–66.

69 Assignments of debts at common law were void, though the rule might be circumvented by use of a bill of exchange or warrant of attorney, see Joseph Chitty, *A Practical Treatise on Bills of Exchange, Checks on Bankers, Promissory, Bankers' Cash Notes, Bank Notes* (5th edn, Butterworth & Son; Clarke & Son; C Hunter; T Hamilton; W Walker and G Wilson; H Butterworth 1818) 7–9.

70 Eg *Ex p Harvey* (1825) B 1/171, pp 84–109; *Ex p Pyke* (1825) B 1/171, pp 257–60.

of the others, or to have the stock of the concern sold off.[71] If all the partners of a firm wished to retire they might agree to appoint a receiver to wind up the concern, and undertake to pay that receiver any money they later received in respect of the partnership's business.[72] Templates for partners seeking to draft a dissolution agreement in these terms were commonly featured in contemporary textbooks.[73] While it was uncontroversial that the retiring partner could sue his former partners for breach of the covenant,[74] difficulties arose as to the effect of this covenant on the old partnership's creditors. The creditors of a partnership which dissolved might be prejudiced in that the capital might be tied up in a new and potentially more risky trade, reducing their chance of having their debts honoured. Likewise, when the trade was continued by new partners, the partnership property would vest in them, drastically reducing the value available for distribution amongst creditors of the old concern.[75] The problem was exacerbated by the fact that, as above, partnerships were fragile and easily dissolved. The details of these issues will be considered in Chapter 7, but the point for present purposes is that creditors of a partnership could find themselves with only limited access to the business assets.

3.2 Jurisdiction over Partnership Disputes and Dissolution.

The fragility of partnership was compounded by the fact that the only court capable of hearing disputes between partners, the Court of Chancery, typically refused to do so unless the partners also sought to liquidate the business. Partnership disputes could not be dealt with by the courts of common law. Disputes between a partner and his firm would technically involve a partner suing himself, as the partnership had no legal personality. Common law procedure would not allow a man to sue himself.[76] Further, as above, determining a partner's share of his firm's assets required an account to determine any surplus which would remain of the joint stock after joint creditors were paid. This would require a Master, a specialised type of Chancery (and bankruptcy) judge, to take accounts: a court of common law could only have resolved such a question of fact using a jury, and cases involving complicated accounts would have been too complicated for a jury to resolve.[77]

[71] Eg *Ripley v Waterworth* (1802) 7 Ves Jun 425, 32 ER 172, Eldon Notebook 1802 pp 144–48, 176–77.
[72] As, for instance, in *Worth v Read* (1805) C 33/536, ff231v–232v.
[73] Cary (n 26) 332–35; Gow (n 7) 392–94.
[74] Eg *Musson v May* (1814) 3 V&B 194, 35 ER 452 (Ch).
[75] Though where the joint estate totally emptied, the joint creditors would be able to claim as separate creditors of the partners, see Chapter 7, text to (n 8).
[76] Eg see *Neale v Turton* (1827) 4 Bing 149, 130 ER 725 (KB). Nor could there be an action at law between two partnerships with a common living partner, *Bosanquet v Wray* (1815) 6 Taunt 597, 128 ER 1167 (CP). See Partnership Select Committee (n 14).
[77] *De Tastet v Shaw* (1818) 1 B&A 664, 106 ER 244 (KB).

While Lord Eldon's Chancery did have some jurisdiction over extant partners and would give directions on the meaning of a partnership's articles,[78] or rectify the partnership deed,[79] it by and large rejected claims brought in relation to going concerns.[80] In *Forman v Homfray* (1813),[81] Lord Eldon refused to allow a suit for account bought by one partner of an extant firm against another on the basis that dissolution was not sought.[82] Likewise, in *Cofton v Homer* (1818)[83] Lord Eldon ruled that a partner could only seek an account in Chancery to ascertain his share upon dissolution. Although in *Marshall v Colman* (1820),[84] Lord Eldon acknowledged that Chancery might intervene by injunction to force partners to comply with the particular terms of a continuing partnership, he made clear that it would only do so in cases of studied, intentional, prolonged, and continued inattention to the calls of one party upon the other to observe the partnership agreement. Given the ease with which partnerships could be dissolved, it is hard to imagine that such behaviour would not have effected dissolution.

The reason Lord Eldon refused relief to partners of going concerns was pragmatic, and does not seem to have been based on his reputed hostility to joint stock enterprise,[85] or the Roman rule providing that litigation between partners would dissolve the concern.[86] Lord Eldon's Chancery came under heavy public criticism for severe delays, and increasing backlog of work.[87] Cases were all heard by one of three judges, Lord Chancellor Eldon himself, the Master of the Rolls or, from 1813, the Vice Chancellor. Lord Eldon sought to prevent further congestion, by refusing

[78] *Baldwin v Lawrence* (1824) 2 S&S 18, 57 ER 251 (Ch).
[79] *Hodgson v Hancock* (1827) 1 Y&J 317, 148 ER 692 (Ch).
[80] Partnership Select Committee (n 14) 3.
[81] 2 Ves & B 329, 35 ER 344 (Ch).
[82] Note that in *Harrison v Armitage* (1819) 4 Madd 143, 56 ER 661 (Ch), Sir John Leach V-C argued that *Forman* applied only to cases of interim management, and that partners were entitled to suits for account in equity against one another for they had no other remedy *even where no dissolution was sought*. Michael Lobban sees Sir John's view as anomalous, and the contrary view as generally prevailing, Michael Lobban, 'Joint Stock Companies' in William Cornish and others (eds), *Oxford History of the Laws of England*, vol XII (OUP 2010) 614. Also see Story (n 22) 333–38.
[83] 5 Price 537, 146 ER 687 (Ch).
[84] 2 J&W 266, 37 ER 629 (Ch).
[85] Discussed in Chapter 2, text from (n 75) to (n 78).
[86] Note that in classical Roman law bringing a claim on the partnership agreement would generally dissolve the concern. That rule though was seen as rooted in the 'brotherly' nature of partnership in its origins governing family property, see D.17.2.65.pr, Buckland (n 13) 506–07, 512. English partnership law had no such origins, and Lord Eldon's actions are best understood on the basis of contemporary concerns.
[87] See Michael Taylor, *Substance of the Speech of Mr Michael Angelo Taylor in the House of Commons on Wednesday the 30th of May 1821 on the Delays in the High Court of Chancery of England and in the Appellant Jurisdiction of the House of Lords* (T Egerton 1821). For modern discussions see Henry Horwitz and Patrick Polden, 'Continuity or Change in the Court of Chancery in the Seventeenth and Eighteenth Centuries?' (1996) 35 J Brit Stud 25; Patrick Polden, 'The Court of Chancery 1820–1875' in William Cornish and others (eds), *Oxford History of the Laws of England*, vol XI (OUP 2010) 646–60; Ron Harris, *Industrializing English Law: Entrepreneurship and Business Organization, 1720–1844* (CUP 2000) 163–64; Victoria Barnes and James Oldham, 'Carlen v Drury (1812): The Origins of the Internal Management Debate in Corporate Law' (2017) 38 JLH 1, 19–25.

to allow it to be used to regulate the internal disputes between partners who remained on good enough terms to be willing to trade together. The point was made clearest in cases where Lord Eldon refused to grant relief to extant partnerships which had not first made use of dispute resolution mechanisms in the partnership articles.[88] In his own words 'if [a case] can be kept out of a Court of Equity, it should; and, therefore, the Court will not be astute to assist those who will not avail themselves of provisions in their deed'.[89]

Whatever Lord Eldon's motivations, it is clear that the courts would seldom provide redress to partners of a going concern involved in a dispute with one another. In this sense the rules cannot be said to have facilitated trade. Legally informed prospective partners would draw no comfort from the fact that, if a dispute later arose between the partners, litigating would require the dissolution of the firm. That being said, there is no evidence that this caused commercial parties to avoid entering into partnership with one another—especially given the lack of other forms of joint stock trading.

4. How Effective Was the Law of Partnership?

The partnership law of the Regency era did allow assets to be bonded to a particular business during its continuance, and so was able to act as organisational law. Its effectiveness was limited by the ease with which partnerships could be dissolved, and the fact the courts would only resolve partnership disputes where the parties sought to wind up the firm. It is therefore easy to see why modern commentators have by and large rejected the ability of partnerships to act as sufficient substitutes for corporation, and seen partnership law simply as a step towards later law's proper and inevitable recognition of the superior form of trading.[90] Partnership's tie to the personality of the partners limited its effectiveness as a means of raising and locking in capital, and so corporations and depersonalised markets for shares were needed in the nineteenth century as capital demands increased with the scale of production.[91]

However, it should be emphasised that this view is very much one formed in hindsight, turning on the tendency of modern corporate governance theorists and historians of management to regard functional separation of powers between

[88] *Waters v Taylor* (1807–08) 15 Ves Jun 10, 33 ER 658 (Ch); *Carlen v Drury* (1812) 1 V&B 154, 35 ER 61 (Ch); *Ellison v Bignold* (1821) 2 J & W 503, 37 ER 720 (Ch).

[89] *Ellison v Bignold* ibid 511, 723.

[90] See for instance Bishop Hunt, *Development of the Business Corporation in England, 1800–1867* (Harvard University Press 1936); Patrick Atiyah, *The Rise and Fall of Freedom of Contract* (Oxford 1979); Harris (n 87).

[91] Margaret Blair, 'Locking in Capital: What Corporate Law Achieved for Business Organizers in the Nineteenth Century' (2003) 61 UCLA L Rev 387.

owners and managers as necessary for optimal risk allocation in an economy.[92] Discontent with the stability partnership law offered is not apparent from contemporary sources: as Martin Daunton puts it, when general incorporation was eventually introduced 'Industrialists did not rush to adopt joint-stock organization, and did not appear to be aware that the law of partnerships imposed any serious constraints.'[93] While partnership's lack of stability compared to corporations may have made it hard to raise large amounts of fixed capital, the fixed capital requirements early in the nineteenth century were generally modest—raising such sum posed no problem for partners.[94] Indeed, the identification of the partnership with the personality of the partners could help the firms raise credit, as James Taylor argues.[95] In the typical case, partners were both owners and managers of the business, traded for their collective benefit on their own reputations, and were liable for the firm's debts personally. This was not regarded as problematic: indeed, it meant that partners were incentivised to trade responsibly and check each other's behaviour. In turn, this helped responsible partners to obtain credit,[96] especially in the early nineteenth century when 'capital markets were essentially local and personal rather than national and institutional'.[97] Although the corollary of partnership's dependence on the personality of the partners and their good relation were the unstable features examined above, those same features were thought to encourage good governance.

Corporations were seen as less trustworthy, for two main reasons. First, corporate privileges in the Regency era generally required an Act of Parliament, and the founders of a business would generally need parliamentary contacts to procure one.[98] For that reason, corporations were linked with corruption, and seen as 'smacking of monopolies and privilege'.[99] Secondly, because corporations involved a split between management and ownership, their directors were incentivised to

[92] Alfred Chandler, *The Visible Hand: The Managerial Revolution in American Business* (Harvard University Press 1977); Eugene Fama, 'Agency Problems and the Theory of the Firm' (1980) 88 J Pol Econ 288; Eugene Fama and Michael Jensen, 'Separation of Ownership and Control' (1983) 26 J L & Econ 301; John Wilson and Andrew Thomson, *The Making of Modern Management: British Management in Historical Perspective* (OUP 2006); Brian Cheffins, *Corporate Ownership and Control* (OUP 2008); Freeman, Pearson, and Taylor (n 5) 4–5.

[93] Martin Daunton, *Progress and Poverty: An Economic and Social History of Britain 1700–1850* (OUP 1995) 239; see also Ron Harris, 'The Private Origins of the Private Company: Britain 1862–1907' (339) 33 OJLS 2013.

[94] Daunton (n 93) 236–46; Michael Postan, 'Recent Trends in Accumulation of Capital' (1935) 6 Economic Hist Rev 1; see also William Cornish and others, *Law and Society 1750–1950* (Hart 2019) 250–52. Note that canal companies and overseas trading companies, which presumably required relatively large sums of fixed capital, were able to incorporate, see Introduction, text to (n 15).

[95] James Taylor, *Creating Capitalism: Joint Stock Enterprise in British Politics and Culture, 1800–1870* (The Boydell Press 2006) 23–32.

[96] On the link between personal reputation and credit see Thomas Gisborne, *An Enquiry into the Duties of Men in the Higher and Middle Classes of Society in Great Britain*, vol 2 (5th edn, J White; Cadell and Davies 1800) 237–38, 241–43.

[97] Daunton (n 93) 245.

[98] Taylor (n 95) 1 and 2, especially at 32–37; Freeman, Pearson, and Taylor (n 5) 77–78.

[99] Daunton (n 93) 238–39; Taylor (n 95) 122–25.

trade less responsibly than partners would have been—and so they were less competitive. As Adam Smith put it:

> The directors of [joint stock] companies, however, being the managers rather of other people's money than their own, it cannot well be expected that they should watch over it with the same anxious vigilance with which the partners in a private copartnery frequently watch over their own. Like the stewards of a rich man, they are apt to consider attention to small matters as not for their master's honour, and very easily give themselves a dispensation from having it. Negligence and profusion, therefore, must always prevail, more or less, in the management of the affairs of such a company. It is upon this account that joint stock companies for foreign trade have seldom been able to maintain the competition against private adventurers.[100]

The same point was made by others. The journalist and political philosopher William Godwin saw company directors as 'men fattened on the vitals of their fellow citizens',[101] while the Anglican clergyman and reformer Thomas Gisborne thought the only way to ensure directors of corporations acted responsibly was to ensure they had a large shareholding in the concern to give them a personal interest in its success—to make them more like partners.[102]

Contemporaries thus did not see partnership simply as a 'second best' for corporation: it was seen as the more commercially effective form because it provided both incentives to partners to trade responsibly *and* asset partitioning features—albeit asset partitioning features less extensive than those general incorporation and limited liability would allow for later in the century.

[100] Adam Smith, *An Inquiry into the Nature and Causes of the Wealth of Nations* (RH Capmbell and AS Skinner eds, OUP 1976 (first published 1776)) Part 1, Book 5, Chapter 1.

[101] Quoted in Roy Porter, *Enlightenment: Britain and the Creation of the Modern World* (Penguin 2009) 344.

[102] Gisborne (n 96) 376–77.

2
The Use of Trusts in Business Structures

Regency era traders did not solely have to rely on the default rules of partnership law to bond trade assets to a business. Although partnership rules by default did do this, and there were perceived advantages of firms run by manager partners, partnership agreements could be created which modified or excluded many of the default partnership rules to create more stable business entities. For instance, the rules providing that partners were to have management powers and inalienable shares could be excluded by express drafting. Further, the problems caused by the de facto dissolution of the partnership upon the death or retirement of any partner could be mitigated by settling business assets on trust. This meant settling legal title to the assets of the business on a fixed body of trustees, who acted as its legal personality, and held the assets for the benefit of the business owners. The device was commonly used in large partnerships, as shown by empirical work undertaken by Freeman, Pearson, and Taylor. Of the 224 large partnerships they examine between 1720 and 1840, 209 made use of trusts in their articles of association.[1]

This chapter explores the way that traders could make use of this device to try and emulate some of the benefits of incorporation, despite the business's lack of its own legal personality, and in the face of the perception of the owner-run partnership as the most stable and moral form of trading. In that way, it examines the extent to which the law of trusts met the needs of traders in the Regency era and so facilitated trade. In so doing, it will show that Regency era trusts were not simply part of the law of real property, as has commonly been supposed, but could be used in two forms of business: the deed of settlement company and the testamentary trading trust.

1. The Traditional View of Regency Era Trusts

Talking about 'commercial trusts' in the Regency era is unorthodox, and contradicts the dominant narrative concerning the evolution of the trust. According to this narrative, trustees in the late eighteenth and early nineteenth centuries typically held fixed assets, usually land, on trust for beneficiaries as part of a family

[1] Mark Freeman, Robin Pearson, and James Taylor, *Shareholder Democracies? Corporate Governance in Britain & Ireland before 1850* (University of Chicago Press 2012) 54. The partnerships they look at are all those with more than thirteen partners, ibid 14.

Capitalism Before Corporations. Andreas Televantos, Oxford University Press (2020). © Andreas Televantos.
DOI: 10.1093/oso/9780198870340.003.0003.

settlement. Following the rise of a wealthy Victorian middle class, the rise of commerce, and later changes in tax law in the early twentieth century, trusts came instead to encompass shifting funds of personal property, forcing trustees to take on a much greater managerial role than hitherto. These socio-economic changes caused trusts law doctrine to change, and prompted the development of more sophisticated fiduciary law, less strict restrictions on trustee remuneration, and more liberal default delegation and investment powers for trustees. Trusts became increasingly separated from land law and conveyancing law and played a greater role in the commercial context. This view is set out by Michael Chesterman.[2] Chantal Stebbings adopts a near identical narrative arguing that the burdens of trusteeship increased in Victorian England, brought about a shortage of gentlemen trustees, and gave rise to the professional trustee, and more investor-friendly trusts law.[3] Further, John Langbein uses this narrative to support his argument that the nature of trusts as agreements or bargains, though always present, has come to the fore in modern law.[4] Richard Nolan suggests that these same Victorian developments prompted the development of the notion of a trust as a fund.[5]

Aspects of this narrative are supported by the primary sources. For instance, Horwitz and Polden, in a sample of Chancery litigation as a whole taken from 1818 to 1819, found that 30.8 per cent of cases related to land holding, 32.2 per cent of cases related to the administration of estates, and 10.5 per cent of cases related to *inter vivos* trusts, the majority of which concerned marriage settlements.[6] This is consistent with the sample of Chancery orders examined by this author, which shows that the vast majority of cases concerning testamentary estates and marriage settlements involved real property, whilst the majority involved a trust of realty too. This focus on land is echoed in contemporary trusts law treatises. Sanders' treatise on trusts and uses, which went through four editions between 1790 and 1827, is essentially a book on trusts of realty and conveyancing.[7] Edward Sugden's edition of *Gilbert on Uses*,[8] and John Fonblanque's edition of *Ballow's Treatise on Equity*,[9] have a similar focus. However, drawing implications from structure of the

[2] Michael Chesterman, 'Family Settlements on Trust: Landowners and the Rising Bourgeoisie' in GR Rubin and David Sugarman (eds), *Law, Economy And Society, 1750–1914: Essays in the History of English Law* (Professional Books 1984).

[3] Chantal Stebbings, *The Private Trustee in Victorian England* (CUP 2002), echoed by Stuart Anderson, 'Trusts and Trustees' in William Cornish and others (eds), *Oxford History of the Laws of England*, vol XII (OUP 2010) 268–94.

[4] John Langbein, 'The Contractarian Basis of the Law of Trusts' (1995) 105 Yale LJ 625.

[5] Richard Nolan, 'Property in a Fund' (2004) 120 LQR 108.

[6] Horwitz and Polden, 'Continuity or Change in the Court of Chancery in the Seventeenth and Eighteenth Centuries?' (1996) 35 J Brit Stud 25, 33–34.

[7] Francis Sanders, *Essays on Uses and Trusts* (1st edn, W Walker 1791); Francis Sanders, *Essays on Uses and Trusts* (2nd edn, W Walker 1799); Francis Sanders, *Essays on Uses and Trusts* (3rd edn, W Walker 1813); Francis Sanders, *Essays on Uses and Trusts* (4th edn, W Walker 1824).

[8] G Gilbert, *Law of Uses and Trusts, with a Treatise of Dower* (Edward Sugden ed, 3rd edn, London 1811).

[9] Henry Ballow, *A Treatise of Equity*, vol 1 (John Fonblanque ed, 5th edn, J and WT Clarke 1820).

latter two works is perhaps dangerous, in that they were new editions of old works that were not restructured. On this basis, Holdsworth considered each to reflect the law of an earlier period than the date of publication would suggest.[10]

Further, it appears from this author's sample of the Chancery order books and Lord Eldon's own manuscript reports of eighteenth century cases,[11] that Regency era Chancery cases involving trusts of personalty, though not infrequent, were largely restricted to cases of marriage settlements and wills. Though trusts for the payment of debts generally by way of compromise with creditors were not uncommon in the Regency era, these tended to be litigated in the Bankruptcy court, rather than Chancery.[12] Chancery's focus on realty, marriage settlements, and wills is reflected in the treatise literature of the time. Henry Maddock's treatment of trusts in his 1815 treatise on Chancery deals principally with marriage settlements and legacies.[13] Further, while George Jeremy's treatise on equity does have a section on trusts of personalty, most of the section is spent distinguishing such trusts from those of realty, on which the author concentrates. Indeed, while Jeremy sets out the uses of trusts of realty, there is no similar treatment of trusts of personalty, and his section on point seems to presume that such trusts will simply relate to dispositions of personalty by will.[14]

Stebbings' supposition that trusts early in the nineteenth century did not usually give trustees the power to invest in businesses is supported by the court record too: none of the trusts in the examined sample of the Bankruptcy and Chancery order books contained investment powers of this kind.[15] Chancery's order books from the Regency era show that trust assets and trustee investment powers were usually limited to public funds and government securities,[16] Bank of England

[10] William Holdsworth, *A History of English Law*, vol xii (AL Goodhart and HG Hanbury eds, Methuen & Co 1952) 186–93.

[11] *Trial Notes*, Mss 26–36, Lord Eldon Collection, Georgetown Law Library.

[12] The Bankruptcy Court's order books show that it was not uncommon for an indebted trader to settle his assets (typically personalty) on trust for his creditors by way of composition, to thereby seek to avoid formal bankruptcy. The cases before the court involved cases where the settlor had become bankrupt after settling the trust, eg see *Ex p Gibb* (1805) B1/107, pp 16–17 (a partnership's assets had been settled on trust for partnership creditors, and the partners later went bankrupt. The creditors petitioned that the trustees be allowed to sell the assets for their benefit, this was allowed); *Ex p Hutchinson* (1825) B1/170, pp 374–88 (claim post-bankruptcy, that the trustees of the composition had acted in breach of trust, reference made to a Master); *Ex p Barker* (1825) B1/171, pp 118–21 (the joint and separate creditors of the partners had agreed that their personal and business assets were to be split up rateably as part of a composition and, after the bankruptcy of the partners, the creditors successfully petitioned that the court would administer the bankrupt estate on this basis). For a discussion see Thomas Gisborne, *An Enquiry into the Duties of Men in the Higher and Middle Classes of Society in Great Britain*, vol 2 (5th edn, J White; Cadell and Davies 1800) 248–50; John Fonblanque, *Observations on a Bill Now before Parliament for the Consolidation and Amendment of the Laws Relating to Bankrupts* (Philips and Yard 1824) 16–19.

[13] Henry Maddock, *In a Treatise on the Principles and Practice of the High Court of Chancery* (1st edn, J and WT Clarke 1815); Henry Maddock, *A Treatise on the Principles and Practice of the High Court of Chancery* (2nd edn, J and WT Clarke 1820).

[14] George Jeremy, *A Treatise on the Equity Jurisdiction of the High Court of Chancery* (J and WT Clarke 1828) 62–76 (personalty), 33–62 (realty).

[15] Stebbings (n 3) 128–62.

[16] *Kent v Mason* (1794) C 33/488, ff 66v–68r; *Smith v Francis* (1825) C 33/736, ff 1769r–1774v.

stock[17] and annuities,[18] stock[19] and annuities[20] of other banks, South Sea stock and annuities,[21] East India bonds,[22] and real property (including mortgages), though the 1825 sample also shows instances of trusts of Navy Annuities,[23] canal company shares,[24] London Assurance Company stock,[25] and London Dock Company stock.[26] Without exception these trusts involved little management discretion by trustees: trustees at most were required to buy a particular type of asset, and to distribute its income. Trustees rarely had discretion about what to invest in.[27] This would seem to disprove Martin Daunton's supposition that 'executors and trustees of marriage settlements had wide discretion in the use of large amounts of personal wealth', and that wide trustee investment powers in the early nineteenth century meant that trust assets were 'available for investment in a variety of outlets' and so played an important role in making credit available and meeting fixed capital needs early in the century.[28]

The widespread acceptance that trusts before the nineteenth century were devices for static property holding has encouraged modern judges to draw distinctions between 'traditional trusts', identified as analogous to the family settlements common at the start of the nineteenth century, and 'commercial trusts' which developed later. In particular, it is argued that some trusts law principles relating to equitable compensation for breach of trust,[29] and the requirement that a trustee not have free use of the assets he is given, which evolved in relation to 'traditional trusts', should not automatically be applied to 'commercial trusts'.[30]

[17] *Barclay v Wainewright* (1807) 14 Ves Jun 66, 33 ER 446; Eldon Notebook 1805–1807 pp 29–32, 38–40.

[18] *Barber v Barber* (1794) C 33/488, f 73r–75r.

[19] *Elwin v Scott* (1808) Eldon Notebook 1807–1809, p 79.

[20] *Holmes v Tring* (1794) C 33/488, ff 231v; *Dousberry v Johnson* (1794) C 33/488, f 38r; *Chirac v Maseres* (1794) C 33/488, ff 34v–37r.

[21] *Chirac v Maseres*, ibid; *Andrews v Andrews* (1794) C 33/488, ff 212v–214r.

[22] *Blondell v Preston* (1815) C 33/613, ff 1111r–1112r.

[23] *Palmer v Noble* (1825) C 33/736, ff 1538v–1540r.

[24] ibid.

[25] *In the Matter of Church* (1815) C 33/613, ff 1048r–1048v.

[26] *Pieschel v Paris* (1825) C 33/737, ff 2067v–2070v.

[27] For a very rare example of a trust where trustees had power to change investments see *Lord v Godfrey* (1819) 4 Madd 455, 56 ER 773 (Ch).

[28] Martin Daunton, *Progress and Poverty: An Economic and Social History of Britain 1700–1850* (OUP 1995) 244, 258–60, 488–89.

[29] See *Target Holdings v Redferns* [1996] AC 421; *AIB Group (UK) plc v Mark Redler & Co Solicitors* [2014] UKSC 58, [2015] AC 1503; Richard Nolan, 'A Targeted Degree of Liability' [1996] LMCLQ 161, 162; David Hayton, 'Unique Rules for the Unique Institution, the Trust' in S Degeling and J Edelman (eds), *Equity in Commercial Law* (Lawbook Company 2005).

[30] *Lomas v RAB Market Cycles* [2009] EWHC 2545, All ER (D) 313 (Ch D); *Pearson v Lehman Brothers Finance SA* [2010] EWHC 2914 (Ch); EWCA Civ 1544. Lord Briggs, writing extra-judicially, has argued that this principle is 'part of the common law of trusts which originated in the context of family estates and succession as far removed from the modern world (or jungle) of investment banking as it is possible to get', Michael Briggs, 'Has English Law Coped with the Lehman Collapse?' [2013] BJIBFL 131, 132.

2. The Deed of Settlement Company

2.1 Deed of Settlement Companies and the Bubble Act

The idea that trusts are primarily devices for landholding in the eighteenth and early nineteenth centuries, though widely held, is at odds with the literature on deed of settlement companies, also known as joint stock companies. These were unincorporated partnerships which made use of trusts to emulate some of the benefits of incorporation. In company archives, contemporary journals, and records of the opinions of counsel there is a wealth of evidence of such entities in the eighteenth and early nineteenth centuries, and they have been commented upon since Maitland.[31] Understanding their propagation turns on recognising the legal and economic circumstances of their origins.

In the late seventeenth and early eighteenth centuries there was a boom in investment of shares in corporations, which reached its height in 1720. One such corporation, the South Sea Company, which converted government debt into private shares in a putative overseas trading monopoly and needed inflows of fresh capital to maintain its share price, was concerned about competition from other entities which raised funds by selling shares. The South Sea Company was authorised to raise funds in this way by its Charter, granted in 1711, but many of its perceived competitors did so without Royal Charter, patent, or Act of Parliament. Others had charters, but had issued more shares than the charter allowed. The South Sea Company had taken on much of the national debt, more than £30 million, and wielded significant influence in Parliament.[32] To stymie competition, it was ultimately able to procure the passing of what has become known as the Bubble Act 1720.[33] The statute provided that it was a criminal offence to purport to act as a corporation, or to raise capital by issuance of transferable stock, without Act of Parliament, Royal Charter, or Patent.[34] Almost two months after the passage of the Act, the market crashed and the value of South Sea Shares plummeted.[35] In the

[31] Frederic William Maitland, 'Trust and Corporation' in HAL Fisher (ed), *The Collected Papers of Frederick William Maitland*, vol 3 (CUP 1911); Bishop Hunt, *Development of the Business Corporation in England, 1800–1867* (Harvard University Press 1936) 3-90; DuBois, *The English Business Company after the Bubble Act 1720–1800* (The Commonwealth Fund 1938); CA Cooke, *Corporation, Trust, and Company* (Manchester UP 1950) 7–126; Daunton (n 28) 239–40; Kam Fan Sin, *The Legal Nature of the Unit Trust* (Clarendon Press 1997) 7–27; Ron Harris, *Industrializing English Law: Entrepreneurship and Business Organization, 1720–1844* (CUP 2000); Henry Hansmann, Reiner Kraakman, and Richard Squire, 'Law and the Rise of the Firm' (2006) 119 Harv L Rev 1333; Michael Lobban, 'Joint Stock Companies' in William Cornish and others (eds), *Oxford History of the Laws of England*, vol XII (OUP 2010) 613–625; Freeman, Pearson, and Taylor (n 1) 21–32; Victoria Barnes and James Oldham, 'Carlen v Drury (1812): The Origins of the Internal Management Debate in Corporate Law' (2017) 38 JLH 1.

[32] Helen Paul, *The South Sea Bubble: An Economic History of Its Origins and Consequences* (Routledge 2010) 43–45.

[33] Cooke (n 31) 82–83; Harris (n 31) 60–78; Paul (n 32) 48.

[34] 6 Geo I c 18, s 18,

[35] Cooke (n 31) 82–83; Harris (n 31) 66; Paul (n 32) 50–53.

aftermath of the crisis, the Attorney General brought writs of *scire facias* against a number of corporations, forcing them to prove that their activities were within the terms of their charters.[36] By mid-1721 the economy had begun to recover,[37] and the criminal offence created by the Bubble Act was not much acted upon. An examination of the King's Bench rolls from the period of 1720 to 1730 by Armand DuBois reveals evidence of only a single prosecution under the Bubble Act, *Rex v Caywood* (1722). This appears to be the only prosecution on the Act during the century.[38]

While the Bubble Act was not rigidly enforced in the eighteenth century, it had two significant effects. First, consciousness of both the crash and the Act's provisions prompted officers of the Crown to became more reluctant to grant corporate status by Royal Charter. They would seldom do so for private domestic enterprise, and where they did grant incorporation, the terms would include strict clauses to (i) the limit the capital they might raise by issuing shares, (ii) restrict their transferability, and (iii) make clear the terms of the charter were not to be construed in any way which would infringe the Bubble Act.[39] In the early eighteenth century Royal Charter had been the main means of acquiring corporate status, and traders were driven to seek incorporation by Act of Parliament,[40] or simply to use unincorporated business forms: particularly from the middle of the century when advances in technology created a demand for capital for manufacturing.[41] Secondly, it caused traders more regularly to consult counsel on how to set up large joint stock businesses, because of fears about the Act's possible scope.[42]

Counsel involved responded to this challenge by creating 'deed of settlement' companies, partnerships with elaborately drafted articles—typically in collaboration with company promoters and officers.[43] In an in-depth study making extensive use of company archives, Armand DuBois has shown that businesses using such structures included the London corn factors, fire insurance companies, metal companies in Birmingham and the Midlands (including Matthew Bolton's), and the Birmingham Flour and Bread Company.[44] Such entities would exclude default rules of partnership in providing that: partners could alienate their shares;[45]

36 For details see DuBois (n 31) 5–10.
37 Paul (n 32) 52–53, 104–07.
38 DuBois (n 31) 10–11. The case is reported as *Rex v Caywood* (1721) 1 Strange 472, 93 ER 641.
39 ibid 12–41.
40 ibid 36–37.
41 TS Ashton, *The Industrial Revolution* (OUP 1964) 58–126. See also Harris (n 31) 168–98, 297–300 for an examination of which industries required joint stock trading to meet capital demands in the period 1721 to 1810.
42 DuBois (n 31) 3–5, 39–40.
43 Freeman, Pearson, and Taylor (n 1) 58–66.
44 DuBois (n 31) 215–80. See also Freeman, Pearson, and Taylor (n 1) 23.
45 In the eighteenth century this right was usually qualified in some way so as to avoid the Bubble Act, but in the early nineteenth century such qualifications became less common. Directors were typically given a veto over transfers of shares. See Freeman, Pearson, and Taylor (n 1) 200.

shareholder-partners would have no individual powers of management over the concern; control of the business was vested in a mixture of directors, a general court consisting of proprietors, and a fixed body of trustees who held the circulating partnership assets.[46] The use of the trustee device is less surprising than the orthodox account of the trading trust form's development suggests. In the eighteenth century, directors of corporations were often treated as trustees for their shareholders[47] and corporations were not seen as distinct from their shareholders.[48] Further, despite having legal personality, corporations such as the Bank of England often settled their property on trustees,[49] though this became less common.[50] That deed of settlement companies typically settled property on trust in this way is strong evidence that eighteenth-century lawyers were comfortable with the notion of trusts of circulating trade assets to be used in a business. Drawing from this phenomenon, historian Boyd Hilton argues that 'equity had developed [by the late eighteenth century] largely to protect business rights ... equity ... became *the* law for protecting the personal, associational, and institutional rights of the middling classes'.[51]

The use of trustees made sense for unincorporated companies and offered clear practical advantages. First, because the trustees held company assets for shareholders, this facilitated the transfer of shares simply by entry in the company's books, which acted as an assignment of equitable interests by a direction to hold to the use of another.[52] Secondly, any conveyance of land owned by the company required only the trustees to partake in the conveyance. Thirdly, although the device

[46] For the most detailed examination of the drafting of such deeds, with examples, see DuBois (n 31) 213–345; Freeman, Pearson, and Taylor (n 1) Ch 3. Also see Cooke (n 31) 86–87; Sin (n 31) 13–19. Sin argues that trustees had no decision-making role in a typical company, citing only the example of a precedent for an ale brewing company in John Collyer, *A Practical Treatise on the Law of Partnership* (London 1832) 734–59, 751, clause 98. However, DuBois shows that the role and powers of trustees varied between companies looking at a range of real examples of deeds of settlement. The trustees of the Phoenix Fire Office, for instance, managed the business alongside the directors, see DuBois (n 31) 238.

[47] Eg see *Child v Hudson's Bay Co* (1723) 2 P Wms 207, 208–09; 24 ER 702, 'The legal interest of all the stock is in the company, who are trustees for the several members', per Lord Macclesfield C; *Harrison v Pryse* (1740) Barnard Ch 324, 326; 27 ER 664, 665, per Lord Hardwicke. See Cooke (n 31) 69–76. Company directors were also treated as 'trustees' in respect of their duties to the corporation, *Charitable Corporation v Sutton* (1742) 2 Atk 400, 26 ER 642; 9 Mod 349, 88 ER 500, per Lord Hardwicke.

[48] Paddy Ireland, 'Capitalism without the Capitalist: The Joint Stock Company Share and the Emergence of the Modern Doctrine of Separate Corporate Personality' (1996) 17 JLH 40, 45–47.

[49] DuBois (n 31) 115–16. The practical reason for this is not clear. DuBois speculates that this was not for practical advantage, but the use of trustees was associated with security. John Scott, the later Lord Eldon, suggested the Bank of England may have done this to allow it to transfer government funds more freely than the Acts of Parliament creating the bank would otherwise allow, John Scott, *Opinion of March 21, 1794, Opinion Book III f.149*, Bank of England records, cited at DuBois ibid 190.

[50] Freeman, Pearson, and Taylor (n 1) 56.

[51] Boyd Hilton, *A Mad, Bad, & Dangerous People? England 1783–1846* (OUP 2006) 122 (emphasis as in the original).

[52] *Ashby v Blackwell and Million Bank* (1765) Amb 503, 505–06; 27 ER 326, 326–27; 2 Eden 299, 28 ER 913 (Ch). See DuBois (n 31) 360–61; Cooke (n 31) 70–71; Sin (n 31) 16–17. Freeman, Pearson, and Taylor suggests that trusts did not affect this issue, but cite no authority for the point, and do not explain the argument, Freeman, Pearson, and Taylor (n 1) 54.

was not perfect (as will be shown), the deed of settlement would usually provide that company litigation need be carried out in the name of the trustees only and did not require the participation of all the shareholder partners. After all, trustees would have legal title to both company property and debts owed to the business, and so could sue in the common law courts[53] for such debts in their own names without reference to the fluctuating body of shareholder-partners.[54] As Maitland imagined, the trustees could litigate at common law to protect the company's rights to these assets without reference to its ownership structure, which was hidden behind the trust.[55] Indeed, vesting partnership assets in trustees was designed to insulate the company from the effect of the rules effecting mandatory partnership dissolution upon any change of partners, which could have been particularly troublesome in concerns with hundreds or even thousands of shareholder-partners.[56] Trustees thus acted as the legal personality for the firm, typically three were appointed, and they often played no role in the management of the business.[57] However, it should be noted that deed of settlement companies could face difficulties in both finding and replacing trustees, especially in light of the restrictive law governing trustees' duties, remuneration, delegation powers, and unlimited liability.[58]

All in all, the advantages of deed of settlement companies have led commentators to argue that trusts therefore allowed firms the main advantages of incorporation free from state regulation, giving British traders an advantage over their foreign counterparts.[59] They operated largely outside the purview of Parliament and the courts in the eighteenth century, which did not endorse such entities per se, but pursued no policy of attacking them, especially as the Bubble Act came to be forgotten in the final decades of the century.

The position began to change in the early nineteenth century, and deed of settlement companies began to attract official attention. Newspapers and journals were filled with promotions for shares in companies, many of which appeared to be dubious;[60] use of company articles purporting to create limited liability and transferable shares had become more common;[61] and the Bubble Act had been largely forgotten. The flurry of economic activity seems to have been prompted by the

[53] But not in Chancery, see below at section 2.2.2.

[54] *Metcalf v Bruin* (1810) 12 East 400, 405; 104 ER 156, 158 (per Lord Ellenborough CJKB, 'We could not, indeed, invert the rules of law to enable persons to sue as a body or company who are not a corporation; but here the bond has been given to trustees [ie not in the name of the shareholder-partners], who are under no difficulty of suing upon it in their own names ... '). The point is not mentioned in Campbell's shorter report of the same case, (1810) 2 Camp 422, 170 ER 1204.

[55] Maitland (n 31).

[56] DuBois (n 31) 217.

[57] Freeman, Pearson, and Taylor (n 1) 55–57.

[58] DuBois (n 31) 222; Harris (n 31) 137–59.

[59] Daunton (n 28) 238–40, 243–46, 486–88; John Morley, 'The Common Law Corporation: The Power of the Trust in Anglo-American Business History' (2016) 116 Colum L Rev 2145.

[60] Hunt (n 31) 15–19.

[61] DuBois (n 31) 222–23; Cooke (n 31) 86–87.

suspension of the gold standard in 1797, the printing of money, and the stimulus to domestic investment which resulted from Napoleon's imposition of a blockade in 1806, which increased the demand for domestic production.[62] Concerns that this economic activity would result in another bubble and financial collapse led the Attorney General to present informations for the prosecutions of two companies acting contrary to the Bubble Act in November 1807.[63] In the period 1808 to 1812, there were two reported prosecutions under the Bubble Act, both of which were unsuccessful[64]—as well as one case where using an agent to buy shares in a deed of settlement company was found to be illegal;[65] and another where an indictment for conspiracy to deprive an individual of his office failed because the office was in a company found to be illegal under the Bubble Act.[66] There were also two (unsuccessful) attempts by company debtors to avoid liability by pleading the illegality of an unincorporated creditor company.[67] Although the Bubble Act was interpreted only as governing businesses which purported to create freely transferable shares, its revival nevertheless caused fear amongst the commercial classes.[68] The position is perhaps illustrated through the reaction to Lord Abbott CJKB's judgment in *Josephs v Pebrer* (1825).[69] Lord Abbott refused to allow a claim by a stockbroker against a client for unpaid shares, on the basis that the shares were in a company which was illegal under the Bubble Act. As shown in Figure 2.1, the decision was satirised in a contemporary cartoon showing Lord Abbott—with a large stick in one hand and the Bubble Act in another—poking a large bubble labelled 'speculation', as investors outside the stock exchange sink into quicksand with cries of despair.[70]

Matters came to a head during the boom of 1824 to 1825, during which 624 companies were floated with a total capitalisation of £372,173,300.[71] The wave of promotions began with ventures seeking to raise money to loan to the new governments of South America, but soon developed a domestic dimension also.[72] These developments were accompanied by a rush on Parliament by joint stock companies seeking incorporation, encouraged by the Bubble Act's revival in the

[62] See Introduction, text to (n 24) and from (n 24) to (n 28).

[63] Hunt (n 31) 17–18.

[64] *R v Dodd* (1808) 9 East 516, 103 ER 670 (KB); *The King v Webb* (1811) 14 East 406, 104 ER 658 (KB).

[65] *Buck v Buck* (1808) 1 Camp 547, 170 ER 1052 (CP) (an agent employed to purchase shares in an unincorporated company overcharged his principal, the claim to recover the sum failed due to the illegality of the company and the transaction under the Bubble Act).

[66] *R v Stratton* (1809), reported in Campbell's report to *Buck v Buck* ibid.

[67] *Pratt v Hutchinson* (1812) 15 East 511, 104 ER 936 (KB); *Brown v Holt* (1812) 4 Taunt 587, 128 ER 460 (CP).

[68] Hunt (n 31) 17–21; Cooke (n 31) 95–99; Harris (n 31) 235–41.

[69] 3 B&C 639, 107 ER 870.

[70] 'The bubble burst—or the ghost of an old act of parliament', BM 14765, *English Cartoons and Satirical Prints, 1320–1832*, see James Taylor, *Creating Capitalism: Joint Stock Enterprise in British Politics and Culture, 1800–1870* (The Boydell Press 2006) 116.

[71] Hunt (n 31) 45–47; Ashton (n 41) 155–56; Taylor (n 70) 106–08.

[72] Hunt (n 31) 31–32.

Figure 2.1 The Bubble Burst or the Ghost of an Old Act of Parliament

courts. Indeed, empirical work by Freeman, Pearson, and Taylor shows that from 1824 it became for the first time common for unincorporated companies to include clauses in their articles of association promising to seek incorporation through an Act of Parliament.[73] This ultimately prompted Parliament, led by a liberal conservative ministry, to repeal the Bubble Act altogether.[74]

It should be emphasised that abolition of the Bubble Act, while it may have eased pressure on Parliament for private acts of incorporation, did not reflect a widespread acceptance of large joint stock companies with transferable shares as valuable—as discussed in Chapter 1 such concerns were seen as less well managed than partnerships.[75] Lord Eldon expressed concerns, from the Bench[76] and in the House of Lords,[77] that allowing joint stock companies to raise large sums by selling freely transferable shares involved usurping privileges properly belonging to the Crown and Parliament, and were dangerous in creating opportunities for fraud and speculative bubbles.

[73] Freeman, Pearson, and Taylor (n 1) 52–53.

[74] Repealed by 6 Geo IV c 91 (1825). See Hunt (n 31) 30–41; Cooke (n 31) 102–06; Boyd Hilton, *Corn, Cash Commerce: The Economic Policies of Tory Government* (OUP 1978) 310–14; Harris (n 31) 250–68; Hilton, *A Mad, Bad, & Dangerous People* (n 51) 301–02, 325–28; Taylor (n 70) 117–21.

[75] See Chapter 1, Section 4.

[76] *Kinder v Taylor* (1824–25) LJR Ch 68; *Van Sandau v Moore* (1826) 1 Russ 441, 38 ER 171; 4 LJR Ch 177; *The Times* 16 August 1826 col 2f (Ch). For discussion see Harris (n 31) 241–45.

[77] Hunt (n 31) 34–42; Cooke (n 31) 103–04; Harris (n 31) 256–68; Taylor (n 70) 108.

Although Lord Eldon's views are often portrayed as conservative, reactionary, and exceptional, others made very similar observations. There was wider concern that the flurry of speculation was another Bubble, which like that of 1720, would burst. As James Taylor has pointed out, *The Times* was convinced that the speculation would mark the end of England's 'commercial greatness' and 'national power',[78] though the paper ultimately thought the Bubble Act was not enough to deal with the problem,[79] while Parliamentary condemnation of bubble schemes was also common.[80] The Prime Minister Lord Liverpool made clear in the House of Lords that 'the spirit of speculation was going beyond all bounds, and was likely to bring the greatest mischief on numerous individuals', and that as a result the government was 'determined not to give relief, or listen to any claims made on account of distress, arising from such sort of speculations', were investors to lose their money.[81] Sir William Haygate MP,[82] a prominent Merchant Taylor and partner in a banking partnership, expressed concerns in the House of Commons about 'those projects which had grown out of the high price of stock, and which, if stocks fell again, would disappear like the South Sea bubble'.[83] The merchant banker Alexander Baring MP[84] went further in denouncing the promotion of dubious joint stock companies. Baring's own bank had largely avoided investing in the new spate of joint stock companies appearing in the 1820s,[85] and in the House of Commons he made his worries about dubious companies selling shares plain:

> It was deplorable to see the gambling mania that was at present abroad; it had seized upon all classes, and was spreading itself in all parts of the country. If it was to be lamented that men of the first rank and family in the country haunted gaming-houses at the west-end of the town, it was still more to be lamented, that merchants at the east-end of it should imitate their example, and make a gaming-house of the Royal Exchange. He saw no difference between the gambling of the nobleman in the hells of St. James's-street, and the gambling of the merchant on the Royal Exchange; except that the latter kept earlier hours and more respectable company than the former. The evil was certainly one which deserved to be checked; though he hardly knew how the check could be applied . . .
>
> It was ridiculous to see the objects for which joint-stock-companies were forming every day. We heard first of a milk company—then of a bread

78 5 November 1825.

79 *The Times*, 4, 5, 8 February 1825, see Taylor (n 70) 117.

80 Taylor ibid 113–17.

81 HL Deb 25 March 1825, vol 12, col 1194–95.

82 Margaret Escott, 'Heygate, William (1872–1844)' in DR Fisher (ed), *The History of Parliament: The House of Commons* (CUP 2009) <http://www.historyofparliamentonline.org/volume/1820-1832/member/heygate-william-1782-1844#footnoteref2_0ey8i3p> accessed 18 March 2020.

83 Hansard ns xi 99 (2 April 1824).

84 John Orbell, 'Baring, Alexander' in Sir David Cannadine (ed), *The Oxford Dictionary of National Biography* (OUP 2008) <https://doi.org/10.1093/ref:odnb/1380> accessed 18 March 2020.

85 Philip Ziegler, *The Sixth Great Power: Barings, 1762–1929* (Collins 1988) 97–98; Orbell (n 84).

> company—then of a brick-bat company, and last of all a lime company, which was to have a joint stock of 150,000*l.*, to work eleven acres of chalk. What to do with these companies he knew not; but that something should be done was quite indispensable.[86]

Ultimately, the nay-sayers proved right, and the boom of 1824 to 1825 was followed by a market crash in 1825 to 1826, most of the companies created during boom did not survive the crises, and all appear to have dissolved by 1843.[87] Country banks—private banks which traded outside of London—were equally hard hit: fifty-seven had declared bankruptcy between January 1825 and February 1826.[88]

For this reason, the repeal of the Bubble Act did not serve to legitimise large joint stock corporations which sold shares, in either the eyes of the public or the courts. Company promoters hawking fraudulent schemes had induced the public to set aside hard work in favour of gambling, and so contributed to the rising bankruptcy rates and more frequent market crashes of the early nineteenth century.[89] It is no coincidence that Ralph Nickleby, the avaricious villain of Dickens' *The Life and Adventures of Nicholas Nickleby* (1839), had been a stock jobber for a dubious enterprise before the deep market crash of 1825–26.

Politicians too bore the blame—particularly given the willingness with which Parliament had granted acts allowing the very joint stock companies which caused the crash to sue and be sued in their own names. As James Taylor puts it, the crisis:

> reaffirmed the link in the public mind between companies and corruption. One key aspect of this corruption stemmed from the relationship between companies and parliament. There was enormous potential for corruption in the procedure by means of which acts of incorporation were sought. Promoters of joint-stock schemes were quite willing to bribe MPs with shares or directorships in order to secure a favourable hearing for their companies. The temptations held out to MPs to become the agents of outside economic interests was [sic] huge.[90]

MPs were thus seen as having colluded with company promoters to confer privileges upon them in return for personal benefit, and so encouraging the public to advance money towards projects which had no chance of being brought to fruition. Discontent was made apparent at the ballot box. Of the thirty-one MPs who had

[86] Hansard 1063–1064 (16 March 1825).

[87] Hunt (n 31) 47; Harris (n 31) 41–42; Taylor (n 70) 121–22.

[88] *Return of Number of Country Banks issuing Notes which became Bankrupt 1816–1826*. HC Papers 27 February 1826, vol 22, p XXII.5 (Paper 94).

[89] Boyd Hilton, *Age of Atonement: The Influence of Evangelicalism on Social and Economic Thought, 1785–1865* (Clarendon Press 1997) ch 4; Taylor (n 70) 93–125.

[90] Taylor (n 70) 122.

held at least three company directorships, fifteen were either defeated or did not stand for election in 1826. Ten of these MPs never returned to Parliament.[91]

It is perhaps unsurprising then that judges continued to threaten to declare joint stock companies with transferrable shares illegal, even after the repeal of the Bubble Act. Lord Eldon thought that raising sums by selling freely alienable shares without Act of Parliament or Royal Charter remained an offence at common law.[92] He had insisted that the Act which repealed the Bubble Act included the clause that such 'undertakings should be adjudged and dealt with according to the common law', to preserve the possibility that such companies could be declared illegal.[93] Although this view is often attributed to Lord Eldon's particular hostility to such companies, the same view had been expressed in 1720 when the Act was passed,[94] as well as in *The Times* in 1825.[95] Although unincorporated joint stock companies were not uncommon in the period 1790 to 1827, their numbers only really surged again in the 1830s, and it was only in the 1840s that Parliament, the public, and the judiciary adopted a different approach.[96] This change was not so much due to an acceptance that the corporate form was the most economically advantageous, but a belief that such entities would cause less mischief if registered, regulated, and brought within the law, rather than being allowed to operate on the borders of legality as they had done since the eighteenth century.[97]

2.2 The Limitations of Deed of Settlement Companies and Partnership Law

Threats of illegality under the Bubble Act and the common law were not the only obstacles to deed of settlement companies acting as effective substitutes for limited liability corporations with legal personality. The main reason was that courts of the Regency era, especially Lord Eldon's Chancery, refused to treat deed of settlement companies as anything other than partnerships: the trust played only a minor role in their constitution, and did not oust most of the partnership law rules. Although CA Cooke has asserted that deed of settlement companies were not treated as partnerships in the eighteenth and nineteenth centuries, and were recognised by equity as separate, he cites no authority for that assertion from before 1852.[98] Early

[91] ibid.

[92] See *Kinder v Taylor* (n 76). Also see ibid 118.

[93] See Hunt (n 31) 41–42; Cooke (n 31) 99–100; Harris (n 31) 245.

[94] Sergeant Thomas Pengelly, a leading lawyer engaged to advise on the Bubble Act in the wake of its enactment, took the view that the Act simply put a pre-existing offence at common law on a statutory footing, see DuBois (n 31) 5.

[95] 4, 5, 8 February 1825. See Taylor (n 70) 117–18.

[96] Hunt (n 31) 43–44, 56–89; Cooke (n 31) 106–26; Harris (n 31) 247–49; Taylor (n 70) 125–34.

[97] Taylor (n 70) 4.

[98] Cooke (n 31) 86–87, 95–96. The case is *Hallett v Dowdall* (1852) 21 LJQB 98, 104.

nineteenth century treatises[99] and even Henry Bellenden Ker's *Report on the Law of Partnership* (1837)[100] treated joint stock companies simply as partnerships. As DuBois explains:

> One is not justified … in regarding this hybrid of the times [the deed of settlement company] as something new or even *sui generis*, for the eighteenth century specialist, be he financier or solicitor, saw it only as a partnership, and the courts had yet to wrestle with the theories that eventually were to accord it a particular status in the hierarchy of business units.[101]

It would only be later in the nineteenth century with the development of impersonal markets in shares, that companies would come to be seen as legally distinct from partnerships.[102]

The fact that deed of settlement companies were treated by the courts as large partnerships formed two obstacles to their effectiveness as a surrogate for limited liability corporations. First, shareholders faced unlimited liability for the debts of the firm. Secondly, deed of settlement companies and their shareholders struggled to make use of the courts, Chancery in particular.

2.2.1 Unlimited Liability of Shareholders.

Shareholders of a deed of settlement company were in law partners of the firm, and this meant that they were personally liable without limit for the firm's debts.[103] While shareholders would not be typical partners, in that a deed of settlement would provide for a split in the firm's ownership and management, they were by definition partners in having pooled assets for the purpose of running business of which they were to receive a profit.[104] The point is made clearest by the law on silent partners—investors in partnerships who were to play no role in the business's management and whose names were not used by the trade. Despite having no power to bind the firm's stock or credit under the partnership agreement, such partners were

[99] N Gow, *A Practical Treatise on the Law of Partnership* (1st edn, C Hunter 1823) 3 ('The laws respecting these companies or societies [large companies which issued shares] when not confirmed by public authority, are the same as in ordinary partnerships; but the articles of agreement between the parties are usually very different.'); Charles Wordsworth, *The Law of Joint Stock Companies* (5th edn, W Benning & Co 1845) 15–16.

[100] Henry Bellenden Ker, 'Report from the Select Committee on the Law of Partnership' (HC 1837, 530-XLIV).

[101] DuBois (n 31) 40. See also Ireland, 'Capitalism without the Capitalist' (n 48) 42–47; Paddy Ireland, 'Company Law and the Myth of Shareholder Ownership' (1999) 62 MLR 32, 39–41; Paddy Ireland, 'Finance and the Origins of Modern Company Law' in Grietje Baars and Andre Spicer (eds), *The Corporation: A Critical, Multi-Disciplinary Handbook* (CUP 2017) 239–40 ('In short, there was nothing at this time resembling a developed and comprehensive corporate legal form for joint stock companies clearly distinguishable from that provided by the law of partnership').

[102] Ireland, 'Capitalism without the Capitalist' (n 48).

[103] See *R v Dodd* (1808) 9 East 516, 527; 103 ER 670, 674 (per Lord Ellenborough CJKB).

[104] See Chapter 1, Section 1.

fully liable to partnership debts, and (in the absence of provision to the contrary in the partnership agreement) were entitled to a rateable share of the partnership stock upon dissolution, after the creditors had been paid.[105]

Although a company's deed of settlement might provide that the shareholders had limited liability,[106] such clauses were not fully effective. As with a typical partnership, the effect of such a clause was that each shareholder could demand that the company's property be used to pay its debts. If the firm's assets were not sufficient to meet its liabilities, its creditors could personally sue the shareholders, unless the creditors had agreed not to do this.[107] The fact that shareholders of a company personally were liable for its debts explains why Lord Eldon proposed creating a register of shareholders of companies which were authorised by Act of Parliament to sue in the corporation's name. The point of the proposal was that creditors of the company could identify and sue the shareholders more easily, where the company defaulted on payment of its debts.[108]

It should be noted some modern commentators have instead argued that the use of trusts in the deed of settlement company did create limited liability for shareholders. The argument is developed most by John Morley. Morley contends that only the trustees of a deed of settlement company were liable for its debts, and that Chancery would sometimes allow a claim for the debts against the trustees without the beneficiaries being added as parties.[109] He recognises that in the 1820s shareholders were seen as partners, and so fully liable to a firm's debts, but sees the development as no earlier than that.[110]

The argument would have surprised contemporaries. While Morley rightly points out that trustees would be liable personally to debts they entered into as such—and so creditors would not need to sue beneficiary-shareholders—this did not limit the liability of beneficiary-shareholders. There is authority from the 1780s that a beneficiary of a trust of a business was liable to be sued upon the business's debts, having had a share of the profit as a partner.[111] In *R v Dodd* (1808),[112] Lord Ellenborough discussed the liabilities of shareholders of a large deed of settlement company in the following terms:

[105] Gow (n 99) 14–18.
[106] This varied considerably by sector, see Freeman, Pearson, and Taylor (n 1) 190–98.
[107] DuBois (n 31) 222–23; Cooke (n 31) 87; Freeman, Pearson, and Taylor (n 1) 53–54.
[108] Hansard NS xi 1456–57 (18 June 1824) (Lord Eldon also suggests that creditors of such companies should be able to recover the full amount of any debt by suing only some of the partner-shareholders, and that, to preserve the register's efficacy, transfers of shares should be null until registration). See also Taylor (n 70) 108.
[109] Morley (n 59) 2174–79, esp 2176–77, citing *City of London II* (1702) 1 Bro Parl Cas 516, 518; 1 ER 727, 728 (HL). See also Daunton (n 28) 239–40; Freeman, Pearson, and Taylor (n 1) 53–54.
[110] Morley (n 59) 2176.
[111] *Hankey v Hammock* (1786), sometimes referred to as *Hankey v Hammond*. A note of the case is contained in a footnote to *Ex p Richardson* (1818) 3 Madd 138, 56 ER 461 (BC), which is taken from Chancery's order book at C 33/467, ff 84v–85v. For further discussion of the point see Section 3.1 below.
[112] (n 64).

> As to the subscribers themselves, indeed, they may stipulate with each other for this contracted responsibility; but as to the rest of the world it is clear that each partner is liable to the whole amount of the debts contracted by the partnership.[113]

In short, it is clear that throughout the Regency era that shareholders of deed of settlement companies were simply partnerships. The use of the trusts in their constitution did not change this, and so could not protect shareholders from liability for the firm's debts. It would only be much later in the nineteenth century—after the introduction of general incorporation and limited liability—that courts would come to see the use of a trust as excluding the existence of a partnership.[114] Even then, there was authority that a trustee could sue the beneficiary personally for expenses where the trust assets were exhausted.[115] The use of a trust would not have given beneficiary-shareholders limited liability.

2.2.2 Making Use of Chancery

Perhaps more significantly, deed of settlement companies struggled to make use of Chancery throughout the long eighteenth century. Although they might use the common law courts,[116] opinions of counsel, and arbitration, the inability to use Chancery was problematic. A Chancery suit would have been necessary in complex matters where a Chancery Master was needed to take accounts, which would not have been possible at common law, as well as in disputes between a joint stock company and one of its shareholders—who was technically a partner in the concern.[117] Although a number of commentators have suggested that deed of settlement companies did successfully bring Chancery suits throughout the eighteenth century, they put forward relatively little evidence to support the claim. Armand DuBois cites a single unreported case,[118] while CA Cooke cites no examples at all.[119]

[113] ibid 527, 674. For later authority see *Ex p Low* (1825) B 1/170, pp 230–38.

[114] *Cox v Hickman* (1860) 8 HLC 267 (HL); *Smith v Anderson* (1880) 15 Ch D 247 (Ch).

[115] *Hardoon v Belilios* [1901] AC 118. As regards the Regency era, *Myler v Fitzpatrick* (1822) 6 Madd 360, 56 ER 1128 (Ch), Sir John Leach V-C appeared to suggest that a trustee de son tort could personally claim against beneficiaries for expenses where the trust assets were exhausted, but there was no direct decision on point. However, Lord Nottingham in *Pollard v Downes* (1682) 2 Ca in Ch 121, 22 ER 876 (Ch), appears to have ordered a trustee to account to the beneficiary, without the beneficiary accounting the trustee first (presumably for his expenses), but the case is very briefly reported and there is no record of it in Yale's edition of Nottingham's Chancery cases. In 1837, Lewin inclined to the opinion that where the trust failed, the trustees would have a personal claim for their expenses against the beneficiaries, T Lewin, *The Law of Trusts* (1st edn, A Maxwell 1837) 455.

[116] See for instance *Metcalf v Bruin* (1810) 2 Camp 422, 170 ER 1204; 12 East 400, 104 ER 156 (KB); *Pratt v Hutchinson* (1812) 15 East 511, 104 ER 936 (KB); *Brown v Holt* (1812) 4 Taunt 587, 128 ER 460 (CP); *R v Ramsbottom* (1818) 5 Price 446, 146 ER 660; (1819) 7 Price 540, 146 ER 1064 (Ex).

[117] See Chapter 1, Section 3.2.

[118] *Hollis v Childer*, C 12/807/22 (1756), DuBois (n 31) 227–28.

[119] Cooke (n 31) 96.

John Morley cites two cases.[120] The first, *Lynch v Dalzell* (1729)[121] concerned a claim on an insurance policy: the managers and trustees of the firm who had personally entered into the policy were sued. The only reason the claim was brought in Chancery was because the policy had been assigned: and contractual rights not being assignable at law, the only way such an assignment could have been effective was in equity. *Horsley v Bell* (1778)[122] concerns a statutory company set up by Act of Parliament to make a river navigable. Lord Thurlow LC ruled that the commissioners appointed to carry out the concern were liable personally for the debts contracted by the company, as trustees—despite the fact the firm had been given corporate status by an Act of Parliament. The judgment is the very opposite of evidence that trusts were used by private parties to emulate corporate privileges: it is an example of Lord Thurlow's Chancery using trusts law reasoning to deny corporate privileges to an entity created by Act of Parliament. Indeed, both *Lynch* and *Horley* involved joint stock companies being sued rather than bringing claims, and so are not good evidence of joint stock companies making use of Chancery. There is very little evidence that they were able to do so.

Although Morley suggests 'that the most likely explanation for the dearth of reports is simply that Chancery reporting was inconsistent during this period, recording only a fraction of the cases decided', the explanation only goes so far. It does not explain why there is not a single case involving a large joint stock company in Lord Eldon's extensive collection of manuscript reports of eighteenth century Chancery cases.[123]

It also does not explain why in the late eighteenth and early nineteenth centuries—a time when there is plenty of other evidence that such entities existed and were trading—there is little trace of them, either in printed materials, the records of Chancery and the Bankruptcy Court, or Lord Eldon's judicial notebooks. In this author's own sampling of court orders, the largest partnership mentioned in a Chancery case had only 10 partners,[124] whilst there was no reference to any large partnerships in a Bankruptcy case.[125] There are only two references to large deed of settlement companies in Lord Eldon's judicial notebooks.[126] Although there are

[120] Morley (n 59) 2172 at note 181.

[121] IV Brown 431, 2 ER 292 (HL).

[122] *Horsley v Bell* (1788) Amb 770, 27 ER 494 (Ch); reported also in the note to *Cullen v Duke of Queensberry* (1781) 1 Bro CC 101, 28 ER 1011 (Ch).

[123] (n 11).

[124] *Hanson v Green* (1815) C 33/613, ff 1731r–1736r.

[125] The lack of bankruptcy cases requires a different explanation, because it shows creditors of deed of settlement companies did not sue out commissions of bankruptcy against them. It might be speculated that this was because (i) such entities tended to raise funds through issue of stock rather than borrowing money, (ii) issuing a joint commission against hundreds or thousands of shareholders would be disproportionately costly and difficult, (iii) the joint credit of so many shareholders meant that creditors were paid without the need for bankruptcy proceedings. DuBois suggests that such companies might have procedures for dissolution, sometimes obtained Acts of Parliament for a formal dissolution, or compromised with creditors by issuing them with stock, DuBois (n 31) 373–75.

[126] *Redfearn v Somervail* (1813) I Dow 50, 3 ER 618 (HL, appeal from Scotland); Eldon Notebook 1813 pp 16–19; *Bond v Campbell* (1812) Eldon Notebook 1812–21 pp 9–10 (unreported). The 1811

more reported cases involving such entities suing or being sued, the numbers again are relatively few—even after Chancery reporting became continuous.[127] In sum, the balance of evidence suggests that throughout the long eighteenth century joint stock companies made little use of Chancery.

There are two potential explanations for these findings, which are not inconsistent. The first is simply that deed of settlement companies avoided courts in the eighteenth century due to concerns about the Bubble Act and were further incentivised to keep away in the Regency era because of the costs and delays in Chancery's procedure during that time.[128] After all, such companies had made extensive use of arbitration in the eighteenth century, and Chancery's increasing backlog would have formed little incentive to change this practice.

A second explanation is revealed by the cases themselves, which represent early instances of judicial scrutiny of business organisational forms which had developed extra-judicially in the eighteenth century. These show that the way Chancery's procedure applied to partnerships could form a significant obstacle to court use by deed of settlement companies.

First, as stated in Chapter 1,[129] Lord Eldon would refuse to interfere with the internal workings of ongoing partnerships where the partners had any other avenue of redress open to them, and the general partnership rules on point were decided in cases concerning deed of settlement companies.[130] In particular, in *Ellison v Bignold* (1821)[131] he made clear that the rule applied to a deed of settlement company of 2,000 people on the basis that it was a 'general partnership'.[132] The rule could make it difficult for shareholders to call managers to account.

Likewise, Chancery's rules concerning joinder of parties to a suit—namely who had to be named when bringing a claim or being sued—could cause problems for deed of settlement companies. As above, companies sought to avoid having to add shareholders as parties to any litigation concerning them, by providing that trustees alone had to conduct the firm's litigation. As regards common law

pleadings and an 1812 Bill of Revivor for *Bond v Campbell* are in the national archives at C13/138/8, but there appears to be no indexed entry in the court's orderbooks for a case involving any party named *Bond* or *Campbell* and a Joint Stock Corporation between 1811 and 1820. The case may never have proceeded to judgment.

[127] *Carlen v Drury* (1812) 1 V&B 154, 35 ER 61 (Ch); *Waters v Taylor* (1807–08) 15 Ves Jun 10, 33 ER 658; 2 V &B 299, 35 ER 333 (Ch); *Bond v Campbell* (n 126); *Ellison v Bignold* (1821) 2 J&W503, 37 ER 720; *Jones v Garcia del Rio* (1823) T&R 297, 37 ER 1113 (Ch); *Natusch v Irving* (1824) 2 CTC 358, 47 ER 1196 (Ch). Neil Gow, *A Practical Treatise on the Law of Partnership* (3rd edn, C Hunter and J Richards 1830) 398; *Kinder v Taylor* (n 76); *Blain v Agar* (1826) 1 Sim 37, 57 ER 492 (Ch); *Van Sandau v Moore* (n 76); *Eyre v Everett* (1824) 2 Bing 166, 130 ER 269 (CP); (1826) 2 Russ 381, 38 ER 379 (Ch). Also see Lord Eldon's observations in *Redfearn v Somervail* (n 126).

[128] Chapter 1, text from (n 86).

[129] Chapter 1, Section 3.2.

[130] *Waters* (n 127); *Carlen* (n 127); *Ellison* (n 127).

[131] 2 J & W 503, 37 ER 720 (Ch).

[132] ibid 723.

litigation, this would be effective. However, such large companies often would have required Chancery's accounting procedures to resolve disputes which would have been too complicated for a jury,[133] or otherwise involve disputes internal to the firm.[134] Chancery's procedures instead required all those beneficially interested in a suit—that is all the shareholder-partners of a firm—to be added as parties. The only exception was where an Act of Parliament had been granted to allow the company to conduct litigation in the name of its secretary or treasurer:[135] though even then Chancery treated the issue of whether all the shareholders had to be added in any litigation as relating to its discretion to set aside joinder requirements, rather than as a natural consequence of corporate personality granted by an Act of Parliament.[136]

The joinder requirements could create problems for deed of settlement companies and those that dealt with them.[137] Lord Eldon as early as *Lloyd v Loaring* (1802)[138] made clear that he did not think that partners should be able to sue in a corporate capacity. Chancery did have discretion to dispense with the requirement that all shareholder-partners be added as parties to a claim concerning a firm,[139] and Eldon himself did so on occasion,[140] though Morley's claim that such dispensation was automatic goes too far, at least as the Regency era.[141] Defendants continued to demur to bills brought by shareholder-partners on the basis that not all the shareholder-partners had been added as claimants.[142] For instance in *Jones v Garcia el Rio* (1823)[143] and *Blain v Agar*

[133] For a detailed account of such a dispute and its complexity see Barnes and Oldham (n 31).

[134] These could not be heard at common law, in that a shareholder in suing the firm (or vice versa) would technically be suing himself. This was not allowed under common law procedure, see Chapter 1, text to (n 76).

[135] Lobban (n 31) 616–17. Note such an Act would only allow the company to conduct normal litigation in the treasurer or secretary's name, not to sue out a commission of bankruptcy against a company debtor, *Guthrie v Frisk* (1824) 3 B&C 178, 107 ER 700 (KB).

[136] *Meux v Maltby* (1818) 2 Swan 277, 36 ER 621 (MR).

[137] DuBois (n 31) 220–21.

[138] 16 Ves Jun 773, 777; 31 ER 1302, 1304 (Ch).

[139] John Mitford, *A Treatise on the Pleadings in Suits in the Court of Chancery by English Bill* (J and WT Clarke 1827) 164–81. For older examples see *City of London v Richmond* (1701) 2 Vern 421, 23 ER 870 (Ch) (all the assignees of shares in a lease did not need to be added to a claim for rent by the lessor); *Chancey v May* (1722) Pec in Ch 592, 24 ER 265 (Ch) (some partners allowed to seek an account against their co-partners, without adding themselves as defendants, though note that the partners as claimants were parties to the claim).

[140] *Adair v The New River Company* (1805) 11 Ves Jun 429, 32 ER 1153 (Ch) (the claimant had a right to rents from the holder of a moiety of the profits of the New River Company. That moiety had itself been split into shares and assigned to various parties, only some of whom were sued. The claim did not fail for want of parties); *Waters v Taylor* (n 127) (a claim by a mortgagee of shares to enforce the security against the firm did not fail though not all the shareholders were added as parties); *Cockburn v Thompson* (1809) 16 Ves Jun 321, 33 ER 1005 (account claim bought by some shareholder-partners against the solicitors and bankers of the firm allowed); *Pearce v Piper* (1809) 17 Ves Jun 1, 34 ER 1 (some subscribers to an annuity fund brought a claim to force the fund's directors to make distributions. The fact not all the subscribers had been added as parties to the claim did not cause it to fail.). For a very early example see *Harrison v Lucas* (1639) 1 Ch Rep 125, 21 ER 527.

[141] Morley (n 59) 2185–87.

[142] *Bond v Campbell* (n 126); Mitford (n 139) 163–81.

[143] *Jones v Garcia del Rio* (n 127).

(1826),[144] several shareholders brought claims on behalf of the collective to have their subscriptions returned to them: Lord Eldon and Sir John Leach V-C respectively refused to allow the claims because not all the shareholder-partners had been added as parties. Likewise in *Baldwin v Lawrence* (1826),[145] Lord Eldon refused to allow a bill for direction as to the meaning of a deed of settlement company's articles of association on the basis that it was not brought by *all* the shareholder-partners.

Conversely, a large partnership could sometimes frustrate Chancery suits brought against it by insisting that in such litigation each of the partner-shareholders be added as defendants, and file separate defences, racking up costs and causing huge delays. In *Van Sandau v Moore* (1826),[146] Lord Eldon rejected the argument that this practice would amount to an abuse of the court's process, refusing to treat large companies differently from small partnerships. Although Morley treats the decision as essentially designed to lock capital into deed of settlement companies, by preventing shareholders from liquidating the firm, there is no hint of this in Lord Eldon's reasoning.[147] First, he made clear that the court had never before intervened to prevent defendants filing separate defences, and that nothing about the nature of the deed of settlement company induced him to do something so drastic as interfere with defences in this way. Second, he saw the difficulty of suing large deed of settlement companies as a sign of why they were illegal when formed without an Act of Parliament to sue and be sued in the name of their treasurer:

> There were some (and many too, whose opinions were very well deserving of attention) who declared,—that, if [deed of settlement companies were formed without Act of Parliament], that they could not, in the Courts of this country and according to the laws of the country, effectually demand what they had a right to demand, or be effectually sued for that for which they were liable—the very circumstance of the existence of that inability or incapacity, and the inconvenience or impracticability of dealing with them in a court of justice, proved bodies of that kind to be illegal at common law.[148]

In other words, Lord Eldon saw the difficulties that deed of settlement companies had in using the courts as a sign of why statutory and common law bars on their legality were sensible. For this reason, his court would not routinely set aside joinder requirements in cases concerning such companies, which meant that they could not reliably sue or be sued in Chancery. This did mean that shareholders could not

144 *Blain v Agar* (n 127).
145 2 S & S 18, 57 ER 251 (Ch).
146 (n 76).
147 Morley (n 59) 2174.
148 *Van Sandau* (n 76) at 1 Russ 462, 38 ER 178.

easily use the courts to dissolve or withdraw their capital from such concerns.[149] However, that was a by-product of what was, in effect, a rejection of jurisdiction over such companies, rather than a substantive rule of law.

Why then did Lord Eldon's Chancery deny jurisdiction over deed of settlement companies in this way? His refusal, particularly in the 1820s, to waive joinder requirements may of course have been motivated by a desire not to encourage what he regarded as irresponsible and illegal forms of trade. However, the decisions are not fully explained by Lord Eldon's hostility to deed of settlement companies because in doing so he tacitly allowed them to continue existing and trading, as Michael Lobban has observed.[150] It is submitted that the decision made sense on a pragmatic basis. Complicated cases concerning large joint stock companies would wreak chaos on an overworked Chancery. Lord Eldon was heavily criticised for delays in Chancery and refused to aggravate the problem by allowing the court to become a forum for company account taking,[151] and this might explain in part why he never brought his proposed bill to make it easier to sue joint stock corporations into law.[152]

2.3 How Effective Were Deed of Settlement Companies Created Using Trusts?

Deed of settlement companies drafted using trusts offered some clear advantages over more typical partnerships and show that lawyers were familiar with trusts of circulating business assets from the eighteenth century. The use of trusts in the constitution of such firms allowed them to act through trustees in the common law courts, facilitated the transfer of shares through adjustment to the company's own books, and prevented the need for shareholders to join in any conveyance of the company's land. However, in two major respects care is needed when assessing the significance and usefulness of trusts in the constitution of large joint stock businesses.

First, deed of settlement companies were partnerships and many of their features were simply the result of partnership law, even if the company assets were settled on trustees. After all, it was partnership law which meant that the company's assets were available to business creditors in priority to the separate creditors of shareholder-partners: the use of the trust made no difference. Conversely, the fact that shareholders faced unlimited liability and companies struggled to make use

[149] Freeman, Pearson, and Taylor (n 1) 201–02.

[150] Michael Lobban, 'The Politics of English Law in the Nineteenth Century' in *Judges and Judging: in the History of the Common Law and Civil Law* (CUP 2012) 125–26.

[151] Chapter 1, text from (n 86) to (n 89).

[152] Text from (n 107) to (n 108).

of Chancery also were rooted in the fact that they were unincorporated partnerships: though the difficulty shareholders had in suing such entities de facto acted as a capital lock-in mechanism.

Secondly, the deed of settlement company with transferable shares, operating without Act of Parliament, only existed on the fringes of legality. Lord Eldon's Chancery insisted that deed of settlement companies were to be treated as partnerships, and refused to develop a separate body of principles to deal with such concerns. Although it is sometimes asserted that this was contrary to a more flexible approach taken in eighteenth-century Chancery, and rooted in Lord Eldon's belief in the economic ill effects of such concerns, those conclusions are far from clear. As above, there are few eighteenth-century examples of Chancery interacting with deed of settlement companies, and Lord Eldon's refusal of jurisdiction over such entities can be explained by concerns about adding such difficult business to an overburdened court's workload. There was no great innovation, but simply a continuation of the eighteenth-century policy of begrudgingly allowing such entities to exist, though refusing to encourage them. It reflected the popular belief that the directors of large corporations, in trading under a corporate name with money advanced from often uninformed shareholders, were unaccountable, and so traded recklessly in a way which ultimately resulted in bubbles and financial crises.[153] The story is not one of judicial sympathy to the needs of traders, nor of a conservative judicial class resisting the call of progress, but of judges mirroring popular political economic ideas in refusing to encourage what was perceived as a dangerous and immoral form of trading. Through use of established doctrinal forms, those lawyers who drafted deeds of settlement for companies were able at least to elicit bare tolerance of their existence: that was their principal achievement. Only in the 1840s, after another heavy crash in the 1830s, would Parliament decide that allowing deed of settlement companies to operate without regulation had allowed them too much freedom, and so encouraged reckless trading and fraud. Parliament passed the Joint Stock Companies Act 1844 to force large partnerships to incorporate by registration, bringing them within the law and the jurisdiction of the courts in the hope of regulating their activities better, and so stabilising the economy.[154] The aim was promoting economic stability, not to encourage the accumulation of capital or economic growth.[155]

[153] Taylor (n 70) chs 1 and 3.
[154] 7 & 8 Vict c 110 (Joint Stock Companies Act 1844).
[155] Taylor (n 70) ch 4.

3. Testamentary Trading Trusts

Trusts were not only used in the constitution of joint stock companies, but also by traders seeking to leave a business as a legacy.[156] A trader in his will could provide that business assets were to be settled on trustees, who were to carry out the business for the benefit of the testamentary estate. Unlike deed of settlement companies, these testamentary trading trusts were fully enforced by the courts and the use of trusts in such businesses was central to their operation.

A business owner making his will might make provision to allow the business to be carried on for the benefit of his wife and children. The most basic form of such a device would simply involve a gift of the stock in trade and book debts of the business.[157] Such a gift might be conditional, as in *Smith v Starkey* (1825)[158] where a testator's disposition of property to his nephews to carry on a trade was made on the condition that they enter into partnership with one another, and allow no woman any role in the management of the business. However, the use of a trust in such bequests seems to have been common and there are a number of instances of such trusts in the Regency era, particularly in Chancery order books.

Creating a trust gave additional control to the settlor over what happened to his property. Whereas a legatee of a testator's stock in trade would have unrestricted control over the business, where the property was held on trust a testator could give the trustees power to prevent an unprofitable business from continuing. For instance, in *Glanvill v Hakewill* (1815)[159] a testator allowed his son and residuary legatee to carry on his business for the son's own benefit, and made clear that the son was to be given property for this purpose by the executors, provided that the trustees of the will thought that this was for his advantage.[160] Such trusts could also provide that a testator's trade was to be continued and the profits thereof be used to provide for his family. A very early example is *Humble v Bill* (1703),[161] where a testator had directed that his executor was to carry on his business as a printer and raise £2,000 for his daughter and children out of the profits. Similarly, in *Coffin v Cooper* (1815)[162] a testator had provided that his business was to be settled on trustees for the benefit of his estate, and managed by his wife (who was not one of the trustees).

156 See Stebbings (n 3) 9–10; Alistair Owens, 'Inheritance and the Life-Cycle of Family Firms in the Early Industrial Revolution' (2002) 44 Business History 21; Aleksi Ollikainen-Read, 'Creditors' Claims against Trustees and Trust Funds' [2018] Trusts and Trustees 177.

157 See for instance *Caffrey v Darby* (1801) 6 Ves Jun 488, 31 ER 1159 (Ch); *Hedges v Blicke* (1815) C 33/613, ff 1645r–1647v.

158 C 33/736, ff 1761r–1765v.

159 C 33/613, ff 1084r–1084v.

160 Also see *Sharpe v East* (1825) C 33/736, ff 1769r–1774v; *Stodhort v Ryle* (1825) C 33/736, ff 2762r–64v, C 33/737, ff 2025r–2026r.

161 2 Vern 444, 23 ER 884 (Ch); *Savage v Humble* (1703) 3 Brown 5, 1 ER 1140 (HL).

162 C 33/613, ff 1100r–1100v.

Trusts were also used where a testator wished an infant son to enter the business upon reaching majority. They were drafted as follows.[163] First, the will would appoint trustees to hold legal title to the assets set aside for running the business, usually the stock in trade, the business premises,[164] a sum of money,[165] and potentially other property too.[166] This property was held on trust for the testator's estate. Secondly, the will would provide that either the trustees, the testator's widow, or a manager,[167] were to carry on the testator's trade until his eldest son reached twenty-one.[168] Thirdly, the will would provide that until the son reached twenty-one the profits of the estate were to be used to discharge pre-existing trade debts,[169] and then used to provide an income for the testator's widow[170] and for the maintenance and education of his children. Fourthly, it would be provided that upon the son reaching twenty-one he would have the option to purchase the stock in trade and book debts from the testamentary estate, typically on credit,[171] and the trustees might have a discretion to lend further sums to the sons for running the business.[172] Finally, the purchase price and the repayments (including interest) on any loans would be used to provide marriage portions or annuities for daughters, and to make provision for younger sons.

There were variations on this model. In *Wilkinson v Stafford* (1789)[173] the testator provided that his sons-in-law, and two clerks he had employed, were to run his share of a colliery for the benefit of his grandchildren until they reached twenty-one. In *Jackson v Jackson* (1802, 1804)[174] the business assets were settled on trust for the testator's sons, so long as they wished to continue the business, but were charged with the payment of legacies to the testator's daughter and an annuity to his widow. Further examples are provided by the two settlements in *Haddon v*

[163] This form of settlement, and variations of it, can be seen in *Wilkinson v Stafford* (1789) 1 Ves Jun 32, 30 ER 216 (Ch); *Ex p Garland* (1804) 10 Ves Jun 110, 111; 32 ER 786, 786 (BC); B 1/105, pp 306–10; *Saunders v Saunders* (1805) C 33/539, ff 1130v–32v; *Hedges v Bilicke* (n 157); *Crawshay v Maule* (1818) 1 Swans 495, 36 ER 479; 1 Wils Ch 181, 37 ER 79 (Ch); *Gordon v Rutherford* (1823) T&R 373, 37 ER 1144 (Ch); *Sharpe v East* (n 160); *Ex p Low* (1825) B 1/170, pp 230–38.

[164] Eg *Smith v Starkey* (n 158).

[165] Eg *Garland* (n 163); *Smith* ibid.

[166] Eg money from annuities or rents, see *Sharpe v East* (n 160).

[167] The terms of the will would typically provide that the manager had to give security, and so would be subject to the control of the trustees. Note, though, that he or she might be allowed a share of the profits in addition to expenses and a salary, see *Stodhort* (1825) (n 160).

[168] Note that in all these cases the business was settled on trust, but that a widow or manager who ran the business was not necessarily one of the trustees.

[169] The testator's trade was to be carried on solely for this purpose in *Alley v Deschamps* (1806) 13 Ves Jun 225, 33 ER 278 (Ch).

[170] As was typical for settlements of property on a widow by her husband's will, this interest would often end upon the wife's remarrying, eg see *Caffrey* (n 157); *Saunders* (n 163).

[171] Eg *Wilkinson* (n 163).

[172] Eg *Saunders* (n 163).

[173] *Wilkinson* (n 163).

[174] (1802) 7 Ves Jun 535, 32 ER 215 (MR); (1804) 9 Ves Jun 591, 32 ER 732 (LC); Eldon Notebook 1803–1804 pp 166–69. The litigation concerned when the property in the capital and profits was to pass to the sons, and whether they would take as joint tenants or tenants in common.

Silverlock (1815).[175] In the first of these a testator provided that his trade was to be continued for the benefit of younger children until they reached twenty-one, at which time marriage portions were to be raised from them out of the profits for his daughters, and the business assets were to vest in the son and those with whom he was intended to carry on the business. The second settlement was contained in the testator's son's own will, and provided that the trade was to be continued to pay off pre-existing debts, then for the benefit of his wife for her life or until remarriage, and then for the benefit of his children. *Sharpe v East* (1825)[176] involved a similar settlement, but provision was made for two of the testator's sons ultimately to take over the trade upon reaching twenty-five, while in *Ex p Garland* (1804)[177] the trustees were to decide when the testator's sons were ready to take over the trade.

3.1 Limited Liability Trading and the Rights of Trust Creditors

Testamentary trading trusts did not simply allow a testator control over how his business was run after his passing, but allowed that business to trade with limited liability. This is significant given the law's general refusal to recognise limited liability, and given the contemporary view that it was crucial that traders be fully liable for their debts, so as to incentivise responsible trading. Nevertheless, trusts law provided a highly technical means of achieving this end. This is because a testator could provide that only a portion of his testamentary estate was to be settled on trust to run the business, and that only this money would be available to its creditors, while any profits could wholly go to the estate itself.

The matter is best explained as follows. Where a trustee contracts a debt on behalf of the trust, the trustee is personally liable for that debt. However, a trustee is not beneficially entitled to trust assets: the creditor could therefore not levy judgment against the trust assets, and the trust assets would not vest in a bankrupt trustee's estate.[178] This means a creditor who had advanced money on behalf of the trust prima facie had no claim to trust assets where the trustee had defaulted on repayment. The point was made by Lord Eldon in *Worrall v Harford* (1802).[179] The claimant was the solicitor to a trustee in bankruptcy, whose fees were outstanding. The solicitor, presumably concerned about the trustee's solvency, argued that as a creditor of the trust he had a direct claim on the trust assets. Counsel argued that this was the effect of a provision in the trust deed, which gave the trustee an indemnity for expenses. Lord Eldon dismissed the claim. He affirmed that '[i]t is in the nature of the office of a trustee, whether expressed in the instrument, or not, that

[175] C 33/614, 1632r–1634r.
[176] (n 160).
[177] (n 163).
[178] See Chapter 6, Section 2.
[179] 8 Ves Jun 4, 32 ER 250 (Ch); Eldon Notebook 1802–1803 p 1.

the trust property shall reimburse him all the charges and expenses incurred in the execution of the trust'.[180] However, Lord Eldon rejected counsel's argument that this gave the creditors of the trust a direct claim on the assets. Such a rule would impede management of the trust and the proper distribution of a bankrupt estate. In the words of his notebook:

> I thought that Clause was merely for the Indemnity of the Trustees, that the Attorney's demand [was] like that of any other person with whom [the] tr[ustees] incurred charges[, the clause] was merely payment of the Trustee—that the contrary w[oul]d be very dangerous & that the effect of the Charge as he insisted is not expressed. There was nothing sufficiently special in the terms of the deed as was insisted at the Bar to distinguish this from the general case. In Bankruptcy the Attornies would be constantly filing bills & presenting Petitions for costs if they were held to have this Lien on the funds in relation to which the charges were incurred.[181]

Accordingly, Lord Eldon held that the creditors of a trustee had no direct claim upon the trust assets, at least if not specially granted such rights by the terms of the trust. He justified this both as a matter of doctrine and policy. As regards doctrine, Lord Eldon made clear that the court would not interpret a clause in a trust deed giving the trustee a right to expenses as also giving him the power to grant charges over the trust assets to trust creditors. That would be to read too much into the terms of the trust. As regards policy, Lord Eldon was keenly aware that *Worrall* involved a claim against a trustee in bankruptcy, and he was worried about the effect of ruling that solicitors to bankrupt estates had direct claims to the bankrupt's assets. This would encourage such solicitors to litigate *against* the bankrupt estate they were hired to serve: both causing delays in bankruptcy administration and reducing the total sum available for distribution amongst the bankrupt's creditors—as the bankrupt estate would end up paying the litigation costs.

This limitation was significant for testamentary trading trusts, as it ultimately allowed them to trade with limited liability. The principal case was *Ex p Garland* (1804),[182] which concerned a trust of a business set up in a will of the type considered above. A testator's widow and executrix was to run his business on trust for the benefit of his estate until other trustees appointed by the will thought that the

[180] ibid 8, 252. This confirmed Lord Macclesfield C's decision in *Trott v Dawson* (1721) 1 P Wms 780, 24 ER 612 (Ch) that a beneficiary could not enforce the trust without making the trustee an allowance for his expenses, though the decision was reversed by the House of Lords on other grounds in *Danson v Trott* (1729) 7 Bro PC 266, 3 ER 173 (HL), see Lewin (n 115) 453. Lord Eldon's rule was accepted by treatise writers, see Henry Maddock, *A Treatise on the Principles and Practice of the High Court of Chancery* (n 13) 159 (1820 edn); George Hampson, *Means by Which Trustees May Perform Their Duties without Incurring Responsibility* (1st edn, A Maxwell 1825) 16–17; Lewin (n 115) 453.

[181] Eldon Notebook 1802–1803 p 1.

[182] (n 163).

sons were ready to take over, at which point the sons were to purchase the assets used in the trade from the estate. The wife was given £600 from the testator's personal estate to run the business on trust and carried it on until 1801 when she was declared bankrupt. At this time, she was indebted to the estate in respect of £1351. 5s. 0d. of stock and in respect of £768. 12s. 4d. of money owed to the estate as executrix. This was significant, because she had used more of the estate than she was permitted to in running the business; in other words the sums beyond £600 taken from the testamentary estate were misapplied by the widow as executrix in breach of her custodial duties as a trustee and executrix.

The surviving trustee, acting on behalf of the testamentary estate, successfully petitioned the Master of the Rolls to be admitted as creditors of the bankrupt widow's estate on the basis of the claims for breach of custodial duty.[183] However, the bankrupt widow's estate appealed the decision to Lord Eldon, and argued that the testamentary estate's claim should not be allowed. It argued that:

> ... inasmuch as the s[ai]d Trades or Businesses of a Farmer & Miller were carried on by the s[ai]d Margaret Ballman [the bankrupt executrix] in pursuance of the directions of the s[ai]d Will of the s[ai]d Test[at]or and the profits the[re]of were to have been applied to the gen[era]l p[ur]poses of the s[ai]d Test[at]or[']s Will the whole of the s[aid] Test[at]or[']s property ought to be considered as liable to make good & satisfy the debts contracted by her in such Trades or Business.[184]

In other words, the widow's bankrupt estate argued that:

(i) The testator's personal estate had received the profits of the business, as a beneficiary of a trust of the business;
(ii) By receiving the business' profits, the testator's estate was in effect a partner in that business and so fully liable to its creditors;
(iii) Because the testamentary estate was indebted to the business' creditors, it could not be allowed to claim a share of the bankrupt widow's assets. If it did so, it would illegitimately reduce the total value available for distribution amongst the business creditors—who were also creditors of the testamentary estate.[185]

In other words, this issue was whether the testamentary estate was fully liable to the business creditors, and so prohibited from seeking a share of the bankrupt widow's estate for breach of custodial duty.

[183] B 1/105, 309.
[184] ibid.
[185] Such competition was not allowed, see Chapter 7, Section 2.

The complication on the facts of *Garland* was the fact that the testator had only settled £600 on trust for running the business. In the absence of such a limitation, the testamentary estate would straightforwardly have been liable for the business debts, as ruled by Lord Thurlow LC in *Hankey v Hammock* (1786),[186] and so could not have claimed a share of the bankrupt widow's estate. Counsel for the bankrupt widow's estate argued that the same rule should be applied in *Garland*. The testamentary estate had shared in the profits of the business, and so should be liable to its debts. The mechanism here was the same as with a typical partnership. As discussed in Chapter 1, partners acquired rights of indemnity and lien in respect of debts contracted on behalf of the partnership and partnership creditors could ultimately claim partnership assets by taking the benefit of those rights.[187] Likewise, the trustee of a testamentary trading trust, who contracted debts on behalf of the trust,[188] acquired rights of indemnity and lien, but these covered the *whole* of the testamentary estate—even if a limitation had been placed on the sums to be used in the trade. The creditors of the trade could take the benefit of these rights to reach through into all the assets of the testamentary estate. To rule otherwise would make it harder to find trustees by limiting the value of their indemnity regarding against trust debts. It would also recognise limited liability trading, in that the testamentary estate would get the profits of the business without being liable to its debts. This would be illegal: 'the general opinion, that by the law of England there cannot be a partial liability in respect of a particular fund, is strong against the rule, upon which the opposition to this petition must rest'.[189]

For the testamentary estate, it was instead argued that only the £600 settled on trust for running the business could be claimed by its creditors, and so that the testamentary estate was not indebted to the trade creditors beyond this. There was in effect a £600 limit on the value of the trustee's indemnity and lien for expenses, and the only way business creditors could claim testamentary assets was through that right to expenses (ie by subrogation). This protected the estate from the full extent of the trade's debts: after all, even partnership creditors could only claim partnership assets through the rights of indemnity and liens of the partners.[190] A limit on the trading trustee's indemnity and lien would thus frustrate creditor claims to the testamentary estate. This did not prejudice creditors: those who had no notice of the trust only ever relied on the executor's personal credit, while those who did have notice of it could inspect the trust deeds for its terms. Further, the

[186] (n 111).

[187] See Chapter 1, Section 2.2 and 2.4.

[188] The personal liability of an executor-trustee for the debts of a business run for the benefit of infant beneficiaries, without authorisation under the will, was recognised by the King's Bench in *Wightman v Townroe* (1813) 1 M&S 412, 105 ER 154. Chancery would take no notice of the 'trust' when considering the trustee's liability in such circumstances, as affirmed in *Pemberton v Oakes* (1827) 4 Russ 154, 38 ER 763 (Ch).

[189] 10 Ves Jun 10, 32 ER 786.

[190] For a fuller discussion see Chapter 1, Section 2.4 and Chapter 7, Section 4.2.

natural implication of holding that the business creditors had a claim on the estate in priority to legatees was that legacies already paid would have to be recalled—disrupting the orderly and speedy administration of testamentary estates whenever the will created a testamentary trading trust.

Lord Eldon accepted the testamentary estate's arguments. First, he ruled that the rights of a trust creditor were limited to taking the benefit of the trustee's right of indemnity and lien in respect of the debt owed to that creditor. If the trustee went bankrupt before the debt was paid, this allowed the trust creditor to claim the sum owed from the trust assets. To paraphrase in modern terminology, the only rights the trust creditors had to the trust assets were by way of subrogation to the trustee's right of indemnity and lien. Secondly, he ruled that the widow-trustee's right of indemnity on the facts was limited to the £600, and therefore that the testamentary estate was not liable to the trade's debts beyond this sum. He justified this second point by building on the estate's counsel's submissions about recalling legacies. Lord Eldon realised that if the whole of the personal estate was liable to the business creditors in the first instance, and only then to legatees, the whole administration of the estate would have to be frozen until such liabilities were met:

> it is impossible to hold, that the trade is to be carried on, perhaps for a century; and at the end of that time the creditors, dealing with that trade, are, merely because it is directed by the Will to be carried on, to pursue the general assets, distributed perhaps to fifty families.[191]

Accordingly, Lord Eldon held that the trustee's right of indemnity for expenses, and thus the rights of the creditors to the personal estate, were limited to the amount set aside for running the business:

> They [ie the business creditors] have something very like a lien upon the estate, embarked in trade [ie the £600 the trustee was permitted to use to indemnify herself for payment of trade debts]. They have not a lien upon any thing else: nor have creditors in other cases a lien upon the effects of the person with whom they deal; though, through the Equity, as to the application of the joint and separate estates to the joint and separate debts respectively, they work out that lien. If it is to be determined upon the convenience, it is not so inconvenient to say, those, who deal with the executor, must take notice, that the testator's responsibility is limited by the authority given to the executor.[192]

The limitation of the trustee-manager's indemnity in this way was justified on the basis that the trustee could always refuse to take up the office. The ruling was

[191] *Ex p Garland* (n 163) 122, 970.
[192] ibid 120, 789.

affirmed in *Ex p Richardson* (1819) on similar facts.[193] The decision is not only significant as an example of how trusts could create limited liability trading entities, but as the root of the modern rules governing how trust creditors can claim trust assets.

4. Conclusion

In sum, although aspects of the law of trusts were ill suited for use in commerce, trusts were used in business structures in the Regency era to emulate some of the benefits of incorporation, despite contemporary hostility to transferable shares and limited liability for private enterprise. Joint stock traders could vest business assets in a body of trustees to create large joint stock enterprises, able to raise capital from shareholder-beneficiaries—though the Bubble Act, contemporary hostility, and difficulties using the courts formed significant obstacles for such entities. Further, testators could use trusts to create limited liability businesses for the benefit of their testamentary estates, ultimately to provide for their widows and children. To this extent, the law of trusts helped meet the needs of traders and so facilitated trade.

This not only antedates developments in the history of organisational law, but sheds light on the development of trusts law thinking. It debunks the myth that the commercial trust was the product of Victorian thought. The testamentary trading trusts cases in particular show that circulating trusts of personalty were seen as orthodox by lawyers in the early nineteenth century: it would be dangerous to draw this conclusion from deed of settlement companies alone because they were seen as partnerships. Modern trusts lawyers who seek to distinguish nineteenth- and late eighteenth-century authorities simply on the basis that the trusts law of that age was uncommercial therefore need to exercise extreme care. The institution's commercial roots stretch back over 250 years into cases which continue to govern the rights of creditors of all trusts—whether 'traditional' or 'commercial'.

[193] Buck 202; 3 Madd 138, 56 ER 461 (VC); (1819) Buck 421 (LC).

PART II

BINDING BUSINESSES ASSETS

3

Ostensible Authority and the Ordinary Course of Business

As seen in Part I, the legal structure adopted for the creation of a business determined the degree to which business assets would be made available to business creditors and shielded from the personal creditors of its owners. In other words, a business's structure determined the extent to which business assets would be dedicated to business purposes. The following chapters look at this same issue from the perspective of an ongoing concern: when could a trader or his agent bind the assets of the firm? When could one business partner or agent bind his co-partner(s) or principal(s) to a contract or dispose of their assets?

The point mattered most in cases where a partner, or agent, of a business fraudulently acted for his own benefit, whilst purporting to act on behalf of his trade. Imagine that A and B are partners, and B takes out a loan from C apparently on behalf of the partnership. B then disappears without repaying the loan, and C seeks to be repaid from the partnership assets. Where A has authorised the loan—either by agreeing to partnership terms which gave B this power or on the instant—it made sense to allow C's claim. However, the courts faced a more difficult problem in circumstances where B acted without authority, should A be bound by C's actions? Was A or C more at fault?

1. Traders and Fault

1.1 Self-regulating Markets and the 'Natural Level' of Trade

Before considering the legal rules governing unauthorised transactions by agents and partners, it is useful to first examine Regency era ideas of responsible trade. Understanding contemporary ideas of the difference between 'good' and 'bad' trade will help show how judges conceived of 'fault' in commercial cases, and how technical legal rules fitted into political economic and moral thinking in the Regency era.

In the Regency era, writers drew a strong distinction between valuable trade and mere speculation, a distinction rooted in deeper ideas about the economy's

Capitalism Before Corporations. Andreas Televantos, Oxford University Press (2020). © Andreas Televantos.
DOI: 10.1093/oso/9780198870340.003.0004.

self-regulation. The notion of self-regulation was put forward most influentially by Adam Smith in the *Wealth of Nations* (1776):

> As every individual, therefore, endeavours as much as he can both to employ his capital in the support of domestic industry, and so to direct that industry that its produce may be of the greatest value, every individual necessarily labours to render the annual revenue of the society as great as he can. He generally, indeed, neither intends to promote the public interest, nor knows how much he is promoting it. By preferring the support of domestic to that of foreign industry, he intends only his own security; and by directing that industry in such a manner as its produce may be of the greatest value, he intends only his own gain, and he is in this, as in many other cases, led by an invisible hand to promote an end which was no part of his intention. Nor is it always the worse for the society that it was not part of it. By pursuing his own interest he frequently promotes that of the society more effectually than when he really intends to promote it. I have never known much good done by those who affected to trade for the public good. It is an affectation, indeed, not very common among merchants, and very few words need be employed in dissuading them from it.[1]

In other words, individuals acting in their own interests will naturally tend to bring about collective good. Although Smith himself conceived of this mechanism in secular terms,[2] Regency era Christian thinkers came to associate this mechanism with divine providence. For instance, the Anglican clergyman and reformer Thomas Gisborne[3] wrote that:

> [W]hile the Government is attending to solely to national interest and the individual to private emolument; they will in most cases manifestly promote, however unintentionally, the divine plan of universal good.[4]

Likewise, Thomas Chalmers,[5] a Scottish minister who in 1823 would accept Chair of Moral Philosophy at St Andrews, wrote that:

[1] Adam Smith, *An Inquiry into the Nature and Causes of the Wealth of Nations* (Roy Capmbell and Andrew Skinner eds, OUP 1976 (first published 1776)) Book IV, ch II. For an account of other eighteenth century writers who advanced similar ideas, and Smith's earlier articulation of the same point, see Donald Winch, *Riches and Poverty: An Intellectual History of Political Economy in Britain 1750–1834* (CUP 1996) chs 3 and 4. For an examination of the complexities of the metaphor see Elizabeth Rothschild, 'Adam Smith and the Invisible Hand' (1994) 84 Am Econ Rev 319.

[2] See Winch (n 1) 239–40.

[3] Robert Hole, 'Gisborne, Thomas' in Sir David Cannadine (ed), *The Oxford Dictionary of National Biography* (OUP 2014) <https://doi.org/10.1093/ref:odnb/10782> accessed 18 March 2020.

[4] Thomas Gisborne, *An Enquiry into the Duties of Men in the Higher and Middle Classes of Society in Great Britain*, vol 2 (5th edn, J White; Cadell and Davies 1800) 200.

[5] Stewart Brown, 'Chalmers, Thomas' in Sir David Cannadine (ed), *The Oxford Dictionary of National Biography* (OUP 2007) <https://doi.org/10.1093/ref:odnb/5033> accessed 18 March 2020.

> God may combine the separate interests of every individual of the human race, and the strenuous prosecution of these interests by each of them, into a harmonious system of operation, for the good of one great and extended family.[6]

The point was developed by the clergyman and influential political economist Thomas Malthus, most famous for the 'population principle'—the theory that the fast-growing population would ultimately depress wages and raise food prices, first set out in 1798. From the second edition of his essay, Malthus directly sought to reconcile his fears about the growing population with his belief in a benevolent deity who had set down laws to regulate the economy, ultimately by arguing that 'evil exists in the world not to create despair, but activity'.[7] As Donald Winch explains, according to Malthus' theology:

> [A] beneficent Deity, anxious to maximise happiness and minimise vice, had attached pleasure to those activities that were conducive to happiness and pain to those that were vicious. This constituted a fixed system of laws of nature designed to place man under sufficient tension between needs and resources to ensure that he did not fall backward along the sliding scale of civilisation ... The goad of necessity acted as the spur to invention, without which God's original purpose in wishing the world's resources to be cultivated optimally would remain unfulfilled.[8]

This meant that, for Malthus, the risk of economic hardship which followed certain actions was designed to give incentive to men to behave as God wished. If men did not exercise restraint in procreating, then labour prices would fall, food prices rise, and famine would result. Likewise, if agriculture or factories produced too much this would have harmful economic effects; as seen in 1815–16 where a good harvest had the effect of depressing agricultural workers' wages, which in turn reduced demand for manufactured goods, resulting in a reduction in factory labourers' wages and a general down turn.[9] For Malthus, then, economic crises were part of the laws governing the economy as set out by God—necessary for the economy to correct itself as the consequence of having been set off-kilter by trading beyond its 'natural' level.[10] As Chalmers, a disciple of Malthus, put it:

[6] Thomas Chalmers, *The Application of Christianity to the Commercial and Ordinary Affairs of Life* (5th edn, A Constable; Blackwood; W Whyte; Olivery & Boyd; W Oliphant; Fairbairn & Anderson; Manners & Miller; and James Robertson 1820) 77.

[7] Thomas Malthus, *An Essay on the Principle of Population* (1st edn, J Johnson 1798) 395. See also Thomas Malthus, *An Essay on the Principle of Population* (2nd edn, J Johnson 1803); John Sumner, *A Treatise of the Records of Creation* (J Hatchard 1816).

[8] Winch (n 1) 260–61.

[9] ibid 359–61.

[10] Piero Sraffa (ed), *Works and Correspondence of David Ricardo*, vol IX (Liberty Fund 2005) 18–22 (Malthus to Ricardo, 16 June 1821); Boyd Hilton, *Corn, Cash Commerce: The Economic Policies of Tory Government* (OUP 1978) 307; Boyd Hilton, *Age of Atonement: The Influence of Evangelicalism on Social and Economic Thought, 1785–1865* (Clarendon Press 1997) 67.

> An affection for riches beyond what Christianity prescribes, is not essential to any extension of commerce that is at all valuable or legitimate; and, in opposition to the maxim, that the spirit of enterprise is the soul of commercial prosperity, do we hold, that it is the excess of this spirit beyond the moderation of the New Testament, which, pressing on the natural boundaries of trade, is sure, at length, to visit every country, where it operates with the recoil of all those calamities, which in the shape of beggared capitalists, and unemployed operatives, and dreary intervals of bankruptcy and alarm, are observed to follow a season of overdone speculation.[11]

This notion of trade having a natural level was voiced by other writers too, even those who disagreed with Malthus on other points. Samuel Taylor Coleridge, the poet and critic, in his *Lay Sermon* (1817)[12] treated the 'overbalance of the commercial spirit' as the 'immediate occasion of the existing distress', arguing that commercial expansion and 'desperate speculation'[13] needed to be contained:

> At the best of times this [commercial] spirit may be said to live on a narrow isthmus between a sterile dessert and a stormy sea, still threatened and encouraged on either side by Too Much or Too Little"[14]

Further, as Boyd Hilton has shown, the idea that economic hardship was created by improper trade beyond its 'natural level' was not confined to religiously minded essayists, but was widespread enough to influence economic policy in the 1810s and the 1820s.[15] The notion of trade having a proper level, for instance, ultimately dictated the government and Bank of England's position in the Bullionism debate—which concerned whether the gold standard should be restored, following its suspension during the Napoleonic Wars.[16] Such a measure would necessarily be deflationary by reducing the value of currency in circulation.

Throughout 1819 though many Parliamentarians argued that the economic growth which had followed the move to a paper currency was not the product of legitimate commerce, but speculation. The move to paper currency had made credit easier to obtain and, in turn, this encouraged traders to borrow beyond their means for the sake of investing rashly. Criticism of those who 'had over-traded themselves—men who, without capital had embarked in speculations for

[11] Chalmers (n 6) v–vi.

[12] Samuel Taylor Coleridge, *A Lay Sermon Addressed to the Higher and Middle Classes on the Existing Distresses and Discontents* (Gale and Fenner; JM Richardson; J Hatchard 1817).

[13] ibid 102.

[14] ibid 84.

[15] Hilton, *Corn, Cash, Commerce* (n 10) 2 and 6; Hilton, *Age of Atonement: The Influence of Evangelicalism on Social and Economic Thought, 1785–1865* (n 10) 4; Martin Daunton, *Progress and Poverty: An Economic and Social History of Britain 1700–1850* (OUP 1995) 352–57.

[16] Hilton, *Corn, Cash, Commerce* (n 10) 2.

the purpose of taking money from anybody that had it',[17] of 'rash and improvident speculators' who traded 'not upon their own capital',[18] was common.

Cabinet ministers took the same view. In 1819 the Prime Minister, Lord Liverpool, drew a direct link between 'the dangers of a periodical revulsion every three or four years' and the 'system by which fictitious capitals might be ... created and extended', allowing the 'appearance of prosperous trade, without the reality'.[19] Sir Robert Peel MP,[20] then the Home Secretary, argued that although 'manufacturing and commercial transactions were on a scale of immense magnitude' in 1819, that 'they were not sound, because the manufacturers depended on a state of currency that gave no security'.[21] Sir Robert was chair of the Parliamentary Secret Committee which recommended a return to the gold standard.[22] As one director of the Bank of England put it, the measure would 'Improve the quality, but diminish the quantity of Trade'.[23] The gold standard was readopted—in an attempt to stabilise the economy, by killing off irresponsible trade.[24]

The response to the economic crash of 1825–26 can also be seen as the product of the distinction between good and bad trade, and the Malthusian view of the function of bankruptcy.[25] When the crisis first appeared the initial instinct of government ministers was not to intervene: it was seen as the economy's natural response to trade beyond its natural level—including the mania in company promotions discussed in Chapter 2.[26] In March 1825, the Prime Minister, Lord Liverpool, made clear that those who had invested heavily in dubious joint stock companies ought not to expect help from the government should there be a crash—if investors suffered losses, that would be their own fault.[27] In December of that same year Robert Peel went further in suggesting that the crisis would ultimately do 'some good' in

[17] George Tierney MP, HC Deb 2 Feb 1819, vol 39, col 217. Tierney had himself been a merchant, DR Fisher, 'Tierney, George' in Sir David Cannadine (ed), *The Oxford Dictionary of National Biography* (OUP 2008) <https://doi.org/10.1093/ref:odnb/27439> accessed 18 March 2020.

[18] Frankland Lewis MP, HC Deb 2 Feb 1819, vol 39, col 239. For more details see Peter Mandler, 'Lewis, Sir Thomas Frankland, First Baronet' in Sir David Cannadine (ed), *The Oxford Dictionary of National Biography* (OUP 2004) <https://doi.org/10.1093/ref:odnb/16605> accessed 18 March 2020.

[19] HL Deb 26 May 1820, vol 1, col 583. Like the above quotes, this referred not just to paper bank of England notes, but the willingness of country banks to extend credit through creating their own notes and bills of exchange, discussed in Chapter 6 text from (n 83) to (n 92).

[20] Later Prime Minister. See John Prest, 'Peel, Sir Robert' in Sir David Cannadine (ed), *The Oxford Dictionary of National Biography* (OUP 2009) <https://doi.org/10.1093/ref:odnb/21764> accessed 18 March 2020.

[21] HC Deb 18 Feb 1822, vol 6, col 492.

[22] Joint Secret Committee to enquire into the State of the Bank of England, with respect to the Expediency of the Resumption of Cash Payments (1819, HL 291-III, HC 282-III).

[23] William Ward, ibid 57.

[24] Resumption Act 1820, 59 Geo III c 49 (restoring convertibility to bullion); Bank of England Act 1821, 1 & 2 Geo IV c 26 (restoring convertibility to gold coins).

[25] Hilton, *Corn, Cash, Commerce* (n 10) 7; Boyd Hilton, *A Mad, Bad, & Dangerous People? England 1783–1846* (OUP 2006) 325–27.

[26] See Chapter 2, Section 2.1.

[27] HL Deb 25 Mar 1825, vol 12, col 1194–95.

killing off irresponsible businesses and the unstable economic growth that reckless trading caused:

> I anticipate more inconvenience from the glut of every article of consumption [ie overproduction] than I do from the recent failures.
>
> I fear we have been working too fast—building too fast—importing too fast and that when the confidence in Banking establishments (at least those that ought to be confided in) shall have been restored, we shall still find that there will have been less demand for labour than there has been ... ultimate good after some suffering will result.[28]

For this reason, during the crisis William Huskisson, President of the Board of Trade, called in the House of Commons for country banks 'not to lend their money to the encouragement of crude and hasty speculations',[29] and the Bank of England deliberately caused deflation (with government approval) by reducing money supply and refused credit even to large banks in the midst of the crisis.[30] The view taken was that the proper response to economic crisis was not to help firms weather the storm, but to cause deflation to make sure the crisis properly killed off illegitimate forms of trade: 'collapse was therefore seen as a useful corrective, purifying the economy and society'.[31]

1.2 The 'Good Trader' and Judicial Treatment of Unauthorised Transactions

The question of who was a 'good' or 'bad' trader mattered not only to government ministers but to judges in cases involving unauthorised transactions. Again, imagine A and B are business partners and B, without A's authority, borrows money in the partnership name from C. Should A be bound by B's action? Was A or C to blame for what had happened? In asking this latter question, judges were influenced by the question of whether C, in contracting with B in this way, had entered into the transaction rashly or without asking proper questions. Did C have some reason to know of the limitation of B's authority? In other words, courts in effect asked if C was one of the 'speculators' who entered into commercial transactions too freely, without asking proper questions, who were ultimately responsible for the periodic economic crashes for the period.

[28] Peel to EJ Littleton, 23 Dec 1825, Staffordshire RO, Hatherton MS D260/M/F/5/27/2/110, cited at Hilton, *A Mad, Bad, & Dangerous People* (n 25) 327.

[29] HC Deb 28 April 1825, vol 13, col 288.

[30] Hilton, *Corn, Cash, Commerce* (n 10) 208–10.

[31] Daunton (n 15) 252.

Although the distinction between good and bad trade was never particularised either by government ministers or indeed Malthus and his followers, the Anglican clergyman and reformer Thomas Gisborne explored the matter in depth in his treatise *An Enquiry into the Duties of Men in the Higher and Middle Classes of Society in Great Britain*.[32] The treatise has been described by Hilton as a 'powerful but conventional expression of the new moral majoritarianism'.[33] It was designed as a manual for moral behaviour, and its chapter on those 'engaged in trade and business' particularised contemporary business practices in some detail, as well as the approach a moral trader should adopt. As Gisborne was an Anglican clergyman, it is perhaps unsurprising that he mirrored other Christian thinkers in recommending that traders should only make 'moderate profits', not lay out too large a share of their capital in 'adventurous enterprises', only contract debts they would be able to pay, and to live up to their reputation of creditworthiness. The overall emphasis is on responsible and considered trading: 'Among the moral virtues peculiarly to be cultivated by persons occupied in business or commerce, probity stands foremost.'[34]

For present purposes, what is particularly interesting is Gisborne's treatment of the responsibility of partners and principals for the actions of co-partners and agents. Gisborne makes clear that a partner owes duties in selecting his co-partner: on the basis that an 'ignorant, careless, or adventurous' co-partner could 'impair the credit and bring on the ruin of his associates'.[35] He also made clear that where a partnership became bankrupt through the actions of one partner, all were to blame: 'for each had made himself in a great degree responsible for the conduct of the other'.[36] As regards agents, he makes clear that a 'principal has a joint share in the immorality' of the actions of his agent 'if he does not actively repress [such actions] in his agents'.[37] Gisborne also emphasised the evils that came from a third party colluding with another's agent[38] and from agents making unauthorised profits at their principals' expense.[39]

These ideas of responsible trade fed into judicial reasoning in A–B–C cases of the type described above. Courts decided such cases in effect by asking whether A or C was more to blame for what had happened. On the one hand, circumstances might be such that C was one of the reckless traders responsible for the

[32] Gisborne (n 4).
[33] Hilton, *Age of Atonement: The Influence of Evangelicalism on Social and Economic Thought, 1785–1865* (n 10) 204.
[34] Gisborne (n 4) 223.
[35] ibid 264.
[36] ibid 256.
[37] ibid 327.
[38] ibid 347.
[39] ibid 360–67.

country's economic instability, willing to enter into transactions without the 'probity' Gisborne discussed as central to responsible trading. If C had entered into the transaction blindly, without asking questions despite the presence of circumstances which indicated the limitations on B's authority, A should not be bound by the transaction. Likewise, if C had colluded with B to defraud A, A should not be bound by the transaction. On the other, there was an argument for saying that A should be bound by the transaction despite his lack of consent. A had after all selected B as his partner—in Gisborne's language, aware of the risks involved in going into partnership with an 'ignorant, careless, or adventurous man'. Likewise, if B were instead employed as A's agent, A could be seen as having a 'joint share in the immorality' of B's actions, in having selected B as his agent, and having failed in his duty to monitor B's actions.

That being said, a judge's role in such cases went beyond simply deciding who was at fault—the real issue was who was *more* at fault for the unauthorised transaction, and so who should bear the loss. The need to judge the facts of real cases, meant that judges had to address their minds to the question of exactly what counted as good or bad trade more directly than political economists or even government ministers. For this reason, as we will see, the court in its jurisprudence came to frame its examination of fault within the question of whether A had *created the appearance* of B's authority, a question resolved by asking what the expectation of a commercial party in the normal course of business would have been. After all, if B appeared to have authority to bind A—because A had held out B as having such authority, B was in the habit of binding A in this way, or it was apparently within their joint course of business—C might well be blameless. All the fault would be A's in having created the risk that third parties would treat B as having authority. The analysis was rooted in comparative fault but as a by-product upheld the typical expectations of commercial parties—this was because of the need to have a workable conception of fault which could be applied in cases. Crucially, transactions C entered into in the ordinary course of business would be upheld. In the absence of such a rule, third parties would have been wary of dealing with representatives, and the economic advantages of a principal being able to carry out business through an agent, or a firm through a single partner, would have been lost.

We can see this pattern of reasoning in the case law concerning unauthorised transactions entered into by partners and agents.

2. The Authority of Agents

The first type of legal relation which could create authority problems was agency. In the first agency treatise, written in 1812 by the lawyer William Paley, it was stated that '[t]he relation of Principal and Agent takes place, wherever one person authorises another to do acts, or make engagements, in his name.'[40] In other words, whenever A authorised B to act on his behalf, and B agreed to do so, this gave rise to a relationship—often, a contract—of agency, and B would be A's agent. B would typically be authorised to dispose of title to A's property or enter into contracts in A's name.

The most important types of commercial agents were 'brokers' and 'factors'. A broker was authorised to exercise his principal's power to contract, and typically had no power to receive payment for his principal, to buy or sell on credit, or to contract in his own name on his principal's behalf, but the scope of his authority was determined by the type of brokerage.[41] A factor was an agent who was given possession of his principal's goods for the purpose of arranging sale typically in the factor's *own name*. That is to say, the factor would personally enter into a contract of sale of his principal's property. He might appear to be acting on his own behalf to third parties.[42]

Cases where agents of these types acted beyond their authority created difficulties. Where A (principal) expressly authorised B (his agent) to enter a contract with C (third party), or to dispose of property to C, A would be bound by the transaction in question. B would incur no liability vis-à-vis either A or C, unless C had entered into a contract with B whilst unaware of A's existence: in which case C could elect whether to treat A or B as party to the contract.[43] However, A might be bound even where B acted without express authority, where he had 'implied authority' to act in a particular way. The term could have one of two meanings in the Regency era.

First, 'implied authority' could refer to agency relationships where A impliedly consented to B acting beyond the literal limit of his express instructions. For instance, an agent authorised to purchase for his principal, but not given money, had authority to contractually bind his principal to pay the seller, while an agent given money to purchase for his principal had no authority to do so.[44] Likewise, an agent employed to sell a horse and receive the price had an implied authority to warrant that the horse was sound,[45] and to do all he could to effectuate the sale.[46] This is implied authority as used by lawyers today, and is a species of actual authority.

[40] William Paley, *A Treatise on the Law of Principal and Agent* (1st edn, J Butterworth 1812) 1. This definition drew upon the treatment of agency in the (more famous) philosopher William Paley's *Principles of Moral and Political Philosophy* (1785) 183–88, which in turn drew upon Thomas Rutherford's *Institutes of Natural Law: Being the Substance of a Course of Lectures on Grotius 'De Jure Belli Et Pacis'* (1754–56). Rutherford was Regius Professor of Divinity at Cambridge 1745–71. See Mark McGaw, 'A History of the Common Law of Agency with Particular Reference to the Concept of Irrevocable Authority Coupled with an Interest' (DPhil, Oxford 2005) 115–17.

[41] Neil Gow (ed), *A Treatise on the Law of Principal and Agent* (J and T Clarke 1819) 13; Joseph Story, *Commentaries on the Law of Agency* (CC Little and J Brown 1839) s 109.

[42] Gow (n 41) 13; Story (n 41) 110.

[43] *Paterson v Gandasequi* (1812) 15 East 62, 104 ER 768 (KB).

[44] *Rusby v Scarlett* (1803) 5 Esp 76, 170 ER 743 (KB)

[45] *Alexander v Gibson* (1811) 2 Camp 555, 170 ER 1250 (KB).

[46] *Helyear v Hawke* (1803) 5 Esp 72, 170 ER 741 (KB).

Secondly, 'implied authority' could refer to circumstances in which A was taken to have consented to B's actions as a matter of law, even if as a matter of fact he had not given B permission to act.

'Implied authority' in its second sense is what would today be called ostensible or apparent authority. In cases where A had allowed B to appear to have authority to bind A, and C reasonably relied on the appearance of B's authority to do so, in contemporary terms B would have 'implied authority' to bind A. The doctrine was rooted in the fact that A initiated C's reasonable reliance that B had the relevant authority, and comparatively A was more at fault than C in evoking this false assumption.[47] It is implied authority in the second sense with which this chapter is concerned.[48] Although the term ostensible authority was not used by contemporary lawyers, the term will be used here to avoid the ambiguities inherent in the contemporary term 'implied authority'.[49]

Before moving on to examine these rules more closely, a further word of caution to modern legal readers is necessary. Unlike modern lawyers,[50] Regency era lawyers did not treat 'course of business' and 'ostensible authority' as separate doctrines. The rule was simply that a partner or agent had ostensible authority to bind his principal when he appeared to act in the ordinary course of business.

2.1 B in the Habit of Acting for A

In the Regency era there were two situations in which an agent would be treated as having ostensible authority. The first arose where B had—to the knowledge of any relevant third parties—regularly acted on A's behalf in a particular way. By definition, such cases involved 'general authority'—where an agent had had authority to bind his principal in a number of transactions, rather than 'specific authority' to bind his principle in a single transaction.[51]

B would be able to bind A by continuing to act in that way, even if A had actually prohibited B from continuing to act as his agent, unless A had given notice to third parties that the agency was at an end.[52] The rule is best understood as providing

[47] Story (n 41) 127.

[48] For the modern distinction Peter Watts and Francis Reynolds (eds), *Bowstead & Reynolds on Agency* (21st edn, Sweet & Maxwell 2017) paras 3-001–3-009.

[49] The earliest use of the term (in its modern sense) in a reported case this author has found is *The Montreal Assurance Company v Dame Elizabeth M'Gillivray* (1859) XIII Moore 87, 121, 15 ER 33, 46 (PC).

[50] *Dubai Aluminium v Salaam* [2002] UKHL 48, [2003] 2 AC 366 [28]–[31] per Lord Nicholls (noted by C Mitchell at (2003) 119 LQR 364),

[51] *Whitehead v Tuckett* (1812) 15 East 400, 408; 104 ER 296, 896 (KB).

[52] *Townsend v Inglis* (1816) Holt 278, 171 ER 243 (CP). General standards of business practice could be relevant, and the court would require strong evidence before ruling that an agent had ostensible authority to carry out business in an unusual way, but the real issue was the actual behaviour of A and B (see *Wiltshire v Sims* (1808) 1 Camp 258, 170 ER 949 (KB).

an incentive for A to give notice to the world if he no longer wished B to act as his agent, by allowing B's actions to bind him if he failed to do so. Its purpose was to protect C in circumstances in which C had good reason to believe that B was authorised to act on A's behalf. In such circumstances it would be unjust for C to be bound by the content of private instructions between A and B.

This doctrine was discussed from the end of the seventeenth century. In *Boulton v Arlsden* (1697),[53] Sir John Holt CJKB held that where A had typically allowed B to buy goods from C on credit, then if B decided to keep the goods for himself on one such occasion, A would be liable to C in an action for the purchase price. Further, Holt CJKB ruled that A would be bound by B's actions after the end of the agency if the termination were either secret, or had occurred at so recent a time that C could not have known about it. Holt CJKB's reasoning suggests that the rationale behind the decision was that C should not be bound by the content of private communications between A and B, about which C had no way of knowing.[54] The judgment in *Boulton* was confirmed in *Hazard v Treadwell* (1721).[55] In *Fenn v Harrison* (1790)[56] the King's Bench rejected the *Boulton* rule, but did so in the face of dissent by Lord Kenyon CJKB, who would state that the rule was good law in *East India Company v Hensley* (1794)[57] and *Runquist v Ditchell* (1799).[58] In the latter case Lord Kenyon made clear that where B had been in the habit of acting for A, and A then revoked B's authority without giving notice to third parties, then B would continue to be able to bind A vis-à-vis those third parties.[59] The same principle was the basis of Lord Eldon CJCP's judgment in *Pearce v Rogers* (1800).[60]

It was Lord Ellenborough CJKB who would develop the doctrine of ostensible authority further. In *Hiscox v Greenwood* (1802)[61] B, A's servant, had negligently broken A's chaise without A's knowledge. B hired C to repair it, without informing A. A had never made use of C's services before. C repaired the chaise, and A sought to recover it. C refused to return it to A without payment, claiming a lien over the chaise, and A accordingly brought an action in trover against C.[62] The issue was whether A was bound to pay C, given B's lack of authority to enter into the contract. Lord Ellenborough ruled for A, on the basis that A had not been in the habit of employing C in the past:

53 3 Salk 234, 91 ER 979; (1702) Holt KB 641, 91 ER 797 (KB).
54 *Anonymous v Harrison* (1704) 12 Mod 346, 88 ER 1369 (Ch).
55 1 Str 506, 93 ER 665 (KB).
56 3 TR 757, 100 ER 842 (KB).
57 1 Esp 112, 170 ER 296 (KB).
58 3 Esp 64, 170 ER 539 (KB).
59 ibid 66; 540.
60 3 Esp 214, 170 ER 592 (KB).
61 4 Esp 174, 170 ER 681 (KB).
62 It is not stated in the report, but presumably B was insolvent or had disappeared.

> [T]he defendant had no right to hold the chaise as a lien. Whatever claim of that sort he might have, he must derive it from legitimate authority: that unless the master had been in the habit of employing the tradesman in the way of his trade, it should not be in the power of the servant to bind him to contracts of which he had no knowledge, nor to which he gave his assent. It was the duty of the tradesman, when he was employed [through the agent], to have inquired of the principal if the order was given by his authority; but having neglected to do so here, and the master having never employed him, the master was not liable to the demand; and the detainer of the chaise was unlawful.[63]

In other words, the fact that A had never dealt with C before meant that, in Lord Ellenborough's eyes, C should have been alive to the possibility of B's lack of authority.[64] It was therefore incumbent on C to make inquiries of A, and his failure to do so meant that he could claim no lien over the chaise.

The King's Bench applied the reasoning from *Hiscox* in the commercial context in *Whitehead v Tuckett* (1812).[65] A employed B as his general broker, and B had been in the habit of selling sugar belonging to A more or less freely, though at times B would receive specific instructions from A. B kept a general account with A, which included: entries for the sugar that A consigned to B; the purchase price for sugar received by B on A's account; money advanced by A to B; and money advanced by B to A. On the facts of the case, A claimed that he had sent a letter to B, asking B not to sell a particular consignment of sugar bought in B's name and stored in B's warehouse. B resold it to C, and later went bankrupt. The sugar, being in the warehouse, was delivered to A, and C (the purchaser) brought trover against A for the sugar.

For C it was said that A was bound by the sale. Counsel argued that B was *in the habit* of acting as A's general agent, and as the public could not be aware of any private instructions given by A to B, A had to be bound. After all, A had allowed B to take custody of the sugar, to dispose of it, and to receive the price. James Scarlett[66] argued for A. He contended that A had only consigned the goods to B for the specific purpose of selling them as a broker, that B had never had general authority over the goods, and thus that A could not be bound.

The court found for C, holding that A was bound by B's sale. Although the decision was based in part on the fact that A's letter to B did not countermand B's authority to sell, the majority made clear that, even had the letter done so, their

[63] 4 Esp 174–75, 170 ER 681.

[64] It is not clear from the judgment whether C would have to make inquiries only if he had never dealt with A before at all, or if he had never dealt with A through an agent. On the facts, C had never before dealt with A, so a ruling on point was not required.

[65] 15 East 400, 104 ER 896 (KB).

[66] A barrister who was to be a major opponent of later statutory reforms to the law of agency, see Sean Thomas, 'The Origins of the Factors Acts 1823 and 1825' (2011) 32 JLH 151, 153, 177–78, 182–85. For a discussion of the reforms, see Chapter 4, Section 3.

conclusion would have been the same.[67] Lord Ellenborough first ruled that B, having been in the habit of buying and selling on A's behalf, had had general authority to bind A. He then made it clear that, as a matter of principle, the private correspondence between A and B could not be allowed to affect third parties:

> [A]lthough there was a communication between them [B] and the defendant [A] as to the price and time of sale, yet the world was not privy to that communication, and had therefore no means of knowing that their general authority was controlled by the interposition of any check.[68]

Grose J acknowledged the same point, emphasising that 'it would be very dangerous to hold third persons bound by communications passing behind their back between a principal and his broker',[69] while Bayley J went so far as to say that ruling for A would be a 'fraud on the public',[70] and that as B 'appeared as owners . . . the defendant [A], who entrusted them, and not the plaintiffs, the innocent purchasers, must suffer for it'.[71] In other words, A had created the risk that third parties would enter into an unauthorised transaction with B: A had chosen B as his agent, and left the sugar in B's hands despite countermanding B's authority to sell it. To return to Thomas Gisborne's language, A had a 'joint share' in what had happened. There was nothing to suggest that C had behaved recklessly or irresponsibly—and so A should be bound by the sale. This decision would be affirmed in the 1820s by Lord Abbott CJ in the King's Bench and by the Common Pleas.[72]

2.2 A Holds B out as Having Authority

The second area where B could bind A beyond the terms of his instructions was in cases where A had clothed B with the appearance of having the right to dispose of A's property. This differs from the cases considered above, in that B's authority here was not based on his past conduct, and in most of the cases C was not aware of A. Instead, B's ostensible authority arose from A allowing B 'to hold himself forth to the world as having not the possession only, but the property' in goods which B held as A's agent.[73]

The leading case was *Pickering v Busk* (1812).[74] A employed B to buy hemp. B was both A's agent and a hemp trader on his own account. B, acting on A's behalf

[67] Only Le Blanc J did not consider the issue, regarding it as 'unnecessary', 15 East 411, 104 ER 900.
[68] ibid.
[69] ibid 410; 900.
[70] ibid 411; 900.
[71] ibid 412; 900.
[72] *Todd v Robinson* (1825) R&M 217, 218; 171 ER 999, 1000 (KB); *Gillman v Robinson* (1825) 1 C&P 642, 171 ER 1350 (CP).
[73] *Dyer v Pearson* (1824) 3 B&C 38, 42; 107 ER 648, 650 (KB).
[74] 15 East 38, 104 ER 758 (KB).

with A's permission, bought a parcel of hemp, but did so *in his own name*. B then sold the hemp to C (a third party), without A's consent. C had believed that B was the owner of the hemp and did not know about A. B then went bankrupt. A brought trover for the hemp against C. In the King's Bench, C's counsel were led by William Garrow,[75] and argued that:

> Hayward and Co. [C] who purchased the hemp of Swallow [B], had no means of discovering that the hemp was not the property of the person in whose name it stood, and who took upon him to deal with it as his own. And it would be unjust that, because the broker has turned out to be an unfaithful steward of his employer, the innocent purchasers should suffer rather than the plaintiff, by whose act in suffering the goods to be entered in the broker's name, the latter was enabled to practise the delusion. If the plaintiff had meant to retain his dominion over the property, he should have taken the transfer in his own name instead of the broker's.[76]

Counsel for A argued that B's disposition could not be effective on the basis that it had been made without authority, drawing an analogy with cases which held that a factor could not pledge the goods of his principal.[77] A's counsel contended that A had left the goods with B not for the purpose of B selling them, but for his own convenience. Accordingly, '[t]he world had no right to conclude from the circumstance of the goods being in his [B's] name, that therefore he [B] had the power of disposing of them'.[78]

The King's Bench ruled for C, on the basis that B had 'implied authority' to dispose of the hemp, though not all the judges who considered what the term meant attributed to it the same meaning. Lord Ellenborough opened his judgment as follows:

> It cannot fairly be questioned in this case but that Swallow [B] had an implied authority to sell. Strangers can only look to the acts of the parties, and to the external indicia of property, and not to the private communications which may pass between a principal and his broker: and if a person authorize another to assume the apparent right of disposing of property in the ordinary course of trade, it must be presumed that the apparent authority is the real authority. *I cannot subscribe to the doctrine, that a broker's engagements are necessarily and in all cases limited to his actual authority, the reality of which is afterwards to be tried by the fact. It is clear*

[75] Most famous as a criminal barrister, though he had a civil practice, was an MP, and later became a judge, see JM Beattie, 'Garrow, Sir William' in Sir David Cannadine (ed), *The Oxford Dictionary of National Biography* <http://www.oxforddnb.com/view/article/10410> accessed 18 March 2020.

[76] *Dyer* (n 74) 40; 759.

[77] Discussed throughout Chapter 4.

[78] *Dyer* (n 74) 41; 760.

> *that he may bind his principal within the limits of the authority with which he has been apparently clothed by the principal in respect of the subject-matter; and there would be no safety in mercantile transactions if he could not.*[79]

In other words, Lord Ellenborough ruled that A was bound by the unauthorised sale made by B. B had what would today be called ostensible authority to sell the hemp, rather than implied actual authority. With A's consent, B had bought the hemp in his own name, and kept possession of it with the 'apparent purpose'[80] of selling it, and so to all the world he appeared to have authority to do so. A had created the risk of third parties mistakenly thinking that B owned the hemp, and so could sell it. C had no reason to suspect there was any such limitation on B's power to do so. Accordingly, A was bound by the sale to C: the fact A owned the hemp and B had no actual authority to sell it was irrelevant. The other three judges reported as giving reasons agreed with Lord Ellenborough's conclusion, but only Bayley J agreed as to his reasoning. Grose J treated the issue of authority as a matter of fact for the jury and found that B was *in fact* authorised by A to sell. Le Blanc J too seems to have reached his conclusion on a finding of fact; he thought it inconceivable that A could have left the property with B for any reason other than to sell it.

The decision in *Pickering* would be affirmed by the King's Bench a number of times, and these later decisions affirmed Lord Ellenborough and Bayley J's ostensible authority analysis.[81] In *Boyson v Coles* (1817) Lord Ellenborough made clear that B had authority to bind A, where A had made 'an effectual representation that the property was in [B]'.[82] Lord Abbott in *Dyer v Pearson* (1824)[83] accepted that where A gave B indicia of title, unauthorised sale by B could bind A.

3. Set-off between Principals, Agents, and Third Parties

The courts did not only seek to ratify transactions entered into by an agent in the ordinary course of business through the doctrine of 'implied authority', but also the law of set-off. In the relevant cases C sought to set off sums he was owed by B against a claim by A, and so involved similar policy concerns to those apparent

[79] ibid 43; 760. Emphasis added.
[80] ibid.
[81] James Oldham and Victoria Barnes have argued that the influence of Lord Ellenborough's judgment can be attributed to its adoption in William Paley, *A Treatise on the Law of Principal and Agent* (2nd edn, J Butterworth 1819), which they suggest might be explained by Lord Ellenborough and the author's friendship, James Oldham and Victoria Barnes, 'The Legal Foundation of Apparent Authority' (2019) 44 J Corp L 649. Respectfully, the argument should be treated with caution. The authors appear to have conflated the better-known Archdeacon William Paley, with whom Lord Ellenborough was friends and died in 1805, with the William Paley whose agency treatise was first published in 1812. These are different people. See McGaw (n 40) 122–24.
[82] 6 M&S 14, 18; 105 ER 1148, 1149 (KB).
[83] 3 B&C 38, 42; 107 ER 648, 650 (KB).

in the cases considered already: where B deals with C outside the scope of his authority, should A or C be prejudiced? In this area too, the court asked whether A or C was more to blame for the unauthorised transaction, though here the debate was framed by very technical rules as to when set-off could be pleaded. Before examining the cases on point, it is first necessary to set out the basics of the law of set-off, and in particular the requirement that only mutual debts could be set off against one another.

The law of set-off governs when a debtor can escape liability for paying a debt, in whole or in part, because his creditor is in turn indebted to him. Accordingly, if X owed Y £50, and Y owed X £25, then if Y brought a debt claim against X for £50, X could plead the £25 debt as a defence, thereby preventing Y from recovering more than £25.[84] Matters would be more complicated where X and Y owed each other sums in different capacities, as there was a general requirement in the Regency era that set-off (whether allowed on the basis of equitable jurisdiction,[85] or on the basis of the statutes of set-off[86]) only be allowed in respect of mutual debts, that is to say sums due by the parties in the same rights.[87] By way of illustration, if X was personally a creditor of Y, but Y was a joint creditor of X and Z, prima facie no set-off would be available, on the basis that the debts were not mutual. On the other hand, if X and Y owed each other debts in their personal capacities then the debts would be mutual and set-off would be available.

This rule was of consequence to agency transactions as follows. In general, where A contracted with C through B, then the legal consequences were as if A had dealt directly with C.[88] Accordingly, C would be able to set off a sum due separately from A against a sum due to A under the contract.[89] By the same logic, C would prima facie be unable to set off the value of a debt from B personally against any obligation arising under the contract with A: the debts would not be mutual.[90] Therefore, the state of accounts between A and B, or B and C, would not prima facie affect A and C's rights against one another.[91]

However, difficulties could arise in cases where B had not disclosed A's existence. In such a situation C had trusted B's credit, and may have relied on the availability of set-off in respect to his dealings with B as security. The policy concerns therefore

[84] The procedure varied depending on whether the debt was a judgment debt or not. For more details see Basil Montagu, *Summary of the Law of Set-Off, with Appendix of Cases* (2nd edn, London 1828) 1–9.

[85] Rory Derham, *The Law of Set-Off* (4th edn, OUP 2010) 73–77. Note that there was no 'general' doctrine of substantive equitable set-off until *Rawson v Samuel* (1841) Cr&Ph 161, 41 ER 451 (Ch).

[86] The Statutes of Set-off 1729 (2 Geo II c 22) and 1735 (8 Geo II c 24). For bankruptcy set-off, which was wider and older, see Bankrupts Act 1705 (4 & 5 Ann c 4), s 12, re-enacted by the Bankrupts Act 1732 (5 Geo II c 30), s 28.

[87] Derham (n 85) 471–73.

[88] *Waring v Favenck* (1807) 1 Camp 85, 87; 170 ER 996 (KB).

[89] *Atkyns v Amber* (1769) 2 Esp 493, 170 ER 431 (KB); *Coppin v Craig* (1816) 7 Taunt 243, 129 ER 97 (CP).

[90] *Goode v Jones* (1792) Peake 235, 170 ER 141 (KB).

[91] *Kymer v Suwercropp* (1807) 1 Camp 109, 112; 170 ER 894, 895 (KB).

were identical to those considered in the cases above. The law on this point would be determined by the common law courts, in particular the King's Bench, as Lord Eldon's Chancery refused jurisdiction over agency disputes of this type.[92]

3.1 Hidden Principals

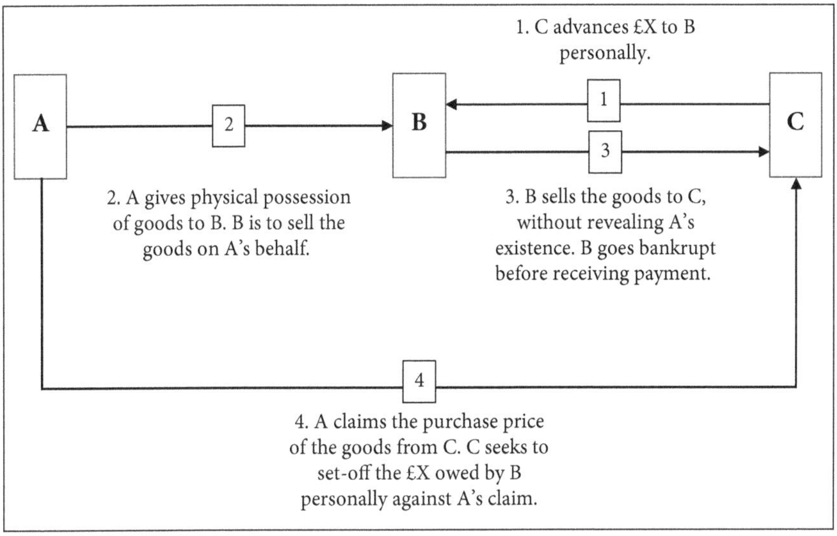

Figure 3.1 Fact pattern: Set-off cases involving hidden principals

The requirement of mutuality for set-off would matter in agency cases which involved hidden principals. This is best explained by example. Imagine a scenario where C is B's creditor. B then sells goods to C, and before C pays the purchase price, B goes bankrupt. It later turns out that the goods sold to C in fact belonged to A, and that B was only A's agent. The question that the King's Bench would have to answer in this scenario was whether to allow C to set off the debt owed to him by B, against A's claim for the purchase price of the goods. C, after all, had thought he was dealing with B, and had imagined that he could set off the sums he was owed by B against an action by B for the purchase price. On normal mutuality rules, C would not have been able to resist an action by A by pleading set-off of a debt owed by B. The conflict here was between A and C's reasonable expectations. This scenario is illustrated in Figure 3.1.

[92] *Dinwiddie v Bayley* (1801) 6 Ves Jun 136, 142; 31 ER 979, 981 (Ch).

The facts described above came before the court in *Rabone v Williams* (1785).[93] A brought a claim against C for the purchase price of goods sold, against which C sought to set off sums due from B. Lord Mansfield allowed the set-off, qualifying the mutuality rules by holding that:

> Where a factor dealing for a principal but concealing that principal, delivers goods in his own name, the person contracting with him has a right to consider him to all intents and purposes as the principal; and though the real principal may appear and bring an action upon that contract against the purchaser of the goods, yet that purchaser may set off any claim he may have against the factor in answer to the demand of the principal.[94]

The decision was upheld by Lord Kenyon CJ in *George v Claggett* (1797)[95] on materially identical facts. The reasoning here is the same as in the cases concerning ostensible authority: C's expectation of set-off should be honoured where A had held out B as beneficial owner of the goods being sold. Later nineteenth-century decisions made the scope of the doctrine in *Rabone* clear, recognising that—as in the ostensible authority cases—C could only have priority over A where (i) C did not know of A *before* it was too late for him to pull out of the contract,[96] and (ii) where A had not held out B as having authority to bind him.[97] The ostensible authority and set-off cases turned on the same concerns, a desire to allocate loss on the basis of relative fault as between A and C. The decisions had the effect of upholding transactions which appeared to occur in the ordinary course of business.

4. The Authority of Partners

4.1. Relationship with Agency Authority Doctrines

Cases where partners acted beyond their authority posed exactly the same issue for Regency era courts as those involving unauthorised agents. The terms of a partnership, like an agent's instructions, determined the power of one partner to bind the

[93] 7 TR 360, 101 ER 1020 (KB). Sometimes spelt 'Raybone'. Cited as a note to *George v Claggett* (1797) Peake 131, 170 ER 219; 2 Esp 557, 170 ER 454; 7 TR 359, 101 ER 1019 (KB).

[94] *Rabone* ibid.

[95] (n 93).

[96] Accordingly, notice to C before delivery under a contract of sale would prevent set-off, *Moore v Clementson* (1809) 2 Camp 22, 170 ER 1068 (KB); *Morris v Cleasby* (1813) 1 M&S 576, 105 ER 215; (1816) 4 M&S 566, 105 ER 943 (KB).

[97] *Baring v Corrie* (1818) 2 B&A 137, 106 ER 317 (KB), (B (a broker) contracted with C on A's behalf in B's own name without authority. C knew B at times acted as a broker, and brokers did not typically have authority to enter into contracts in their own names).

others, and similar issues arose when a partner entered into a transaction, ostensibly on behalf of the firm, without actual authority to do so: should the firm's assets be bound? It is therefore unsurprising that some contemporary treatise writers identified partnership with agency. Some went so far as to assert that 'the law of partnership is but a branch of that of principal and agent',[98] though some partnership rules (such as those governing the rights of partners inter se and partnership bankruptcy) had nothing to do with agency. More moderately, partnership treatise writers such as William Watson, JH Lloyd, and Joseph Story, as well as the philosopher William Paley, wrote that each partner was an agent for his firm, which explained the ability of partners to bind the joint stock and credit.[99] This mirrored the cotemporary civil law position,[100] and is accepted by modern English lawyers.[101]

The statements, though, did not reflect the law as espoused in the reported cases. Although it was possible for a partner expressly to be appointed as an agent of his firm,[102] Regency era courts treated the authority doctrines governing agents and partners as distinct. Contemporary decisions which stated that a partner had the implied consent of his co-partners to bind them made no reference to agency case law.[103] Further, the cases in the period concerning a partner's ostensible authority to bind his partners, he had acted beyond the terms of the partnership agreement and without his co-partners' consent, made no reference to agency.[104] Even on rare occasions when counsel and judges did cite agency decisions in partnership cases, this was clearly by way of analogy to a separate area of law.[105]

Secondly, there was clear authority that the scope of an agent's power to bind his principal was different from that of a partner to bind his partnership. As will be seen in the next chapter, there were restrictions on when an agent could pledge his principal's goods, whereas a partner could pledge his firm's credit and property as security for his own debts under the doctrine of ostensible authority. Indeed, there were cases which made clear that the agency law rules on the point did not

[98] Eg see William Paley, *A Treatise on the Law of Principal and Agent* (JH Lloyd ed, 3rd edn, Saunders and Benning 1833) 164, (the addition was Lloyd's, no such statement appears in the earlier 1812 and 1819 editions); WM Theobald, *The Law of Principal and Surety and Principal and Chiefly with Reference to Mercantile Transactions* (E Hammond ed, Gould, Banks & Co 1836) 230.

[99] William Paley, *The Principles of Moral and Political Philosophy* (London 1785) 149; William Watson, *A Treatise of the Law of Partnership* (2nd edn, J Butterworth 1807) 167; Neil Gow, *A Practical Treatise on the Law of Partnership* (3rd edn, C Hunter and J Richards 1830) 36–38; Story (n 41) 113.

[100] For details, and an account of the development of this position from classical Roman law, see Peter Stein, 'Mutual Agency of Partners in the Civil Law' (1958) 33 Tul L Rev 595. See also Code Civil des Francais, Edition Originale et seule officielle (Paris, 1804) Art 1859, provision 1 and Robert Pothier, *A Treatise on the Contract of Partnership (1765)* (Owen Tudor tr, Butterworths 1854) 45–49.

[101] Roderick Banks, *Lindley & Banks on Partnership* (20th edn, Sweet & Maxwell 2019), Chapter 12, Section 1.

[102] The only clear example of such a case encountered in the reported cases and sampled archival materials was *Parcas v Humphrey* (1805) C 33/537, ff339r–339v. This involved a dispute between former partners over a piece of machinery owned by the firm, and who was entitled to it upon dissolution. The court record states that one partner was to employ another as agent.

[103] Discussed below in Section 4.2.

[104] ibid.

[105] Eg *Whitehead v Tuckett* (1812) 15 East 400, 405; 104 ER 896, 898 (KB).

apply to partners. In *Meyer v Sharpe* (1813)[106] Sir James Mansfield CJCP ruled that an agent could not pledge his principal's goods after his principal's bankruptcy. A partner would have been able to do this in respect of the estate of his bankrupt co-partner.[107] Sir James Mansfield justified his ruling on the basis that an agent had no beneficial interest in his principal's goods, whereas a partner (a co-owner in equity) would have had such an interest in partnership assets. *Meyer* and its reasoning were affirmed and applied by Sir Robert Dallas CJCP in *Raba v Ryland* (1819).[108] Accordingly, there was clear authority to the effect that a partner's ability to bind his co-partners *did not* relate to the fact that he was an agent for his firm.

4.2 Partners Binding the Firm in 'the Course of Business'

If Regency era courts treated the authority doctrines governing agents and partners as distinct, why then did treatise writers assert that partners were agents? The answer seems to be that the ostensible authority doctrine governing partners evolved to resemble closely that governing agents. Courts resolved both sets of cases using very similar notions of comparative fault.

The partnership agreement formed the source of partners' power to bind one another. As above, a partner could bind his co-partners by contract, or dispose of the assets presently owned by the partners jointly, whenever allowed to do so by the terms of the partnership agreement. This latter power was not an incident of their equitable co-ownership of the partnership assets, but the authority conferred by the partnership agreement. It is because the partnership agreement was the source of a partner's authority that he could only bind his co-partners by deed, where the partnership agreement itself was in the form of a deed.[109]

The authority of each partner to bind the partnership was interpreted in light of the partnership's course of business. It should be noted that the terms of the power of a partner to bind his co-partners would be construed broadly. Unlike in cases involving trust deeds, where powers of investment and delegation were construed strictly, the powers of partners to bind one another were construed more broadly, and each partner was treated as having the power to bind the firm when acting within the purposes of the business. The classical formulation of the principle was given by Lord Mansfield CJKB in *Hope v Cust* (1774):

[106] 5 Taunt 74, 128 ER 614 (CP).
[107] See text to (n 125) below.
[108] Gow 132, 171 ER 861 (CP).
[109] For the rule and its exceptions see Gow, *A Practical Treatise on the Law of Partnership* (n 99) 58–60.

> . . . there is no doubt but that the act of every single partner in a transaction relating to the partnership binds all the others. If one give a letter of credit or guarantie in the name of all the partners it binds all.[110]

The point was elaborated upon by William Watson in the first English treatise on partnership:

> Although the general rule of law is, that no one is liable upon any contract except such as are privy to it; yet this is not contravened by the liability of partners, as they may be imagined virtually present at and sanctioning the proceedings they singly enter into in the course of trade; or as each vested with a power enabling them to act at once as principals and as the authorized agents of their co-partners. It is for the advantage of partners themselves that they are thus held liable, as the credit of their firm in the mercantile world is hereby greatly enhanced, and a vast facility is given to all their dealings . . . A due regard to the interests of strangers is at the same time observed; for where a merchant deals with one of several partners, he goes upon the credit of the whole partnership, and therefore ought to have his remedy against all the individuals who compose it.[111]

Both saw partners as impliedly consenting to all transactions entered into by their co-partners in the course of the partnership's business. This made sense. If A and B became partners, of course each intended the other to have authority to bind the partnership when acting within the course of the agreed business. It would have been inefficient to require *every* partner in a firm to ratify every transaction that the firm entered into.

Conversely, this rule meant that prima facie partners would not be bound by errant co-partners acting beyond the scope of the firm's business. An errant partner could not bind the firm by entering into a transaction with a third party who knew, or should have known, about the partner's breach of the partnership agreement. The third party would have such notice where he: had colluded with the partner to defraud the firm;[112] had read a newspaper in which the errant partner's lack of authority had been advertised;[113] had knowingly taken a bill drawn upon the partnership by the errant partner for his private use;[114] had been told that the transaction was to be kept secret from the partnership.[115] The partnership would also not

110 1 East 48, 53; 102 ER 19, 21 (cited from manuscript by Lord Kenyon in *Shirreff v Wilks* (1800) 1 East 48, 102 ER 19), affirmed in *Sandilands v Marsh* (1819) 2 B&A 673, 106 ER 511 (KB).

111 Watson (n 99) 167, repeated almost verbatim in Gow, *A Practical Treatise on the Law of Partnership* (n 99) 36–38.

112 *Hope v Cust* (n 110); *Wells v Masterman* (1799) Esp 731, 170 ER 512 (KB); *Swan v Steele* (1806) 7 East 210, 213; 103 ER 80, 82 (KB); *Bond v Gibson* (1808) 1 Camp 185, 170 ER 923 (KB); *Ridley v Taylor* (1810) 13 East 175, 104 ER 336 (KB); *Bignold v Waterhouse* (1813) 1 M&S 255, 105 ER 95 (KB).

113 *Lord Galway v Matthew* (1808) 1 Camp 403, 170 ER 1000 (KB).

114 *Ex p Agace* (1792) 2 Cox 312, 30 ER 145 (BC); *Green v Deakin* (1818) 2 Stark 347, 171 ER 669 (KB).

115 *Arden v Sharpe* (1797) 2 Esp 524, 170 ER 442 (KB).

be bound where the transaction was of a type which was clearly not within its usual business, such as where a partner in a trading or manufacturing firm guaranteed the debts of a third person in the firm's name.[116] These circumstances were suspicious, and only a dishonest or reckless trader would have entered into such transactions without asking further questions.

However, the King's Bench and the Bankruptcy Court refused to allow firms to escape liability for the unauthorised acts of a co-partner who dealt with a third party in what appeared to be the ordinary course of the firm's business: much as in the agency cases. In *Hope v Cust* (1774),[117] Lord Mansfield had said that those who dealt with errant partners would have their expectations upheld where the transaction was in the course of business unless there was 'covin or such gross negligence to amount to covin, for covin is defined to be a contrivance between two to defraud or cheat a third'.[118] In *Wells v Masterman* (1799),[119] Lord Kenyon CJKB emphasised that this did not mean that a firm would escape from all consequences of a partner acting beyond the terms of the partnership agreement. He ruled that:

> When a man enters into a partnership, he certainly commits his dearest rights to the discretion of everyone who form a part of that partnership in which he engages; and if a bill is drawn upon the partnership in their usual style and form, and it is accepted by one of the partners, it certainly binds the partnership to the payment of it; but if a man has dealings with one partner only, and he draws a bill on the partnership on account of those dealings, he is guilty of a fraud, and in his hands the acceptance made by that partner would be void; but it would be otherwise in the case of a *bona fide* indorsee. In his hands, the acceptance of one of the partners binds the partnership, as he is ignorant of the circumstances under which it was created, and takes it on the credit of the partnership name.[120]

On the facts of the case the partnership was forced to honour a bill of exchange accepted by a partner acting beyond the terms of the partnership agreement. The essence of Lord Kenyon's reasoning was that the partnership had held out the partner as having authority to bind it: exactly like in the agency cases concerning ostensible authority. This meant that the holder of the bill had trusted the partnership's credit and, having no reason to suspect that the partner was acting without authority, was allowed to sue the partnership. Partners generally had the power to accept bills of exchange on the firm's behalf, and it was the other partners

[116] *Crawford v Stirling* (1802) 4 Esp 207, 170 ER 693 (KB); *Duncan v Lowndes* (1813) 3 Camp 478, 170 ER 1452 (KB).
[117] (n 110).
[118] ibid 53; 21.
[119] 2 Esp 731, 170 ER 512 (KB).
[120] ibid 731–32; 512.

who created the risk of the unauthorised transaction—fully aware that a partner 'certainly commits his dearest rights to the discretion of everyone who form a part of that partnership'.

Lord Eldon reached much the same decision in *Ex p Bonbonus* (1803).[121] Unknown to the other partners, a partner pledged partnership credit to secure a private debt, and so for 'his sole use and accommodation'.[122] Lord Eldon set out the law on this point as follows:

> This petition is presented upon a principle, which it is very difficult to maintain; that if a partner for his own accommodation pledges the partnership, as the money comes to the account of the single partner only, the partnership is not bound. I cannot accede to that. I agree, if it is manifest to the persons advancing money, that it is upon the separate account, and so, that it is against good faith, that he should pledge the partnership, then they should shew, that he had authority to bind the partnership. But if it is in the ordinary course of commercial transactions, as upon discount it would be monstrous to hold, that, a man borrowing money upon a bill of exchange, pledging the partnership, without any knowledge in the bankers, that it is a separate transaction, merely because that money is all carried into the books of the individual, therefore the partnership should not be bound. No case has gone that length.[123]

In other words, the mere fact a partner had pledged the partnership's credit for his own benefit, or otherwise in breach of the partnership agreement, did not automatically mean that his co-partners would not be bound. Both Lord Kenyon and Lord Eldon were reluctant to allow third parties who had no reason to know of a partner's breach, to be bound by the terms of the partner's authority. To rule otherwise would force commercial parties to make extensive inquiries every time they dealt with a single partner on behalf of the firm, or to avoid dealing with partners individually. Accordingly, only those third parties with actual or constructive notice of the breach (as above) would be bound. The decisions would be affirmed a number of times.[124] On this basis, the courts would tend to conclude that co-partners had validly bound one another: by trading together each held the other

[121] 8 Ves Jun 540, 32 ER 465 (BC); B 1/103, pp 9–13.

[122] B 1/103, p 10.

[123] 8 Ves Jun 542–43, 32 ER 465–66.

[124] *Porthouse v Parker* (1807) 1 Camp 81, 170 ER 884 (KB); *Grant v Hawkes* (1817) cited in Joseph Chitty, *A Practical Treatise on Bills of Exchange, Checks on Bankers, Promissory, Bankers' Cash Notes, Bank Notes* (5th edn, Butterworth & Son; Clarke & Son; C Hunter; T Hamilton; W Walker and G Wilson; H Butterworth 1818) 42. An apparent exception to this trend is *Ex p Goulding* (1826) 2 G&J 118 in which Sir John Leach V-C held that a partnership was not liable on a bill of exchange accepted by an errant partner in respect of his separate debt, despite the good faith of the holder of the bill. Neither *Wells* nor *Bonbonus* were cited. The report itself gives little clue as to the reasons for this, and there is nothing in the report to suggest the bill holder had constructive notice of the partner's breach of duty.

out as having authority to do so when entering the types of transaction that particular trade involved. Even after dissolution of the concern, partners would continue to bind one another post-dissolution, unless notice were given to third parties: usually by placing a notice on the *London Gazette*.[125]

The reasoning here strongly resembles the agency cases and links into contemporary ideas of responsible trading. A, by taking B into partnership, held out B as having authority to bind him. Although A had not consented to B's actions, B nevertheless had what a modern lawyer would term ostensible authority to bind A's credit. This explains why it was that A and B had ostensible authority to bind one another even when they only *appeared* to the world to be partners, and why contemporary treatise writers came to see partners as agents of their firms. Although partnership authority rules evolved independently of the equivalent agency rules, the considerations informing each type of dispute were the same, and the rules governing each converged. As this happened, English law came to fit neatly within the civilian formulation of a partner as an agent of his firm, and the courts' concern with the relative fault of A and C came to the fore. English courts—of both law and equity—would uphold transactions entered into by an agent or partner which appeared to be in the normal course of business, in circumstances which were not suspicious. Third parties who dealt with agents and partners in good faith, acted responsibly according to contemporary business practices, and had no reason to suspect any lack of authority, could be sure of ultimately being able to claim against business assets.

5. Conclusions

In sum, partners and agents would bind business assets when they were authorised to act or appeared to be acting in the ordinary course of business. This is because courts determined the effect of unauthorised transactions entered into by agents and partners by looking at the comparative fault of A and C. Was C innocently misled by A's having given B, a fraudulent partner or agent, the appearance of authority? Or was C one of the reckless over-traders responsible for contemporary economic instability, who had entered into the transaction with B in suspicious circumstances without making proper enquiries? The analysis had roots in the political economic ideas that reckless trading was responsible for destabilising the economy but developed in the court's own precedents to focus on whether B's

[125] They would not be treated as partners inter se. See *Waugh v Carver* (1793) 2 H Black 235, 246; 126 ER 525, 532 (CP); *Hesketh v Blanchard* (1803) 4 East 144, 102 ER 785 (KB); *Parsons v Crosby* (1805) 5 Esp 199, 170 ER 785 (KB); *Ex p Hamper* (1811) 17 Ves Jun 403, 34 ER 156 (Ch); *Ex p Broome* (1811) 1 Rose 69 (BC); *Geddes v Wallace* (1820) 2 Bligh 270, 300; 3 ER 238, 338 (HL); *Smith v Watson* (1824) 2 B&C 401, 107 ER 434 (KB).

actions would have appeared suspicious to a reasonable commercial party in C's position. It had the side effect of upholding transactions which occurred in the ordinary course of business—in that sense it was commercially efficient and facilitated trade. However, as will be shown in the next chapter, the courts' conception of what constituted reckless trading as opposed to some ordinary course of business, could differ from the assessments of merchants or of legislators in Parliament.

4
Judicial Resistance to Merchant Demands: Factors and Paternalism in the King's Bench

In the 1820s, what counted as an agent's 'ordinary course of business' became a major Parliamentary issue. The dispute was rooted in a profound disagreement between the government, merchants, and the Court of King's Bench—the most important common law court in the Regency period—as to what should properly be considered the course of business of a factor: a commercial agent given possession of his principal's goods to sell in his own name. The controversy arose over whether a factor had authority to *pledge* his principal's property: was it part of B's course of business to give A's property as security for a debt, rather than selling it outright? On the one hand, merchants contended that factors would typically appear as owners of the property, and so pledges made by a factor should bind the principal's business assets under the doctrine of ostensible authority, otherwise C's legitimate expectations would be undermined. The government took the same view—hoping to encourage foreign merchants to store and sell their wares in Britain through agents. However, the King's Bench rejected the argument, fearing that allowing factors to validly pledge their principal's property in respect of their own debts would facilitate widespread fraud and breach of fiduciary duty by factors. In turn, this would encourage the type of immoral trading which caused financial instability. The dispute became a public debate over the proper relationship between legal rules and commercial practice, and whether the courts or traders were better placed to decide which rules would best encourage the right sort of commerce.

1. The Rule in *Paterson v Tash*

The origin of the rule that a factor, with authority to sell his master's goods, had no authority to pledge them was said to be *Paterson v Tash* (1742).[1] A shipped linens to B, his factor. B indorsed an invoice for the linens, and thereby the right to claim

[1] 2 Str 1178, 93 ER 1110 (KB).

Capitalism Before Corporations. Andreas Televantos, Oxford University Press (2020). © Andreas Televantos.
DOI: 10.1093/oso/9780198870340.003.0005.

the linens when they arrived at port, to C, a creditor of B for £800. C believed the linens belonged to B in his own right, and was unaware of A. B went bankrupt, and A sought to recover the property from C. C claimed a lien over the linens for the value of the debt which he was owed by B.

The pleadings show that C's counsel argued that the transaction was a sale in the usual course of business: they stated 'it is usual for merchants and others to sell goods which are consigned to them'.[2] In Chancery, Lord Hardwicke LC seems to have accepted this argument, describing the disposition made by B to C as a sale, albeit a sale 'to secure a debt due' from B to C.[3] The statement that the disposition was a sale to secure a debt is a puzzling one: if B had given A's goods to C by way of sale then there would have been an absolute transfer, discharging rather than securing the debt owed to C, and leaving B with no right to redeem the linens. The point, presumably, is that upon B's failure to repay the debt, the transfer to C would become absolute: a fortiori authority to sell therefore included authority to pledge. For that reason, Lord Hardwicke thought that the transaction was prima facie valid. He saw the question in the case as a factual one: had the disposition by B to C been made after A's bankruptcy? If so, then B's authority to dispose of A's assets would have determined upon A's bankruptcy, and so he could not have given title to C.[4] Being faced with an issue of fact, Lord Hardwicke referred the matter to the King's Bench for determination.

However, Sir William Lee CJKB took a different view of the case. He disagreed with Lord Hardwicke as to the nature of the transaction between B and C, and characterised the transaction as a pledge rather than sale:

> It was held by C. J. Lee, that though a factor has power to sell, and thereby bind his principal, yet he cannot bind or affect the property of the goods by pledging them as a security for his own debt, though there is the formality of a bill of parcels and a receipt. And the jury found accordingly.[5]

Sir William Lee's concern here was to prevent agents using the assets of their principal as security for their past private indebtedness. This was presumably because the risk to a principal was particularly acute in such cases. After all, where B sold A's goods to C without authority, then purchase money came into B's hands, which he would have held on trust for A.[6] However, where B was already indebted to C, and pledged A's goods, then no new value came into B's hands in respect of which A could be secured. That being said, early in the nineteenth century the King's

[2] C 12/2226/7.
[3] 9 Mod 397, 88 ER 531 (Ch).
[4] Unless the doctrine of ostensible authority applied, as discussed in Chapter 3, Section 2.
[5] *Paterson* (n 1).
[6] *Scott v Surman* (1742–43) Willes 400, 125 ER 1235.

Bench would refuse to characterise pledges of goods as sales, and so within a factor's authority, even when the pledge was given in return for *new value* which would have been held on trust for A; though on the facts of those cases there does not appear to have remained any property in specie which could have been the object of a proprietary claim.[7]

One potential explanation for the decisions is the fact that a factor in this period was considered a species of trustee: holding possessory title to his principal's assets on trust and owing what we would today call fiduciary duties.[8] Thomas Gisborne, when discussing the duties of factors and brokers, emphasised that the root of most breaches of duties by agents was the making of unauthorised profits and using their principal's assets for their own benefit.[9] The King's Bench—though a court of common law rather than equity—took the view that allowing factors to give title to their principal's goods by way of security, in the absence of express authority to do so, would pose a particular risk to principals. It would encourage agents to pledge their principal's goods for their own private debts and dis-incentivise third parties from making proper enquiries as to the scope of an agent's authority. The risk of opportunism which a presumption of authority would create could be seen to have prompted the common law courts' restrictive view of a factor's authority to pledge. The attitude is evident from the decision in *Guerreiro v Peile* (1820),[10] where the King's Bench ruled that a factor does not have authority to barter his principal's goods. Lord Abbott CJKB and Bayley J are reported as giving only brief judgments on point, each of which is essentially a point-blank assertion that authority to sell is not equivalent to authority to barter. Of more interest is Holroyd J's reasoning, which centred on the duties of an agent: 'Where a factor sells the goods of his principal, it is his duty to keep that sale wholly unconnected, and not to mix other matters with it to the detriment of his principal.'[11] The point is significant in that Holroyd J saw the rule that a factor could not barter away the goods of his principal as rooted in his duties to keep his own property and interests wholly distinct from his principal's. Similar reasoning could be seen as underlying the King's Bench's refusal to allow factors to pledge their principal's goods as security for the factors' own debts. It was seeking to discourage breach of fiduciary duty by factors: challenging modern perceptions that such duties were exclusively the preserve of equity.

[7] *Graham v Dyster* (1817) 2 Stark 21, 171 ER 559; 6 M&S 1, 105 ER 1143 (KB); *Shipley v Kymer* (1813) 1 M&S 484, 105 ER 181 (KB); *Ducos v Ryland* (1812) 5 Moore 518 (KB); also *Jackson v Clarke* (1827)1 Y&J 216, 148 ER 651 (Ex).

[8] See Chapter 4, text from (n 60) to (n 76).

[9] Thomas Gisborne, *An Enquiry into the Duties of Men in the Higher and Middle Classes of Society in Great Britain*, vol 2 (5th edn, J White; Cadell and Davies 1800) 360–67.

[10] 3 B&A 616, 106 ER 786 (KB).

[11] ibid 618; 787.

2. Challenging the Rule in *Paterson* in the Courts

2.1 C's Lien

The rule in *Paterson* was challenged in the courts by litigants throughout the Regency period, and cases of factors pledging their principal's goods were not uncommon. In the first set of cases counsel sought to challenge the rule technically, by arguing that C had acquired an interest in the property which had priority over A's title. On that basis, A could not assert his title to the pledged property until the debt owed by B to C had been paid.

The first such case was *Daubigny v Duval* (1794).[12] On the facts, as above B, a factor, had pledged A, his principal's, goods to C, a third party, as security for B's own debt. A sought to recover the property from C. C's counsel sought to defeat the claim by focussing on the nature of B's rights in the property—in particular the lien B had over it for his expenses. A factor's lien was his right to retain possession of his principal's assets until he was paid any expenses and commission owed to him by his principal. In technical terms, B could plead sums he was owed by A as a defence to any claim brought by A to recover the property. A could therefore not recover the property from B without first paying B's expenses, and so discharging his lien. In *Daubigny*, C's counsel argued that B's lien was a proprietary right which could be transferred to C. For that reason, they argued that C could plead any sums that C was owed by B as a defence to A's claim to recover the property.

The King's Bench rejected the argument, ruling that a B's lien could not be transferred to a third party, and that A should always be able to reclaim the property once he had paid B's expenses—regardless of whether C was still owed a debt by B. Otherwise, A would be left at the mercy of any bargain struck between B and C, unable to claim the property back until the value of the debt B owed to C had been paid. The decision was affirmed a number of times,[13] though with a significant qualification: A could *not* recover his property from C where sums were still owing to B, despite the supposed impossibility of B transferring his lien.[14]

In other cases, it was contended that C himself had a lien over the property pledged to him by A, which did not depend on transfer of B's lien. The argument was accepted in cases of sub-agency: where B hired C as his agent with A's (implied actual) authority, C would have a lien over A's property for sums owed to him by B.[15] However, where C was *not* a sub-agent in this way, but

[12] 5 TR 604, 101 ER 338 (KB).

[13] *Sweet v Pym* (1800) 1 East 4; 102 ER 2 (KB); *M'Combie v Davies* (1805) 7 East 5, 103 ER 3 (KB).

[14] *Atkyns v Amber* (1796) 2 Esp 493, 170 ER 431 (CP); *Dixon v Purse* (1800) Peake 187, 170 ER 240 (KB); *Castling v Aubert* (1802) 2 East 325, 102 ER 393 (KB).

[15] *Maanss v Henderson* (1801) 1 East 335, 102 ER 130 (KB) (Lord Kenyon); *Mann v Shiffner* (1802) 2 East 523, 102 ER 469 (KB); *Blackburn v Kymer* (1814) 5 Taunt 584, 128 ER 818 (CP) (Sir Vicary Gibbs

was nevertheless aware that B was A's agent, C would acquire no lien over the property.[16]

There was also some authority to the effect that C would have a lien for all the sums he was owed by B in cases where C had been unaware of A. For instance, in *Maanss v Henderson* (1801)[17] Lord Kenyon suggested that C would have succeeded in *Daubigny*, had B disclosed A's existence at the time of making the pledge, though the report of *Daubigny* gives no indication that this was relevant to the court's reasoning in that case, and indeed does not mention whether or not C was aware of A. In *Pulteney v Kymer* (1800),[18] Lord Eldon CJCP ruled that C had acquired a lien with priority over A, on facts where C had been unaware of A's existence at the time B made pledge. A could therefore not recover the property without paying the sums that C was owed by B. It appears from the discussion of the case in the 1823 Select Committee report on the law relating to merchants, agents, and factors, that A ultimately only recovered £500 of the £18,000 sale price of his property, once C's lien had been discharged.[19] However, as discussed below, the King's Bench in the early nineteenth century refused to follow the decision in *Pultney*. The court would always allow A to recover the property from C, regardless of whether C was aware of A's existence at the time of the pledge, and regardless of what obligations B owed to C. The agency law Select Committee recognised that *Pultney* was at odds with the rule later applied by the King's Bench, and on this basis concluded that the rule against factors pledging only came to be strictly applied in the nineteenth century.[20]

2.2 The Actual Scope of a Factor's Course of Business

Following the King's Bench's refusal to allow a factor to pledge his principal's goods on the basis of his lien, the rule that a factor had no authority to pledge was attacked more directly. In a number of cases, counsel argued that it was normal commercial practice for a factor to pledge his principal's good, and so as a matter of fact a factor's authority to sell included an implied actual authority to pledge.

CJCP); *Querioz v Trueman* (1824) 3 B&C 342, 107 ER 760 (KB). The same principle applied where C arranged an insurance policy in his own name for A's benefit, *Westwood v Bell* (1815) 4 Camp 349, 171 ER 111(KB).

16 *Maanss* (n 15); *Snook v Davidson* (1809) 2 Camp 218, 170 ER 1134 (KB); *Lanyon v Blanchard* (1811) 2 Camp 597, 170 ER 1264 (KB); *Querioz* (n 15); *Stierneld v Holden* (1825) 4 B&C 5, 107 ER 961 (KB).

17 *Maanss* (n 15) 337; 131.

18 3 Esp 182, 170 ER 581 (CP).

19 Agency Select Committee, 'Report from the Select Committee on the Law Relating to Merchants, Agents or Factors' (HC 1823, 452-IV) 6.

20 ibid.

However, such arguments were unsuccessful. In *De Bouchout v Goldsmid* (1800),[21] Lord Loughborough C ruled that a power of attorney which included a power to assign and transfer did not in general imply a power to pledge, though he was urged to decide the contrary on the basis that it would be unfair to C, where C lacked notice of A's instructions to B.

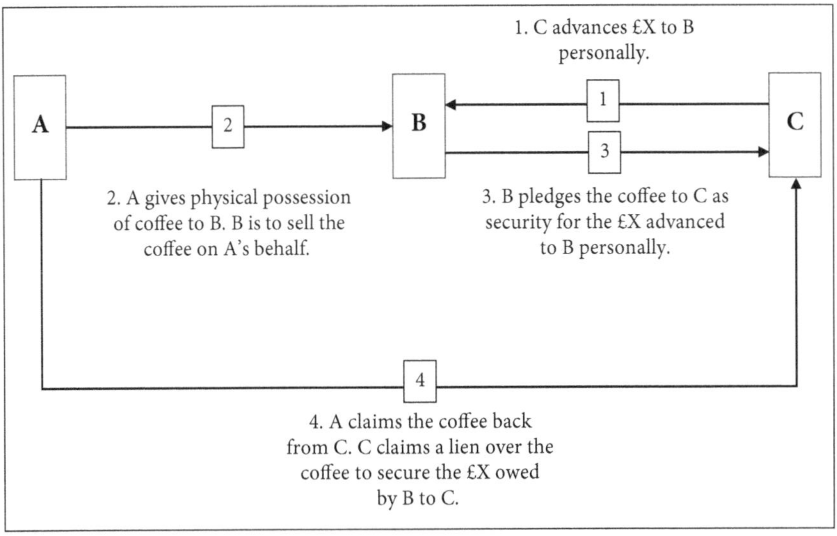

Figure 4.1 Fact pattern: cases concerning a factor's course of business

The matter was considered specifically in relation to factors in *Martini v Coles* (1813),[22] illustrated in Figure 4.1. B owed money to C on a private debt. A owned coffee which he put into the hands of B (his factor). B pledged the coffee to C as security for The prior private debt, and A brought trover to recover the goods from C. C resisted the claim, seeking sums he was owed by B from the value of the goods. C had had no notice that the coffee belonged to A.

For C, it was argued that B's general authority as a factor included actual authority to pledge goods. Principals as a matter of fact, it was argued, intended their factors to have the authority to pledge. As Michael Lobban writes, '[i]n 1811, when the price of colonial produce was low, London factors borrowed large sums by pledging goods in their possession. This allowed them to postpone sales of commodities until prices rose, an arrangement which was generally beneficial to the owners.'[23] Evidence to this effect was given to the 1823 Select Committee on the

[21] 5 Ves Jun 211, 31 ER 551 (Ch).
[22] 1 M&S 140, 105 ER 53 (KB).
[23] Michael Lobban, 'Property Torts' in William Cornish and others (eds), *Oxford History of the Laws of England*, vol XII (OUP 2010) 1122. Note that there was an economic crisis in 1811, and to make credit more available, the Bank of England was temporarily allowed to provide advances on pledges and

reform of the law relating to agents and factors: evidence showing the mercantile community had presumed such pledges were valid.[24] C's counsel therefore urged the King's Bench to recognise contemporary commercial practice, in a way which would ultimately benefit principals.

The King's Bench dismissed C's argument, refusing to give effect to commercial expectations, and affirming that a factor had no general authority to pledge his principal's goods. Lord Ellenborough, who had previously voiced doubts about the rule that factors had no authority to pledge,[25] nevertheless saw it as too well established to be overturned:

> [I]t has been decided ever since the case of *Paterson* v. *Tash*, that a factor cannot pledge. Perhaps it would have been as well if it had been originally decided that where it was equivocal whether a person was authorized to act as principal or factor, a pledge made by such a person free from any circumstances of fraud was valid. But it is idle now to speculate upon this subject, since a long series of cases has decided that a factor cannot pledge.[26]

Accordingly, he ruled that a factor's pledge would not bind his principal, unless—by reasoning analogous to *Pickering v Busk*—it could be shown that the factor had ostensible authority to do so by virtue of his principal having clothed him with some additional indicia of title, a point Lord Ellenborough affirmed in *Boyson v Coles* (1817).[27] In *Martini v Coles*, Le Blanc J reluctantly reached the same conclusion as Lord Ellenborough, again clearly feeling bound by authority on point.[28] It was only Bayley J who defended the rule in *Paterson* as a matter of principle: he rejected counsel's argument that the rule in *Paterson v Tash* was hostile to principals in general, by making the world unable to trust their agents, and emphasised that the rule simply prevented fraudulent agents pledging their principal's goods for their *own* debts. Bayley J expressed the same view in later cases, where he would go so far as to assert that the rule had operated 'much to increase the foreign commerce of this kingdom'.[29] In later cases Abbott J, later Lord Abbott CJKB, would argue that the rule against factors pledging was 'for the benefit of commerce',[30] 'one of the greatest safeguards which the foreign merchant has in making consignments of goods to be sold in this country',[31] and would only harm those who 'blindly

other securities. This change would be revived and incorporated into the Bank's charter in 1826, Sean Thomas, 'The Origins of the Factors Acts 1823 and 1825' (2011) 32 JLH 151, 185–86.

24 These doubts were collectively recognised by the Agency Select Committee (n 19) 3–4.
25 *Pickering v Busk* (1812) 15 East 38, 44; 104 ER 758, 761 (KB).
26 1 M&S 140, 142; 105 ER 53, 54 (KB).
27 6 M&S 14, 17–18; 105 ER 1148, 1149 (KB).
28 (n 22) 149; 56.
29 *Querioz* (n 15).
30 *Graham v Dyster* (1817) 2 Stark 21, 27; 171 ER 559, 561 (KB).
31 *Quiroz* (n 15) 349–50; 763.

advance[d] their money to those who ask for it *without exercising a little caution*'.[32] The decision that factors had no actual authority to pledge was later affirmed by both the King's Bench[33] and the Common Pleas.[34]

The reasoning here is best understood as follows. Although, as seen in Chapter 3, the King's Bench would typically uphold transactions which appeared to occur in the ordinary course of business, their fundamental concern was 'fault'. Fraudulent and reckless trading, after all, caused economic instability—and the courts sought to discourage such behaviour. Although the question of what was fraudulent or reckless in many cases would turn on the normal expectations of commercial parties, in the factors cases Lord Abbott's King's Bench thought that normal commercial practice encouraged fraud, and so they were not willing to uphold the expectations of commercial parties. Upholding such expectations was not the courts' main aim.

3. Statutory Reform of the *Paterson* Rule and Judicial Backlash

By 1820 the rule that factors could not pledge was firmly entrenched, with the principal commercial judges in the King's Bench—Lord Abbott and Bayley J—firmly of the view that the rule was in the interests of commerce, because it discouraged the fraudulent and reckless trading blamed for the financial instability of the period. As Sean Thomas has observed,[35] this judicial refusal to give effect to contemporary business practices rankled merchants,[36] and was seen by both the men of business and by the government of the 1820s as hostile to commerce.[37] In particular, it was argued that many merchants had been unaware of the rule, had taken pledges from agents which they had presumed were good, and had thereby exposed themselves to unforeseen losses.[38] Further—as counsel had contended in *Martini v Coles*— it was argued that a factor needed to be able to pledge goods to raise credit in times of economic downturn when selling would be unfavourable. As above, factors had behaved in this way during the financial crisis of 1810–11, unaware of the state of the law. Such a practice ensured principals ultimately obtained good prices for their goods. Recognising factors as having the authority to pledge then would be as much for the benefit of principals as third parties, and would encourage trade through factors.

32 *Ducos v Ryland* (1812) 5 Moore 518 (KB). Emphasis added.
33 *Graham* (n 30); *Queroiz* (n 15).
34 *Guichard v Morgan* (1819) 4 Moore 36 (CP); *Fielding v Kymer* (1821) 2 B&B 639, 129 ER 1112 (CP).
35 Thomas (n 23).
36 ibid 156–59.
37 Agency Select Committee (n 19) 9–19.
38 ibid 8.

Importantly, Lord Liverpool's government, after a reshuffle of 1821, deliberately pursued free trade policies with an aim of encouraging traders internationally to warehouse their goods in Britain, transforming the country into an international market and clearing house: providing a ready reserve of cash and goods in case of war[39] and generating money to import corn to stave off any threatened famine.[40] 'In short, [the government] was desirous of making this country the general depot, the greatest emporium of the commerce of the world',[41] as William Wallace MP put it.[42]

This explains why the government appointed a Select Committee to investigate the Law Relating to Merchants, Agents, or Factors: those who purchased warehoused stock in Britain would very often purchase it from a factor rather than its owner. Protecting the expectations of those who did business with factors was central to the government's economic plan. Further, as Martin Daunton has argued, British firms in the early nineteenth century relied on factors to access foreign markets. Factors would typically have expert knowledge of those markets which their principals lacked, and selling to new overseas markets helped British firms survive despite domestic overproduction in the early nineteenth century.[43] It is therefore unsurprising that the select committee was dominated by commercial men rather than practising lawyers, and that of the fifty-two witnesses examined by the Select Committee, fifty were merchants, and only two were lawyers.[44]

It is equally unremarkable that the Select Committee Report of 1823[45] criticised the rule that a factor could not pledge as unjustified. The rule insufficiently protected those who dealt with agents who were ignorant of the terms of the agency. James Manning, a barrister, gave evidence to the committee to the effect that he had held a conversation with Sir Vicary Gibbs CJCP shortly before Sir Vicary's death, and that the judge had told him that *Paterson v Tash* had been misreported, and did not in fact stand for the proposition that a factor could not pledge his principal's goods without specific authority to that effect.[46] Though Manning was unable to adduce any further evidence of this, the Select Committee accepted his evidence that the case had been misreported,[47] though the court record itself suggests that

[39] See Gisborne (n 9) 199–200 ('The usual object of even good governments in encouraging trade is merely to replenish the public coffers to strengthen the national marine, and thus to render the state formidable to rival powers').

[40] Boyd Hilton, *Corn, Cash Commerce: The Economic Policies of Tory Government* (OUP 1978) chs 6 and 8.

[41] Thomas Wallace MP, HC Deb 25 June 1821, vol 1, col 129.

[42] Wallace was Vice President of the Board of Trade and Chair of a number of committees appointed to investigate how to promote foreign trade in the 1820s. See George Stronach and HCG Matthew, 'Wallace, Thomas, Baron Wallace' in Sir David Cannadine (ed), *The Oxford Dictionary of National Biography* (OUP 2013) <https://doi.org/10.1093/ref:odnb/28543> accessed 18 March 2020.

[43] Martin Daunton, *Progress and Poverty: An Economic and Social History of Britain 1700–1850* (OUP 1995) 334–38.

[44] Thomas (n 23) 165.

[45] Agency Select Committee (n 19).

[46] ibid 76.

[47] ibid 5.

the case was correctly reported and that the Select Committee was mistaken on this point.[48] Further, the Select Committee argued that removing the rule in *Paterson* would make English common law more consistent with law on the Continent,[49] and with the position in equity under which a pledgee of a trustee could be protected by the bona fide purchaser for value defence.[50] Reversing the rule would also have made the law governing the authority of agents and partners more similar, and assimilated the rules governing pledges of chattels and bills of lading with bills of exchange.[51]

Accordingly, the committee recommended that any person possessing 'a bill of lading, or other apparent symbol of property, not importing that such property belongs to others, shall be considered as true owner, so far as respects any person who may deal with him, in relation to such property, under an ignorance of his real character'.[52] The committee sought to protect principals from abuse at the hands of their agents by recommending no person 'taking security for a prior debt due from a factor or agent, upon goods in the possession of such factor or agent, or of which he holds such symbol of property as is before mentioned, was to acquire any greater interest therein than really belonged to, and might have been enforced by such factor or agent'.[53] Further, the committee recommended that the act of an agent pledging the goods of his principal be made a criminal offence, to discourage agents from exceeding their authority, while at the same time protecting the titles of those who dealt with them.[54] The reforms recommended by the committee were enacted in two stages through the support of merchants and Lord Liverpool's commercially minded ministry, in spite of the objections of a more conservative lawyer class which worried that the reforms in question would encourage fraud.[55]

The Factors Act 1823[56] enacted only a portion of the Select Committee's recommendations. Section 1 provided a defence only to the disponee of a person in whose name goods were to be shipped, while section 2 provided that agents or consignees could, by the act of depositing or pledging their principal's goods, assign any lien they had over those goods to third parties. The Factors Act 1825[57] went

48 See discussion above in Section 1.
49 Agency Select Committee (n 19) 19–21.
50 ibid 28. For the bona fide purchaser defence, see Chapter 5, Section 1.
51 Agency Select Committee (n 19) 7, 78. A bona fide purchaser for value without notice would take good title to bills of exchange (*Collins v Martin* (1797) 1 B&P 648, 126 ER 1113 (CP)), exchequer bills (*Wookey v Pole* (1820) 4 B&A 1, 106 ER 839 (KB)), and bank notes (*Miller v Race* (1758) 1 Burr 452, 97 ER 398; 2 Keny 189, 96 ER 1151 (KB)). A bona fide purchaser of a bill of lading, which gave a right to specific tangible property, would not receive the same protection (*Wright v Campbell* (1767) 1 Wm Bl 628, 96 ER 363; 4 Burr 2046, 98 ER 66 (KB)).
52 Agency Select Committee (n 19) 21.
53 ibid.
54 ibid 22.
55 Robert Winter, *Objections to the Proposed Alteration of the Law Relating to Principal and Factor* (R Stevens and Sons 1823); Thomas (n 23) 160, 183–87.
56 4 Geo IV c 83.
57 6 Geo IV c 94.

further. Section 1 made clear that factors or agents with goods in their possession would be deemed to be owners for the purpose of passing good title to third parties without notice of the agency. Section 2 made clear that anyone who had been entrusted with a bill of lading or other indicium of title could prima facie pledge good title to the property in question, effectively expanding the doctrine of ostensible authority.[58] This appears to have been the provision regarded with most hostility by lawyers in Parliament during the reading of the bill,[59] and later by treatise writers.[60] Section 3 again provided that where an agent gave his principal's property as security for his own *pre-existing* indebtedness, that even a creditor without notice of the agency would not acquire any interest in that property beyond the value of the agent's lien. Section 4 made clear that agents who sold goods in the 'ordinary Course of Business', or with the authority of their principal, would bind their principal. Section 5 made clear that an agent could effectively transfer his lien to a third party with notice of the agency, where he purported to pledge the principal's property to that third party. Section 6 made clear that nothing in the Act would prevent the principal, or his bankrupt estate, from recovering goods from an agent or third party by paying off the advances secured upon them (to that agent or a third party respectively). Finally, section 7 made it a criminal misdemeanour for an agent to 'deposit or pledge any Goods' consigned to them as such 'as a security for any Money or Negotiable Instrument or Instruments borrowed or received by such Factor or Agent', where the agent 'appl[ied] or dispose[d] thereof to his or her own Use, in violation of good Faith, and with Intent to defraud the Owner or Owners of any such Goods'.

Accordingly, the King's Bench's approach to a factor's power to pledge was seen by Parliament as hostile to the government's economic policy and reversed. When faced with a choice between A and C, the King's Bench had leaned in favour of A on the basis that the property had been his originally, A's perceived vulnerability in pledge cases, and a desire to discourage breach of fiduciary duty by factors. However, the Select Committee and those from whom it took evidence took a different view. The point was made most clearly by the reformer and political economist David Ricardo,[61] a member of the 1823 Select Committee, who argued that where an agent acted outside his principal's authority 'it was not desirable that either party [A or C] should lose: but one must suffer, and the sufferer ought to be the individual who did not use proper caution'.[62] Although the reformers were driven by a desire to encourage foreign merchants to warehouse in Britain, they

58 See Chapter 3.

59 Thomas (n 23) 182.

60 William Paley, *A Treatise on the Law of Principal and Agent* (JH Lloyd ed, Saunders and Benning 1833) 227.

61 Terry Peach, 'Ricardo, David' in Sir David Cannadine (ed), *The Oxford Dictionary of National Biography* <http://www.oxforddnb.com/view/article/23471?docPos=1> accessed 18 March 2020.

62 Agency Select Committee (n 19) 161. Also see 78–79 and 170.

also adopted the fault-based reasoning used in Lord Ellenborough's judgments on ostensible authority: reasoning with deeper roots in the contemporary ideas about responsible trade discussed in Chapter 3. Where A used B as his factor, he held B out as having authority to bind him, and thus created the risk that third parties could be misled as to the extent of B's actual authority. Where B exceeded this authority, then A rather than C should have to bear any resulting loss, unless C had actual or constructive notice of the terms of B's authority. As has been seen, the judges and barristers in the common law courts *did* take note of standards of commercial practice, but judges were fearful that giving effect to such standards would encourage fraudulent and reckless trading.

The King's Bench would make its discontent with the Factors Act 1825 evident in its restrictive interpretation of its provisions. In *Thompson v Farmer* (1827),[63] Lord Abbott took a very restrictive view of section 5 of the Factors Act 1825. He accepted that the Act allowed an agent to transfer his lien to a third party with notice of the agency, but ruled that it applied only where the agent purported specifically to *pledge* those goods to C. On the facts of the case B had purported to sell the goods to C without authority, and so the lien had not been transferred.

The King' Bench further cut down the section's scope in *Fletcher v Heath* (1827).[64] A owed several sums to B, which were secured by a lien over such of A's assets as were in B's hands. B had transferred his lien to C, but B had subsequently been paid all he was owed by A. The issue was whether A could discharge the lien transferred to C by making payment to B. The King's Bench ruled that A could. Lord Abbott again accepted that section 5 allowed B to transfer his lien to C, but said that it *did not* prevent the lien being discharged if A later paid B his expenses and commission. A could therefore recover the property from C regardless of any subsisting obligation between B and C. In other words, the King's Bench treated C's rights in such a scenario in exactly the same way as it had before the Factors Act 1825 was passed. The ruling was confirmed in *Blandy v Allan* (1828).[65]

Further, in the 1830s the scope of section 2 was cut down drastically. Although the section was designed to provide that factors had ostensible authority to pledge their principal's goods, the courts prevented it from having its desired effect. The section was ruled only to apply for pledges of new value—and so had no operation in cases where B pledged A's property to C as security for an existing obligation. It was also ruled *only* to be triggered where A had specifically entrusted B with indicia of title, it would not be triggered simply where A had given possession of property to B.[66] Because of the restrictive interpretation of the 1825 Act, many

[63] M&M 48, 173 ER 1077 (KB).

[64] 7 B&C 517, 108 ER 815 (KB).

[65] 3 Car & P 447, 172 ER 495 (KB).

[66] For a review of the case law on point see John Russell, *The Laws Relating to Factors and Brokers* (S Sweet; V & R Stevens & GS Norton 1844) 127–35.

commentators recognised that it was essentially ineffective.[67] Greater protection for those who dealt with factors was only effectively provided by the Factors Act 1842 (5 & 6 Vict c 39).

This case law provides a clear example of the way in which the King's Bench in the early nineteenth century would not simply give effect to commercial practice and expectations—even where statutes so required—where doing so clashed with standards of proper commercial behaviour enshrined in pre-existing rules of the common law. As examined in Chapter 3, the courts' authority doctrines did generally give effect to transactions occurring in the usual course of business. However, those doctrines were *not* formulated simply to give effect to merchant expectations and to encourage trade. They were a product of the court's own weighing-up of the relative fault of A and C: a balancing-up exercise enshrined in its precedents, but also influenced by the ideas of those like Gisborne and Malthus on what constituted responsible trade.

The cases concerning a factor's authority to pledge shows that the King's Bench would not bend its rules when the product of this evaluation differed from merchant expectations and government policy. Apart from Lord Ellenborough and Le Blanc J, who doubted the wisdom of the rule, the King's Bench judges of the Regency era were convinced that the *Paterson* rule was just: principals should be protected from their agents pledging the assets they managed as security for their own debts. Treating factors as having authority to pledge their principals' goods would have encouraged fraud by agents and encouraged third parties to be more reckless in their dealings with factors—in other words exactly the sort of irresponsible trade for which contemporary economic turbulence was blamed. This was the wrong sort of trade, and the law would not encourage it. The restrictive interpretation of the Factors Act 1825 was thus rooted in a notion of what constituted responsible trade as developed in the case law, and a sense of judicial responsibility to promote economic stability.

[67] ibid 140–42; Mark McGaw, 'A History of the Common Law of Agency with Particular Reference to the Concept of Irrevocable Authority Coupled with an Interest' (DPhil, Oxford 2005) 293. Compare with Paley (n 60) 226–37, where the court's restrictive interpretation of section 5 is endorsed.

5

The Authority of Trustees and Executors

Trustees and executors acting beyond their authority posed similar problems for courts as partners and agents—though perhaps more severe. Unlike agents and partners,[1] trustees and executors had legal title to the assets they managed: they did not simply appear to be owners of trust and testamentary property, at common law they *were* the owners. That being said, trustees and executors could not use the assets they managed freely, but their authority in equity to do so was limited by the terms of the relevant trust or will. What then should happen where a third party validly purchased legal title from a trustee or executor, who was acting beyond his authority, in what seemed to be the normal course of business? Should such transactions bind the trust or testamentary assets? Understanding the law's approach to unauthorised transactions occurring in the ordinary course of business therefore involves looking at the treatment of trustees and executors as well as partners and agents.

Ultimately, the courts treated purchasers from trustees and executors in a very similar way to those who dealt with partners or agents. Reckless purchasers would lose out, while those who had no reason to know of the trustee's or executor's breach of duty would typically take good title. In other words, the courts' focus again was on the extent to which the purchaser was at fault vis-à-vis the beneficiary. However, unlike agents and partners, trustees and executors were not governed by the doctrines of ostensible authority, unless they were agents or partners also.[2]

It will be recalled that the ostensible authority of agents and partners came from the fact that partners and agents had been allowed to appear as having authority to bind their co-partners or principal. Thomas Gisborne rooted the responsibility of partners for their co-partners in the fact that partnership was a voluntary commercial relationship.[3] A trust beneficiary, however, would not always choose his trustee—for instance in cases concerning trusts for the benefit of married women, trusts created in wills, or those for the payment of debts by way of compromise

[1] As above, partners would be equitable co-owners of partnership assets, but whether they had a direct legal claim on those assets would depend on the terms of the partnership agreement, see Chapter 1, text from (n 20) to (n 25). The power of the partners to dispose of the assets in the course of the business was rooted in the authority conferred in the partnership agreement, which came to be interpreted as an agency mandate. This is discussed at length in Chapter 3, Section 4.

[2] As in the case of factors (discussed in Chapter 6, text from (n 60) to (n 76) or deed of settlement companies discussed in Chapter 2, Section 2).

[3] Thomas Gisborne, *An Enquiry into the Duties of Men in the Higher and Middle Classes of Society in Great Britain*, vol 2 (5th edn, J White; Cadell and Davies 1800) 264.

Capitalism Before Corporations. Andreas Televantos, Oxford University Press (2020). © Andreas Televantos.
DOI: 10.1093/oso/9780198870340.003.0006.

with creditors[4]—and so would not necessarily hold out his trustee as having power to bind him. This affected how the court weighed up the relative fault of the parties. Whereas partners held each other out as having authority to bind one another by trading under their joint names, a beneficiary was instead the passive recipient of the benefit of managed trust assets, making no representations about his trustee or that trustee's powers. Likewise, a testator had no real choice but to entrust his property to an executor to carry out his will upon his death—the only alternatives were to die intestate or dispose of all his property during his life. The different legal and doctrinal circumstances of trustees and executors meant that the doctrine of ostensible authority did not apply to them.

This chapter examines the doctrines governing the authority of trustees and executors, and the extent to which they could bond the assets they managed where they had no authority to do so under the express or implied terms of the trust or will. As in other areas, the courts of equity and law were concerned to protect innocent purchasers by upholding transactions which appeared to take place in the ordinary course of business, and so to facilitate trade. However, in these cases the courts had to balance that concern with a desire to ensure that trusts and wills could continue to play their respective social functions, and a recognition that testators and beneficiaries were not responsible for creating the risk of the unauthorised disposition in the same way as partners and principals.

1. The Authority of Trustees

Where a trustee disposed of assets with authority under the terms of the trust, his disposition of those assets bound the beneficiaries. Although the word was not used by contemporaries, in modern terms the interest of the beneficiary was 'overreached': exactly like the equitable interest of a partner in the assets of his firm following an authorised disposition of the firm's assets.[5]

As above, third parties who dealt with trustees acting *beyond* the terms of their authority were not protected by the doctrine of ostensible authority. Third parties who purchased from trustees were instead protected by a different doctrine: the plea of bona fide purchase for value. As David Fox has shown, the doctrine began life as a rule which determined when the purchaser of an estate in land, held by the seller to the use of another, would be 'privy' to the seller's estate and so bound by the use. However, by the nineteenth century it had developed into a more general rule governing the priority of legal and equitable interests.[6] Unlike ostensible

[4] Ie many common types of trust at the time, see Chapter 2, Section 1.

[5] See Chapter 1 at text to (n 29).

[6] David Fox, 'Purchase for Value Without Notice' in Paul S Davies, Simon Douglas, and James Goudkamp (eds), *Defences in Equity* (Hart Publishing 2018).

authority, the rule was not based on a holding out, but was based on Chancery's preference for those who gave value, though like ostensible authority it was also rooted in a desire to prevent fraud, recklessness, and lack of proper care.[7] Edward Sugden, like others in a tradition reaching back to Francis Bacon, saw the doctrine as rooted in the fact that 'a court of equity acts upon the conscience',[8] though the doctrine itself pre-dates that rationalisation.[9]

The bona fide purchase plea worked as follows. Purchasers from trustees with notice of the trust would be bound by the trust,[10] though they would owe more limited duties to the beneficiaries than original trustees,[11] but a bona fide purchaser of an interest in trust assets for value without notice would take that interest free of the claims of beneficiaries.[12] In the Regency era, the rule was wider than its modern equivalent: it protected the purchaser of *any interest*, not simply legal title as under modern law.[13] The most extensive contemporary discussion of the defence, particularly what constituted 'notice', is to be found in Edward Sugden's treatise on *Vendors and Purchasers of Estates*.[14] Sugden made clear that a purchaser would be bound by a pre-existing equitable interest where he had 'actual notice', where he had been informed by a party to the transaction of a third party's interest; or 'constructive notice', where there was evidence raising a conclusive presumption that he had such notice.[15] A purchaser who took in suspicious circumstances would have had constructive notice of adverse interests affecting the estate, as Sugden put it 'what is sufficient to put a purchaser upon an inquiry is good notice; that is, where a man has sufficient information to lead him to a fact, he shall be deemed conusant of it'.[16] For example, a purchaser would be bound by an interest he could have ascertained from a fact stated in the deed of sale; an interest created

[7] ibid. Also see Mike Macnair, 'Equity and Volunteers' (1988) 8 LS 172; Joshua Getzler and Mike Macnair, 'The Firm as Entity before the Companies Acts' in Paul Brand, Kevin Costello, and WN Osborough (eds), *Adventures of the Law: Proceedings of the Sixteenth British Legal History Conference* (Four Courts 2005); Stuart Anderson, 'Trusts and Trustees' in William Cornish and others (eds), *Oxford History of the Laws of England*, vol XII (OUP 2010) 262–68.

[8] Edward Sugden, *A Practical Treatise of the Law of Vendors and Purchasers of Estates* (J Butterworth 1826) 713–14.

[9] Fox (n 6) 62.

[10] *Saunders v Dehew* (1692) 2 Vern 271, 23 ER 775 (Ch). ('A purchaser or mortgagee shall not protect himself by taking a conveyance from a trustee after notice of the trust, for by taking such a conveyance he becomes trustee himself.')

[11] The purchaser owed more limited duties than the initial trustee, see Richard Nolan, 'Equitable Property' (2006) 122 LQR 232, 239–48.

[12] For an account of how the bona fide purchaser became 'sacrosanct' see David Yale, *Lord Nottingham's Chancery Cases*, vol II (79 Selden Soc) (Bernard Quaritch 1961) lxvi–lxviii.

[13] Edward Sugden, *The Law of Vendors and Purchasers of Estates* (3rd edn, J Butterworth 1808) 536; Sugden, *A Practical Treatise of the Law of Vendors and Purchasers of Estates* (n 8) 714. In the 1862 edition of the work the matter is put at greater length, see Edward Sugden, *The Law of Vendors and Purchasers of Estates* (H Sweet 1862) 791 and the following discussion. Also see Yale (n 12) 67, 160–63; Getzler and Macnair (n 7) 274–75.

[14] Sugden, *A Practical Treatise of the Law of Vendors and Purchasers of Estates* (n 8) 789–839.

[15] ibid 730, 732.

[16] ibid 743. See also *Taylor v Baker* (1818) 5 Price 306, 146 ER 616 (Ex).

by a registered deed where the purchaser (or his agent) had conducted a search of the register; an interest communicated to the purchaser's agent; or an interest held by a person known by the purchaser to possess the title deeds to property.[17]

From this discussion of constructive notice, it should be clear that although the bona fide purchaser defence and ostensible authority rule were distinct doctrines, both would tend to guarantee the validity of unauthorised dispositions of property which did not appear to be suspicious. Both focussed on the relative fault of the parties and the enquiries a purchaser had made. Of course, which circumstances were suspicious would turn on context—and the case law on bona fide purchase focussed on cases involving sale of land, whilst that concerning ostensible authority tended to involve commercial situations involving unauthorised sale of personalty and contracting debts. Conveyances of land would typically have involved more extensive checks than commercial dealings, meaning that in practice a defence would be easier to make out in commercial cases.[18] The principle, however, appears to have been the same. A purchaser would have no reason per se to be suspicious where he knowingly bought assets from a factor, or from a partner in a firm whose business included buying and selling. One who knowingly purchased from a trustee, however, would presumably only be in the same position where they knew the terms of the trust involved selling property, for example as under a trust for sale, of a business, or for the payment of debts. After all, trustees might expressly be given powers or duties to sell trust assets but had no such power by default.[19] A purchaser from a trustee, who was aware of the trust, would be more likely to have constructive notice of any breach than a purchaser from an agent or partner.

Leaving aside context, the biggest[20] difference between the rules was as follows. Whereas ostensible authority applied to both dispositions of property *and* debts incurred by an agent or partner, the bona fide purchaser defence applied only to dispositions of property by a trustee. The defence was not available to a creditor who had lent money to a trustee in good faith, apparently on behalf of the trust. The creditors of trustees were therefore less well protected than those of agents or partners, and the problem is best explained as follows.[21]

[17] ibid 732–832.

[18] Note that the broad interpretation of 'notice' in the context of land was problematic throughout the nineteenth century, culminating with the legislative reforms of 1925. See Stuart Anderson, *Lawyers and the Making of English Land Law* (OUP 1992); Stuart Anderson, 'Changing the Nature of Real Property Law' in William Cornish and others (eds), *Oxford History of the Laws of England*, vol XII (OUP 2010); William Cornish and others, *Law and Society 1750–1950* (Hart 2019) 173–79.

[19] T Lewin, *The Law of Trusts* (1st edn, A Maxwell 1837) 205–06.

[20] Technically, a purchaser from an agent or partner with ostensible authority acquires good title without giving value. There is no reported example of such a case however, and it is hard to imagine a scenario in which a purchaser could without suspicion expect a commercial agent or partner to have authority to gift the assets they managed.

[21] Debts incurred within an agent or partner's ostensible authority would bind his principal or co-partners respectively, as discussed in Chapter 3.

A trust was not a legal entity, and where a trustee entered into a debt on behalf of the trust, the trustee was liable. A trustee was not beneficially entitled to trust assets, which were treated as separate from his own wealth to prevent them being taken by his personal creditors rather than being used for the purposes of the trust.[22] However, this meant that the creditors of the trust—being at law simply creditors of the trustee—could not prima facie claim trust assets either. However, a trustee who contracted a debt on behalf of the trust would acquire a right to be indemnified for that liability, which would be secured by a lien over the trust fund. If the trustee went bankrupt, the trust creditor could take the benefit of these rights of lien and indemnity, and so claim the trust assets. In modern terms, trust creditors could be subrogated to the trustee's own claim against the trust assets in respect of the debt.

As discussed, a very similar mechanism explained how partnership creditors could claim partnership assets with priority over the partners' separate creditors they would be subrogated to the rights of indemnity and lien the partners could assert against one another in respect of the partnership debts.[23] However, there was a significant difference between partnership and trusts here. Partners would have ostensible authority to enter into contracts on behalf of the firm where they appeared to be acting in the normal course of business—even if a partner had no actual authority to do this. Where a partner contracted a debt without actual authority, which bound the firm under the doctrine of ostensible authority, the co-partners acquired rights of lien and indemnity *exactly as if the debt had been authorised*. This meant that even where it turned out a partnership creditor had advanced money to a partner who had no actual authority to bind the firm, in the event of default, the creditor would usually be able to claim the firm's assets.

The fact that the doctrine of ostensible authority did not apply to trusts meant that good faith creditors of trusts had no equivalent protection. Where a trustee appeared to have authority to borrow money on behalf of the trust, but had no actual authority to do so, the creditor would have no access to the trust assets. In such a case, the trustee would have no right of lien and indemnity in respect of the trust assets, because the debt had been contracted without authority—there was therefore no right to the trust assets to which the creditor could be subrogated. For that reason, in *Ex p Garland* (1804)[24] creditors of a trustee could not claim trust assets beyond a cap imposed on the trustee's indemnity.[25] On those same principles, even where a trustee had borrowed money with authority under the terms of the trust—and so did have a right of lien and indemnity—the creditor might still be unable to claim trust assets where the trustee had committed an unrelated breach

[22] See Chapter 6, Section 2.
[23] See Chapter 1, Section 2.4.
[24] *Ex p Garland* (1804) 10 Ves Jun 110, 32 ER 786 (Ch); B1/105, pp 306–10.
[25] Chapter 2, Section 3.

of trust. In that case, sometimes known today as 'impairment', the beneficiaries could set off the value of the claim against the trustee against the value of the indemnity. For this reason, creditors who dealt with trustees in the ordinary course of business were far more vulnerable than those who dealt with partners or agents. That being said, contemporaries did not pay the point much attention: presumably because clauses authorising trustees to contract debts on behalf of the trust were relatively unusual until later in the nineteenth century—at least outside of trusts of businesses. Indeed, in that context trustees with a power to borrow might well be partners or agents too—if so the doctrine of ostensible authority could apply to protect creditors.

2. The Authority of Executors

2.1 The Beneficial Interest of Executors in the Testamentary Estate

Modern lawyers tend to think of executors as a species of trustee, governed by similar rules. The position throughout the long eighteenth century was not so straightforward. Executors were governed by common law courts, ecclesiastical courts, and Chancery, and the result of this patchwork was that for much of the eighteenth century an executor could use testamentary assets for his own benefit so long as he paid the testator's debts and satisfied the legacies.

In modern terms, neither the common law courts, ecclesiastical courts, nor Chancery treated executors as owing general custodial or fiduciary duties in relation to testamentary assets. The duties owed were more specific and varied by jurisdiction. At common law, an executor was liable for his testator's debts, but could avoid such liability where debts were outstanding by pleading due administration of the estate: accordingly he would not have to indemnify an insolvent testamentary estate.[26] It also meant that, so long as the executor paid off the debts of the estate, at law he would incur no liability—regardless of whether he used his own assets or testamentary assets.

The ecclesiastical courts did have the power to compel an executor to account for the testator's personal estate, in the sense of forcing him to explain what had happened to the property, but could not order him to pay the estate's debts or restore property to the estate.[27] The ecclesiastical court could enforce the payment of legacies of personalty (where there was no trust or other feature governed by

[26] Eg *Erving v Peters* (1790) 3 TR 685, 100 ER 803 (KB); *Mara v Quinn* (1794) 6 TR 1, 101 ER 403 (KB).
[27] Samuel Toller, *The Law of Executors and Administrators* (2nd edn, J Butterworth 1806) 491–95.

equitable jurisdiction the ecclesiastical court lacked), but it was only in respect of those assets specifically bequeathed that it would compel executors to act.[28]

Finally, Chancery did not treat an executor simply as a trustee, with a general duty not to use testamentary assets for their own purposes, either. Executors had been described as having been trusted since at least the sixteenth century,[29] and were chargeable in Chancery for those assets they received or ought to have received as an executor.[30] However, unlike a true trustee, an executor was entitled to the residue of an estate after paying off the testator's debts and legacies, unless the will by 'implication or violent presumption' provided otherwise.[31] For much of the eighteenth century an executor thus differed from a true trustee and was allowed by default free use of the testamentary estate: he could employ the assets for his own benefit without being liable to account for profits.[32] His only duty was to make sure debts and legacies were paid. Lionel Smith has argued that the extent of the executor's powers historically are explained by the fact that an executor was seen as analogous to an heir in civil law, a development shaped by civilian ecclesiastical jurisdiction over wills.[33]

An executor's entitlement to the use of the testamentary estate meant that testamentary assets were not treated as completely separate from his personal wealth. There were rules which partitioned testamentary assets from an executor's personal wealth. For instance, testamentary assets would not be forfeit to the Crown were the executor attainted.[34] Likewise, if the executor were declared bankrupt, or died, the testamentary assets would not vest in his bankrupt[35] or testamentary estate,[36] respectively. However, for much of the eighteenth century testamentary assets would be more available to an executor's disponees and personal creditors than were he a true trustee.

This can be seen in the way the bona fide purchaser defence applied to purchasers from executors. As above, the defence allowed any purchaser for value to take title free of adverse equitable interests *unless* he knew or had reason to know

28 ibid 489–91. Where no will was made, the court could compel an administrator to distribute the intestate's personal property.

29 See Neil Jones, 'Wills, Trusts, and Trusting from the Statute of Uses to Lord Nottingham' (2010) 31 JLH 273, 283–94, esp 290–94.

30 Thomas Wentworth, *The Office and Duty of Executors* (London 1703) ch 10.

31 *Bishop of Cloyne v Young* (1750) 2 Ves Sen 91, 96; 28 ER 60, 63 (per Lord Hardwicke LC); *Bowker v Hunter* (1783) 1 Brown Ch Cas 328, 329; 28 ER 1161, 1162 (per Lord Thurlow LC) ('the fundamental presumption the law makes, is, that the appointment of executors is a gift to them of what is undisposed of') Henry Ballow, *A Treatise of Equity*, vol 2 (John Fonblanque ed, 5th edn, J and WT Clarke 1820) 413–14; Yale (n 12) 147. This right was abolished by statute in 1830, see text to (n 45).

32 *Adams v Gale* (1740) 2 Atk 106, 26 ER 466 (Lord Hardwicke LC); *Treves v Townsend* (1783) 1 Cox Ch Cas 50, 51; 29 ER 1057, 1058 (Lord Loughborough LC).

33 Lionel Smith, 'Scottish Trusts in the Common Law' (2013) 17 Edinburgh L Rev 283, 297–99.

34 Wentworth (n 30) 85.

35 *Ex p Ellis* (1742) 1 Atk 101, 26 ER 66; B 1/17, pp 33–34 (BC); *Ex p Croft* (1786) in *Notes of Cases in Chancery and Exchequer 1780* at 527, part of the Lord Eldon Collection at Georgetown Law Library; William Cooke, *The Bankrupt Laws* (8th edn, W Reed, C Hunter 1823) 160–64.

36 *Heron v Heron* (1701) Prec in Ch 163, 24 ER 78 (Ch).

of the breach. A purchaser for value from an executor would almost always be able to make out the defence even when he knew about the executorship, as there was nothing suspicious about an executor selling or pledging testamentary assets. The executor might simply be raising money to pay the testator's debts or pecuniary legacies as his office required: as Lord Kenyon recognised in *Shirreff v Wilks* (1800)[37] the ordinary course of business of an executor resembled that of a partner in that (in the typical case) each had to exercise extensive powers of disposition to carry out their office. Further, knowledge that the testamentary estate had outstanding debts, or that the executor was disposing of assets for his own purposes, was no notice of fraud: for an executor could legally pay the debts out of his own assets, and so take the testamentary assets beneficially. Accordingly, a purchaser for value from an executor would take good title unless either (i) the purchaser was fraudulently colluding with the executor to deplete the testamentary estate or (ii) the purchaser had notice that the property had been specifically bequeathed, was held on trust, or charged with the payment of a particular debt.[38] As Lord Hardwicke LC put it in *Nugent v Gifford* (1738):[39]

> a purchaser from an executor, has no power of knowing the debts of the testator; and if this court, upon the appearance of debts afterwards, would controul such purchasers, no body would venture to deal with executors.[40]

Lord Mansfield CJKB in *Whale v Booth* (1784)[41] reasoned in similar terms:

> The general rule of law and equity is very clearly settled, that an executor may dispose of his testator's assets; and that they cannot be followed by any creditor [of the testator] whatever. A creditor [of the testator] has no lien upon them. It would be monstrous if the law were otherwise; for no one would deal with an executor (whose duty in general it is to sell) without taking an account of the whole estate of the testator. It is clear that an executor may alien; and it is also clear that when an executor aliens his testator's assets, the purchaser must know them to be assets for the payment of his debts. That is no objection. It is no evidence of fraud: for

[37] 1 East 48, 51; 102 ER 19, 21 (KB).

[38] *Elliot v Merryman* (1734) Barn Ch 78, 27 ER 562; (1740) 2 Atk 41, 26 ER 422 (Ch) (Sir Joseph Jekyll MR); *Nuggent v Gifford* (1738) 1 Atk 463, 26 ER 294 (Ch) (Lord Hardwicke LC); *Taner v Ivie* (1752) Dick 168, 21 ER 233 (Ch) (Lord Hardwicke LC); *Whale v Booth* (1784) 4 Doug 36, 99 ER 755 (KB); 4 TR 624–25, 100 ER 1211–12 (Lord Mansfield CJKB); *Bonney v Ridgard* (1784) 1 Cox CC 145, 147; 29 ER 1101, 1102 (Ch) (Sir Lloyd Kenyon MR). Note that according to the report of *Mead v Orrey* (1745) 3 Atk 235, 26 ER 937 (Ch), Lord Hardwicke allowed a purchaser of a testamentary asset, *with* notice of the a legacy relating to the asset, to take good title: the decision was at odds with dicta in *Elliot*, and expressly rejected later by Sir Lloyd Kenyon in *Bonney v Ridgard* and Lord Thurlow LC in *Scott v Tyler* (1788) 2 Brown CC 431, 29 ER 241; Dick 712, 21 ER 448 (Ch).

[39] 1 Atk 463, 26 ER 294 (Ch).

[40] ibid 464; 295.

[41] 4 Doug 36, 46; 99 ER 755, 760.

> the testator's debts may have been all satisfied. Or, if not, must the purchaser look to the application of the money? It is clear the executors may alien them for a debt of his [sic] own, either absolutely or conditionally, as a security. There is only one qualification and exception: viz. where there is an express contrivance and collusion with the executor to commit a devastavit.[42]

The scope of the 'notice' doctrine concerning purchasers from executors therefore was designed to encourage third parties to deal with executors, just as authority doctrines allowed third parties to deal securely with agents and partners in the ordinary course of business. Both doctrines focussed on whether C had had any reason to suspect the transaction was unauthorised—and if an executor was generally free to make use of the testamentary assets, a sale by an executor would rarely seem suspicious.

The decision in *Whale v Booth* itself forms a more striking example still of the way testamentary assets could be treated as part of an executor's own wealth. Personal creditors of an executor, with the executor's consent, had executed judgment against testamentary assets, which were then sold by the Sheriff. The claim was brought by creditors of the testator who, having later obtained a judgment against the executor, sought to execute judgment against those same testamentary assets. The Sheriff, however, returned *nulla bona testoris*—claiming that there were no remaining testamentary assets from which the testator's creditors could be satisfied. The testator's creditors brought an action for a false return against the Sherriff, arguing that the Sheriff should not have allowed the executor's own creditors to levy judgment against the testamentary assets. Lord Mansfield ruled in favour of the Sheriff, finding that the personal creditors of an executor were entitled to *knowingly* levy judgment against testamentary assets, in the way personal creditors of a trustee could not have done. He saw this decision as the natural corollary of the fact that the executor could have given good title to that property.

2.2. Treatment of Executors as Trustees

The eighteenth century saw the beginning of the end of the beneficial ownership of executors. Although in modern law executors are treated as having the 'whole property' of testamentary assets,[43] and executors were treated as beneficially entitled to testamentary assets for much of the eighteenth century, the scope of this beneficial entitlement was whittled down in different ways, particularly from the 1780s onwards.

[42] ibid 46; 760.
[43] *Commissioner of Stamp Duties v Livingston* [1965] AC 694, 707 (PC, per Viscount Radcliffe).

First, Chancery developed rules of construction whereby executors would be treated as trustees of, rather than beneficially entitled to, the residue of an estate. This would be the case where: a testator devised of his estate in trust for purposes which did not exhaust the estate; the testator had made specific provision in the will for the executor; or the testator's will demonstrated an intention to dispose of the residue of the estate, regardless of whether he had done so effectively.[44] The right to the residue was abolished by statute in 1830.[45]

Next, Regency era courts treated executors as liable for the value of testamentary assets that they had made use of personally. In *Newton v Bennet* (1784),[46] Lord Thurlow held that an executor who made use of the testator's assets in his trade—rather than calling them in to pay the debts and legacies—would be liable to the estate for the sums used as well as interest. Lord Eldon, who owned a manuscript report of the case,[47] adopted the same position. In the unreported case of *Denyer v Billisworth* (1803),[48] recorded in Lord Eldon's judicial notebook, he 'held that money which an ex.[ecut]or placed in his Bankers hands among his other money of his own there for his general business was money which, being the testators[,] the ex.[ecut]or had made use of', and so was liable to the estate for the sum in question.[49] Like trustees, executors had to keep testamentary assets separate from their private wealth, and had to account to the estate for sums disposed of for their own purposes.

The narrowing of an executor's beneficial interest in testamentary assets caused a narrowing in the protection given to disponees and creditors of executors in respect of such assets. After all, if an executor no longer typically had free use of testamentary assets or a right to their residue, then a purchaser could not legitimately expect to take good title to such assets where he knew that the executor was disposing of them for his own purposes. For that reason, from the late eighteenth century it was ruled that a purchaser of an executor who accepted testamentary assets in discharge of what he knew to be the executor's own antecedent debt, would not take good title, especially soon after the executor took up his office.[50]

[44] *Bishop of Cloyne v Young* (1750) 2 Ves Sen 91, 28 ER 60 (Ch) (Lord Hardwicke LC). See *Edwards v Countess Dowager* (1723) 2 P Wms 171, 176; 24 ER 687, 688 (Ch) where Lord Macclesfield LC stated that 'in all cases, where it is a measuring cast betwixt an executor and an heir, the latter shall, in equity, have the preference'; *Nisbett v Murray* (1799) 5 Ves Jun 149, 158; 31 ER 518, 523 (Ch); *Hill v Cock* (1813) 1 V & B 173, 35 ER 68 (Ch), Eldon Notebook 1812–1821 p 50. Also see George Spence, *Equitable Jurisdiction of the Court of Chancery* (Lea and Blanchard 1846) 226; Anderson, 'Trusts and Trustees' (n 7) 242.

[45] 11 Geo IV & 1 Will IV c 40. For the modern position, see Administration of Estates Act 1925, s 49.

[46] 1 Brown CC 359, 28 ER 1177 (Ch).

[47] '*Newton v Bennett*, 26 April 1784' in *Notes of Cases in Chancery and Exchequer 1780–1788* at pp 252–53, Lord Eldon Collection, Georgetown Law Library.

[48] *Billisworth* (1803) Eldon Notebook 1802–1803 pp 107, 109.

[49] Eldon Notebook 1802–1803 pp 107, 109. See also *Raphael v Boehm* (1805) 11 Ves Jun 92, 32 ER 1023 (Ch), Eldon Notebook 1802 pp 73–79; (1805) 13 Ves Jun 407, 590; 33 ER 347 (Ch); and *Sutton v Sharp* (1826) 1 Russ 146, 38 ER 57 (Lord Gifford MR).

[50] *Scott v Tyler* (1788) 2 Brown CC 431, 29 ER 241; (1788) Dick 712, 21 ER 448 (Ch) (Lord Thurlow LC); *Hill v Simpson* (1802) 7 Ves 152, 32 ER 63 (Ch) (Sir William Grant MR).

Lord Eldon emphasised the point in *M'Leod v Drummond* (1810).[51] In that case, an executor (long after his testator's death) pledged bonds belonging to the testator as security for a loan of *new value*, rather than to secure or discharge any 'debt or debts antecedently due', as the court order makes clear.[52] The purchaser was thus not treated as having notice of the executor's breach, and so took good title—from the purchaser's perspective the executor may simply have been raising money as part of managing the estate. After reviewing all the previous authorities,[53] Lord Eldon set out the law as follows. He made clear that an executor's power to dispose of property was very large both at law and in equity, but affirmed that 'that is for the purpose of enabling him to execute his *trust*, and to prevent the general inconvenience of implicating and entangling third persons in inquiries as to the application he may propose to make of the money'.[54] Accordingly, where an executor sells assets in return for new value, 'the vendee can never be affected by proving the executor's *intention* at the time to misapply the produce', or a subsequent intention to this effect. The real issue in the case was:

> whether there must be, what some of the cases import, fraud and circumvention by the person dealing with the executor for his own benefit; or, on the other hand, if there is direct evidence, that the executor is going to misapply the produce, whether the other party can safely deal with him.[55]

In other words, a purchaser for value would not usually be found to have any notice of an executor's intention to breach his duty by keeping the sale money for himself. Such a purchaser would only be aware of such fraud if suspicious circumstances at the time of sale suggested such an intention.

By the end of the Regency era, the rules governing purchasers from trustees and executors had grown more similar. A purchaser from either a trustee or an executor, who realised that he was purchasing property disposed of for the trustee or executor's private purposes, would not take good title. As Williams' treatise on the Law of Executors put it:

> In equity, it seems to be now established (in contradiction, as it should appear, to some former decided cases), that the executor or administrator can make no valid sale or pledge of the assets as a security for, or in payment of, his own debt, on the

51 17 Ves Jun 152, 34 ER 59 (Ch) (Lord Eldon); Eldon Notebook 1810–1811 pp 92, 120–28; C 33/578, f 1504v. On appeal from (1807) 14 Ves Jun 353, 33 ER 556 (Ch) (Sir William Grant MR)

52 C 33/554, ff 1225v, 1226r.

53 Lord Eldon lists them all and goes through them in his notebook, Eldon Notebook 1809–1810 pp 120–27.

54 17 Ves Jun 152, 153–54; 34 ER 59, 60. Emphasis added.

55 ibid.

> principle that the transaction itself gives the purchaser or mortgagee notice of the misapplication, and necessarily involves his participation in the breach of duty.[56]

This was because of the narrowing of an executor's beneficial interest in testamentary assets. When an executor was beneficially entitled to the use and residue of testamentary assets, disposing of those assets to third parties—for the executor's own benefit—would not necessarily have amounted to a breach of duty, and would not have signalled any wrongdoing. That reasoning did not hold good, however, once the law treated executors as trustees. Third parties were left with no good reason for thinking an executor might have the right to dispose of testamentary assets for their own purposes. Those who purchased testamentary assets, and knew they were given for the executor's own purposes, would not get good title without making enquiries sufficient to ascertain that the transaction was authorised.

The assimilation with the law governing executors and trustees was shown just as clearly in the King's Bench decision in *Farr v Newman* (1792).[57] Personal creditors of an executor took steps to levy judgment against (what they knew to be) testamentary assets held in his name, before the debts of the testator's estate had been paid. The testator's creditors had also levied judgment against all the executors and sought also to levy judgment against the testamentary assets. The Sheriff, as in *Whale*, returned *nulla bona testoris*: one of the executor's personal creditors had already had the testamentary assets seized. The testator's creditors brought an action for making a false return, alleging that the Sheriff had no right to seize the testamentary assets in satisfaction of an executor's personal debt. As seen above, Lord Mansfield in *Whale v Boothe* (1784)[58] had ruled in favour of the Sheriff on similar facts.

The majority of the King's Bench allowed the testamentary creditors' claim, distinguishing Lord Mansfield's judgment in *Whale*.[59] Lord Kenyon CJKB and Grose J argued that *Whale* was an exceptional case in that the executor had agreed that his personal creditors could levy judgment against testamentary assets: on that basis Lord Mansfield was right to decide the case on the basis of whether the executor would have been able to give good title to the assets.[60] Lord Kenyon and Ashurst J also distinguished *Whale* on the basis that execution in that case was *completed* by the time of the claim; Ashurst J further argued the testamentary creditors in *Farr* had forfeited their claim by negligently not suing until the executor's personal creditors had already executed judgment.[61] Both also showed that in *Whale*, unlike

[56] Edward Vaughan Williams, *The Law of Executors and Administrators* (London 1832) 612.
[57] 4 TR 621, 100 ER 1209 (KB).
[58] 4 Doug 36, 99 ER 755 (KB).
[59] It should be noted that Douglas' report of *Whale v Boothe* (ibid) was not published until 1831, after *Farr v Newman* was decided. The bench in *Farr* would have had access to the less detailed edition of the case reported in the footnote to the report of *Farr v Newman* itself at 4 TR 624–25, 100 ER 1211–12. I am grateful to Professor James Oldham for this observation.
[60] *Farr* (n 57) 632; 1216.
[61] ibid 645; 1222.

in *Farr*, it was not pleaded that the personal creditors were *aware* that any testamentary debts were still owing, though Lord Mansfield had made clear that in the absence of fraud or collusion an executor's personal creditors could levy judgment against testamentary assets, even if they were aware of outstanding testamentary debts.[62]

Indeed, the reasoning in *Farr* was very different from that in *Whale*. The majority ruled that personal creditors of an executor should not be able to levy judgment against testamentary assets at all. Allowing an executors' personal creditors to levy judgment against testamentary assets would have meant that testators could not be sure that their property would go to their creditors and legatees. In other words, if an executor's personal creditors could take testamentary assets, that would undermine a testator's right to dispose of property by will: the assets might be whisked off by the executor's creditors before the will was carried out. Such a ruling would condone a 'shameful act of injustice' which could 'hardly exist under the name of law'.[63] Lord Kenyon emphasised that if a testator could not make sure that *his* debts were paid, that his widow and children may struggle to raise credit. Further, Ashurst J emphasised that the testator's creditors should have a better claim to testamentary assets than the executor's creditors, as the testator's creditors had never trusted the executor's credit. In other words, whereas the testator's creditors had lent money to the testator, aware that if he became insolvent that he might not be able to pay the debt, they had never voluntarily assumed the risk of the executor's insolvency.

This concern that it was undesirable for an executor's creditors to be able to frustrate the execution of the will, led the King's Bench—despite being a court of common law— explicitly to treat an executor as a species of trustee. This is worthy of note in and of itself, given the personalities involved, and the tendency of later judges to presume that the common law courts would not take notice of trusts before the Judicature Acts.[64] Although there were common law cases recognising trusts in the early eighteenth century the view taken by commentators, with the notable exception of Lionel Smith,[65] is that in the period after Lord Mansfield the boundary between equity and the common law hardened.[66] Holdsworth argued that Lord Kenyon and Lord Eldon worked together 'in securing the rejection of Mansfield's project of fusing the rules of law and equity', though he acknowledged

[62] See text to (n 42) above.
[63] *Farr* (n 57) 627; 1213.
[64] *Sinclair v Brougham* [1914] AC 398, 420; *Re Diplock* [1948] Ch 465, 519.
[65] Lionel Smith, 'Tracing Confusion: Equity in the Court of King's Bench' [1995] LMCLQ 240.
[66] See Douglas Hay, 'Kenyon, Lloyd' in Sir David Cannadine (ed), *The Oxford Dictionary of National Biography* <http://www.oxforddnb.com/view/article/15431?docPos=2> accessed 18 March 2020; EA Smith, 'Scott, John' in Sir David Cannadine (ed), *The Oxford Dictionary of National Biography* <http://www.oxforddnb.com/view/article/24897?docPos=13> accessed 18 March 2020; Tariq Baloch, *Unjust Enrichment and Contract* (Oxford, Portland 2009) 39 (on the relationship between equity and claims for money had and received).

that Lord Eldon would sometimes adopt common law rules.[67] Similarly, Warren Swain has argued that though some judicial rhetoric caused the link between equity and the common law to remain 'superficially strong' in this period, common law judges ceased to use equitable principles.[68] Mark McGaw has also emphasised Lord Kenyon's anti-fusionist attitude and reluctance to borrow from equity, though he recognises that the effect of many of Lord Kenyon's rulings was to allow relief at common law equivalent to what had been long offered in equity.[69] However, he sees Lord Kenyon's reasoning in such cases as rooted in his belief that such relief was available on the basis of the application of the common law *alone*, part of an inherent common law equitable jurisdiction, entirely without reference to the equity administered by Chancery.[70] It is on this basis that McGaw suggests that 'Lord Kenyon had advanced the wider process of articulating the common law courts' equitable jurisdiction',[71] 'infusing law with equity'.[72] Other commentators have suggested that common law courts in that period would only take note of equitable jurisprudence because of bankruptcy considerations.[73]

The facts of *Farr*, however, did not involve bankruptcy and directly involved applying equitable jurisprudence. Lord Kenyon addressed the point directly, ruling that the common law did draw a distinction between goods held by a person in his own right, and goods held as executor, and further that while the decisions upon which such a distinction was based were equitable, the law would grant relief, though his explanation was circular: 'Equitas sequitur legem. Where the law is ineffectual, equity steps in to give redress, following however the rules of law.'[74] Grose J also argued that an executor's power of disposition was not rooted in a beneficial interest in testamentary assets: that power was simply a 'necessary incident of his office: without that power his *trust* cannot be executed', in that he would be unable to raise funds to pay off debts and legacies.[75] Likewise, Ashurst J emphasised that an executor held testamentary property 'only under a trust to apply it for the payment of the testator's debts, and such other purposes as he ought to fulfil in

[67] William Holdsworth, *A History of English Law*, vol xii (AL Goodhart and HG Hanbury eds, Methuen & Co 1952) 583–605; William Holdsworth, *A History of English Law*, vol xiii (AL Goodhart and HG Hanbury eds, Methuen & Co 1952) 627–28.

[68] See Warren Swain, *The Law of Contract 1670–1870* (CUP 2015) 133–35. As Swain notes, the attitudes of treatise writers in the early 1790s on the point varied. Fonblanque and Ballow affirmed that equitable and common law jurisdiction were entirely separate, whereas Woodeson argued that the principles applied in the common law courts and Chancery were similar. See Henry Ballow, *A Treatise of Equity* (John Fonblanque ed, 1st edn, J and WT Clarke 1793) 10; Richard Wooddeson, *A Systematical View of the Laws of England as Treated of in a Course of Vinerian Lectures*, vol 1 (T Payne 1792) 203.

[69] Mark McGaw, 'A History of the Common Law of Agency with Particular Reference to the Concept of Irrevocable Authority Coupled with an Interest' (DPhil, Oxford 2005) 252–56.

[70] ibid.

[71] ibid 114.

[72] ibid 346.

[73] The point is noted at Lionel Smith, 'Taylor v Plumer (1815)' in *Landmark Cases in Restitution* (Hart Publishing 2006) 60. For an example of this see Swain (n 68) 134–35.

[74] *Farr* (n 57) 650; 1225.

[75] ibid 629–30; 1214. Emphasis added.

the course of his office as executor'.[76] Unlike in earlier authorities, an executor was treated as a trustee of *all* testamentary assets, not only those settled for particular purposes. The decision therefore challenges the conventional view that the King's Bench became less willing to apply to apply equitable jurisprudence in the period after Lord Mansfield, supporting Lionel Smith's argument that throughout the long eighteenth century the King's Bench was willing to recognise trusts, and that 'equitable rights could be enforced in courts of law so long as there was nothing contrary to the law in the plaintiff's case'.[77]

The only dissenting judgment given in *Farr* was given by Buller J, who rejected the argument that the King's Bench should apply equitable jurisprudence and recognise an executor as a trustee. Although Buller J was widely considered to be in favour of the application of equitable jurisprudence in courts of common law, in his view the claim should not have been allowed, and the common law should not take notice of the executorship.[78] He argued that it was contrary to common law principles to recognise 'funds' in the way that Chancery did:

> For the plaintiffs several cases were quoted from the Court of Chancery; to which my answer is, that none of them are of the least avail in a Court of Law; because the two Courts act on different principles ... before we adopt the doctrines of Courts of Equity, we must see that we do not act in violation of settled rules of law, and that we have the power of following up the relief given by a Court of Equity to that extent, which makes their proceedings just and reasonable. The Court of Chancery consider the fund as debtor; and therefore they pursue that; collect it all into their own hands, under the notion of taking an account; call all persons before them who have any demand on that fund; and distribute it amongst all, according to their priorities at law (if they have any); or if not, equally ... *This Court cannot call all the creditors together; they cannot compel an account of all the effects, or administer the same relief which equity does; therefore we must not be governed by the rules of equity on this subject. At law there is no such thing as a fund in the hands of an executor being the debtor; but the person of the executor, in respect of the assets which he has in his hands, is the debtor.*[79]

On this basis, Buller J held that as the property was in the executor's name the King's Bench should allow his creditors to levy judgment against it. In discussing the idea that the common law, unlike equity, did not recognise 'a fund in the hands

[76] ibid 645; 1222.

[77] Smith, 'Tracing Confusion' (n 65) 244; Smith, 'Taylor v Plumer (1815)' (n 73) 60. For further examples see *Winch v Keeley* (1787) 1 TR 619, 99 ER 1284; *Gladstone v Hadwen* (1813) 1 M&S 517, 105 ER 193 (KB); and *Taylor v Plumer* (1815) 3 M&S 562, 105 ER 721.

[78] James Oldham, 'Buller, Sir Francis' in Sir David Cannadine (ed), *The Oxford Dictionary of National Biography* <http://www.oxforddnb.com/view/article/3914?docPos=1> accessed 18 March 2020.

[79] *Farr* (n 57) 636–37; 1218.

of an executor being the debtor', Buller J was making the point that a common law court lacked equity's accounting procedures, and so would not always be able to tell which assets an executor had received from the estate. It was inappropriate for the King's Bench to apply equitable jurisprudence—which involved recognising the distinction— given its inability to compel an account. Similar concerns explain why, as Nye Perram has observed, in the nineteenth century administration suits tended to be brought against executors in equity rather than claims at law—even if both courts applied the same principles Chancery's accounting procedures made such suits more useful than a common law claim.[80]

By the end of the Regency era the general rule was that an executor's personal creditors could not levy judgment against testamentary assets. The only exceptions were (i) where the executor had already converted the testamentary assets to his own use, taking them out of the estate[81] or (ii) where *Farr* (as reinterpreted in *Whale*) applied, in cases where the creditors managed fully to execute judgment without becoming aware of testamentary debts. Although executors, due to the nature of their office, retained more extensive powers of disposition than typical trustees, and could even (without specific authority in the will) lend testamentary assets on personal security without facing liability for breach of their custodial duties,[82] executors were seen by both courts of equity and common law as a species of trustee. As Lewin put it in 1837, 'Assets in the hands of an executor are regarded even by the common law as a species of trust property, and in respect of them has engrafted upon itself a *quasi* equitable jurisdiction.'[83]

3. Conclusions

The law governing the authority of trustees and executors was designed to strike a balance between the rights of beneficial owners and purchasers. Purchasers from trustees and executors would prima facie take subject to the rights of the beneficiaries and testamentary estate respectively, helping to ensure that trust and

[80] Nye Perram, 'The Operations and Present Operation of the Action in Devastavit' [2012] Federal Journal Scholarship 23.

[81] *Quick v Staines* (1798) 1 B&P 293, 126 ER 911; 2 Esp 657, 170 ER 488 (KB); *Fox v Fisher* (1819) 3 B&A 135, 106 ER 612 (KB).

[82] *Webster v Spencer* (1820) 3 B&A 360, 106 ER 694 (KB). A typical trustee would have been found to have committed a breach of trust unless specifically authorised to do this by the trust deed or *sui juris* beneficiaries, Anderson, 'Trusts and Trustees' (n 7) 278–94.

[83] Lewin (n 19) 243–44. Note that before the passage quoted above, Lewin refers to a dictum of Ashurst J in *Farr*, stating that a Sheriff who sold testamentary assets of an executor with notice of the executorship, on the demand of a personal creditor of the executor, would commit a tort. He follows this citation with an observation that 'the doctrines which in the last century confounded the legal and equitable jurisdictions have been since overruled', but cites no authority on point. There is no equivalent point made in other contemporary treatises, including Joseph Story, *Commentaries on Equity Jurisprudence*, vol 1 (Hilliard, Grey & Company 1836); Spence (n 44); James Hill, *A Practical Treatise on the Law Relating to Trustees* (V & R Stevens and GS Norton 1845).

testamentary assets were applied to the purposes of the trust or will. Purchasers, however, would take good title where they had given value and had no reason to be aware of the trustee's or executor's breach of duty. This meant that unauthorised dispositions by trustees and executors which seemed to occur in the ordinary course of business would be upheld: the bona fide purchaser defence was in this respect functionally equivalent to the doctrine of ostensible authority which governed partners and agents. What constituted 'the ordinary course of business' depended on the rights and duties of the seller which, as we have seen from the law concerning executors and factors, could change. An agent's course of business would depend on the type of his agency, while a partner's ordinary course of business would depend on the nature of partnership. Likewise, there would be nothing suspicious about a trustee of a business or an executor having a power to sell the assets they each managed, though purchasers would need to exercise greater caution, for instance, when dealing with a trustee of property for the benefit of a married woman.

The unifying principle—that priority and authority disputes should be determined by weighing up the comparative fault of beneficial owners and purchasers when judging the authority of agents, partners, trustees, and executors— was consistent with contemporary political economic thought. Those who recklessly bought property or lent money without making proper enquiries were seen as creating economic instability. Discouraging such behaviour was seen as vital to the country's prosperity. Judges were not concerned per se to encourage trade, but only *responsible* trade.

This overarching idea helps to explain why the focus on comparative fault is evident across a wide variety of doctrines and institutions (partnership, agency, set-off, trusteeship, and executorship) as well as straddling the divide between law and equity. This was one area where each set of courts applied the jurisprudence of the other relatively freely. The most striking example of this is the King's Bench's willingness in *Farr v Newman* to treat executors as trustees. In a similar fashion, the law governing the authority of errant partners also developed through a mix of judgments by courts of common law and equity, which itself came to resemble the common law's rules governing the ostensible authority of agents. There is no hint in the historical cases of the modern distinction sometimes drawn between the common law standard of being 'on inquiry' and an equitable doctrine of 'notice'.[84] The development shows a degree of mutual influence between courts of equity and common law in the period after Lord Mansfield that is greater than has been traditionally supposed.

[84] See *Akai Holdings Ltd v Thanakharn Kasikorn Thai Chamkat* (2010) 13 HKCFR 479.

PART III
BUSINESS FAILURE, RISK, AND INSOLVENCY DISTRIBUTION

6
Trusts and the Risk of Bankruptcy

The Regency era was an economically turbulent time, characterised by unstable growth, rising bankruptcy rates, regular market shocks, and deeper crashes than had been known before. The rising frequency and severity of downturns meant that business failure can never have been far from the minds of business men. Although stabilising the economy was a core concern of Lord Liverpool's government, that same government (influenced by Malthusian ideas) took the view that economic crises were *necessary* to restore economic stability by killing off irresponsible trade: hence the government and Bank of England's unwillingness to ameliorate the threat the crisis of 1825–26 posed to many firms. Viewed in this light the focus on bankruptcy in contemporary writing—both fiction and non-fiction—is unsurprising.[1]

The threat of business failure made it important for creditors to consider the possible default and bankruptcy of their debtors, and ways of protecting themselves should this happen. The natural way of doing this would have been by taking security for debts—a creditor could take an interest in an asset belonging to his debtor, which would typically allow the creditor to keep or sell the asset if the debtor were unable to pay. By doing so, the creditor would be sure of being paid, even if the debtor were declared bankrupt—he would have a 'priority' claim to the proceeds of the asset, which would not be distributed amongst the debtor's other creditors.

However, while the law governing mortgages of land were well established, the statute 21 Jac 1 c 19, s 10 provided that a creditor could not take security over personal property (ie assets other than land), where that property remained in the possession of the debtor. Should the debtor be declared bankrupt, the creditor would *not* be allowed a priority claim to the asset: like the debtor's other creditors, he would only get a rateable share of the debtor's total estate. This prohibition on non-possessory mortgages and charges of personal property was known as the

[1] Thomas Gisborne, *An Enquiry into the Duties of Men in the Higher and Middle Classes of Society in Great Britain*, vol 2 (5th edn, J White; Cadell and Davies 1800) 244–58; Samuel Taylor Coleridge, *A Lay Sermon Addressed to the Higher and Middle Classes on the Existing Distresses and Discontents* (Gale and Fenner; JM Richardson; J Hatchard 1817); Thomas Chalmers, *The Application of Christianity to the Commercial and Ordinary Affairs of Life* (5th edn, A Constable; Blackwood; W Whyte; Olivery & Boyd; W Oliphant; Fairbairn & Anderson; Manners & Miller; and James Robertson 1820) 78–84; Boyd Hilton, *Age of Atonement: The Influence of Evangelicalism on Social and Economic Thought, 1785–1865* (Clarendon Press 1997) 138–40; Barbara Weiss, *The Hell of the English: Bankruptcy and the Victorian Novel* (Bucknell University Press 1986).

Capitalism Before Corporations. Andreas Televantos, Oxford University Press (2020). © Andreas Televantos.
DOI: 10.1093/oso/9780198870340.003.0007.

doctrine of reputed ownership. The key point is that it limited the ability of traders to control what would happen on the bankruptcy of those they did business with, because it restricted when security could be effectively granted over personal property. It therefore limited their ability rationally to plan their affairs. However, the reputed ownership doctrine did not apply to trusts, in that personal property held on trust would not vest in the trustee's bankrupt estate, even if it had been in his possession.

This chapter shows how commercial parties could use trusts to control the effects of bankruptcy and evade the doctrine of reputed ownership. Trusts therefore facilitated trade by improving traders' capacity to pursue their rational self-interest by acting as a surrogate for a charge or mortgage over personal property. The use of mortgages[2] and agency doctrines[3] as security in the late eighteenth and nineteenth centuries have been well documented, but the use of trusts to allow traders to allocate risk has received less attention.[4] By the late eighteenth century a general principle had evolved providing that where A advanced money or personal property to B for a specific purpose, B would hold the asset on trust for A. Where B became bankrupt before the fulfilment of that purpose, A could sue on equitable title to claim the asset from B's estate, whether in the Bankruptcy Court, Chancery, or even the King's Bench. This would allow A to claim the asset with priority to B's unsecured creditors, and so to avoid the effects of B's bankruptcy and the doctrine of reputed ownership. The doctrine resembles so-called *Quistclose* trusts, recognised by modern courts as arising whenever a lender advances a loan to a borrower for a specific purpose only, causing the borrower to hold the money on trust for the lender, subject to a power to use the money for the specific purpose for which it was lent.

This chapter will examine how traders could use trusts to avoid the risk of their debtors' insolvency in the following stages. Section 1 will examine why and how the doctrine of reputed ownership restricted the ability of traders to take mortgages or charges over personal property, and so limited their autonomy. Section 2 will then examine why the doctrine did not apply to trusts law—if a trustee had legal title to trust assets, surely he was their 'reputed owner'? Section 3 will then show the role that trusts played in controlling the risk of insolvency in contemporary finance.

[2] Stuart Anderson, 'Leases, Mortgages, and Servitudes' in William Cornish and others (eds), *Oxford History of the Laws of England*, vol XII (OUP 2010) 132–58. Martin Daunton, *Progress and Poverty: An Economic and Social History of Britain 1700-1850* (OUP 1995) 243–46.

[3] Mark McGaw, 'A History of the Common Law of Agency with Particular Reference to the Concept of Irrevocable Authority Coupled with an Interest' (DPhil, Oxford 2005).

[4] For an exception see F Stolker, 'The Rise and Fall of the Reputed Ownership Clause' (MSt thesis, Oxford 2016).

1. Reputed Ownership, the Changing Bankruptcy System, and Non-possessory Security of Personalty

The 'doctrine of reputed ownership' was shorthand for section 10 of the Bankrupts Act 1623–24, 21 Jac I c 19. This provided:

> And for it often falls out that many persons before they become Bankrupts do convey their Goods to other Men upon good Consideration, yet still do keep the same, and are reputed the Owners thereof, and dispose the same as their own; Be it enacted, That if at any time hereafter, any person or persons shall become Bankrupt and at such time as they shall so become Bankrupt, shall by the consent and permission of the true Owner and Proprietor, take upon them the Sale Alteration or Disposition as Owners, that in every such Case the said Commissioners [of bankruptcy] or the greater part of them [i.e. the bankrupt's estate], shall have power to sell and dispose the same to and for the benefit of the Creditors which shall seek Relief by the Commission, as fully as any other part of the Estate of the Bankrupt.[5]

In other words, the Act provided that if A had title to goods, so was 'true Owner and Proprietor' thereof, and allowed B to appear to have power of 'Sale, Alteration, or Disposition as Owner' over those goods, then if B went bankrupt the property would be sold as part of B's estate, as if B were the owner rather than A. It should be emphasised that the Act did not apply to real property, and so did not apply to mortgages of land, presumably because third parties were less likely to associate possession of land with ownership of it.

The provision was introduced as part of package of bankruptcy reforms which were a response to the crumbling of English cloth exports in the early seventeenth century, part of which was blamed on an ineffective bankruptcy system.[6] It was introduced before discharge provisions where included in the bankruptcy statutes,[7] at a time when bankrupts were *always* regarded as fraudsters whose conduct victimised those around them. As Craig Muldrew has shown, the evolution of a 'culture of credit' from the mid-sixteenth century meant that people of all social strata in the early seventeenth century were indebted to one another. This meant that even a single default on repayment of a debt could cause massive chain

[5] Spelling modernised. Note the provision was re-enacted in the Bankruptcy Act 1825, s 72 (6 Geo IV c 16).

[6] The concern about the clothmakers is stated explicitly in the statute's preamble. For discussion about the Parliamentary Debate see WJ Jones, 'The Foundations of English Bankruptcy: Statutes and Commissions in the Early Modern Period' (1979) 69 Transactions of the American Philosophical Society 1, 20.

[7] 4 & 5 Anne c 17 (1705), s 7.

reactions, and led to a wider association between moral vice and bankruptcy.[8] The reputed ownership doctrine itself seemed to be a restatement of the decision in *Twyne's Case* (1601)[9]—a case concerning actual fraud— that a seller remaining in possession would raise a presumption of fraud as a matter of evidence.[10] This was a doctrine with civilian roots, as Constantin Willem has shown.[11] Unsurprisingly, early cases considering the provision treated it as relating to actual fraud.[12] Its effect in the seventeenth century was muted for two main reasons. First, it applied only in bankruptcy matters, and there were fewer bankruptcies litigated in the seventeenth century than later on,[13] due to the inadequacies of bankruptcy law and procedure[14] and its costs.[15] Secondly, secured lending was not common at the time.[16]

In the eighteenth century things changed, and courts began to consider whether the doctrine had some application outside of cases of actual fraud. The reason for this is not clear, but may be linked to early eighteenth-century reform of the bankruptcy system. In response to a rise in the availability of credit;[17] short periods of economic depression caused by war in 1702 and 1705 in particular;[18] the winter of 1703 which stopped shipping by freezing the Thames and destroyed livestock;[19] and the publicly scandalous bankruptcy of Thomas Pitkin,[20] the legislature again sought to reform the bankruptcy system.[21] It did so by adopting a 'carrot and stick' approach. Bankrupts who co-operated with the process would be discharged from their debts,[22] while those who refused to do so could face the death penalty.[23] Bankrupts were therefore no longer seen as *necessarily* fraudulent—though the

[8] Craig Muldrew, *The Economy of Obligation: The Culture of Credit and Social Relations in Early Modern England* (Macmillan 1998). The position remained similar in the eighteenth century, Tawny Paul, *The Poverty of Disaster: Debt and Insecurity in Eighteenth-Century Britain* (CUP 2019).

[9] 3 Co Rep 80, 76 ER 809; Moore KB 638; William Paley Baildon (ed), *Les Reportes del Cases in Camera Stellata, 1593 to 1609. From the Original MS. of John Hawarde* (London 1894) ix.

[10] A point Coke confirmed in *Stone v Grubham* (1614) 2 Bulstrode 225, 80 ER 1079.

[11] Constantin Willems, 'Coke, Collusion, and Conveyances: Unearthing the Roots of Twyne's Case' [2015] JLH 129.

[12] Eg *Crisp v Pratt* (1634) Car Croke 549, 550; 79 ER 1072, 1073 (KB); March NR 34, 36–38; 82 ER 399, 400–01.

[13] Jones (n 6) 1821; Julian Hoppit, *Risk and Failure in English Business 1700–1800* (CUP 1987) 23–25; Muldrew (n 8) 283–84.

[14] Jones (n 6) 21–35; Emily Kadens, 'The Last Bankrupt Hanged: Balancing Incentives in the Development of Bankruptcy Law' (2010) 59 Duke LJ 1230, 1243–44.

[15] Muldrew (n 8) 284.

[16] ibid 96 (most credit arrangements were informal, witnesses were used, but no security taken).

[17] Julian Hoppit, 'The Use and Abuse of Credit in Eighteenth-Century England' in Neil McKendrick and Brian Outhwaite (eds), *Business Life and Public Policy* (CUP 2002) 64–65, 72.

[18] Thomas Ashton, *Economic Fluctuations in England, 1700–1800* (OUP 1969) 57–58.

[19] Hoppit, *Risk and Failure in English Business 1700–1800* (n 13) 35.

[20] Emily Kadens, 'The Pitkin Affair: A Study of Fraud in Early English Bankruptcy' (2010) 84 ABLJ 483; Emily Kadens, 'The Last Bankrupt Hanged' (n 14) 1255–61.

[21] For an overview see, Daniel Defoe, *Remarks on the Bill to Prevent Frauds Committed by Bankrupts* (London 1706).

[22] 4 & 5 Anne c 17 (1705), s 7.

[23] 4 & 5 Anne c 17 (1705), s 1. Also see Kadens, 'The Last Bankrupt Hanged' (n 14) 1252–70.

association between bankruptcy and fraud continued into the nineteenth century.[24] Commentators like Coleridge and Malthus recognised that those who were bankrupted during financial crises were not necessarily those irresponsible traders that *caused* the crisis.[25] The gradual appropriation of bankruptcy jurisdiction by the Lord Chancellor from Lord Nottingham LC's time onwards also helped supplement the deficiencies of the system, and saw a rise in bankruptcy cases heard by the Lord Chancellor.[26] At any rate, bankruptcy rates rose during the eighteenth century.[27]

In the eighteenth century, then, conditions were in place for counsel to argue that the doctrine of reputed ownership did not only apply to cases involving actual fraud. The debate centred on whether the doctrine would apply to cases where A lent money to B and—without dishonesty or collusion—took a security interest over personal property belonging to B, of which B was to retain possession. The value of such arrangements was that they allowed traders to exploit the capital value of their stock in trade—by borrowing money against it—while retaining use and possession of it. Traders, like shopkeepers for instance, might have limited other means of giving security to borrow money, in that parting with possession of their stock in trade would deprive them of their ability to continue their livelihood. It would be in both A and B's interests that B retain possession of the property then, otherwise how would B pay off the debt? On the other hand, allowing B to grant security rights to assets which were to remain in his possession posed a hazard for third parties. C, for instance, might extend credit to B in the belief that he could execute judgment against B's stock in trade in the event of default. Such an expectation would be frustrated if A's security were enforced by the courts. Similarly, B may purport to give multiple parties security rights over the same property, in that each might take B's possession of the property as evidence of B's absolute entitlement to it. In such a case, A might be understood to have facilitated B's fraud by permitting B to retain possession of the property. It was ruled that such arrangements were not dishonest, and so would not be set aside as fraudulent conveyances under the statute 13 Eliz c 5.[28] What judges had to ask was whether the risk of

[24] Hilton, *Age of Atonement: The Influence of Evangelicalism on Social and Economic Thought, 1785–1865* (n 1) 136–47.

[25] Coleridge (n 1) 103–34; Thomas Malthus, *Principles of Political Economy*, vol 1 (John Pullen ed, CUP 1989 (1st published 1820)) 521–22; Martin Daunton, *Progress and Poverty: An Economic and Social History of Britain 1700–1850* (OUP 1995) 248–49.

[26] DEC Yale, *Lord Nottingham's Chancery Cases*, vol I (73 Selden Soc) (Bernard Quaritch 1954) cxiv–cxx; Jones (n 6) 48–49.

[27] See Hoppit, *Risk and Failure in English Business 1700–1800* (n 13) 45–46.

[28] *Meggot v Wilson* (1697) 1 Raym 286, 91 ER 1088 (KB); *Small v Oudley* (1727) 2 P Wms 427, 24 ER 799 (Ch). Both concerned whether personalty in the possession of a bankrupt would vest in his bankrupt estate, despite his having passed title to it by bill of sale to a creditor as security. In *Small*, counsel for the bankrupt estate argued that the disposition was a fraudulent preference (and do not seem to have relied on reputed ownership), while the report of *Meggot* does not make the basis of counsel's submissions clear. The court in each case ruled that the security would be valid unless made fraudulently.

misleading third parties created by the enforcement of non-possessory security over personal property was justified by its beneficial effects on the availability of credit. In this sense the issue in these cases was the same as that in cases concerning the ostensible authority of agents and partners.

Ultimately, eighteenth century courts ruled that the harm of such arrangements was not justified by their beneficial effects. In *Bucknal v Roiston* (1709),[29] Lord Harcourt LK suggested that where a bankrupt had given a bill of sale over personal property to a creditor, but retained possession of that property, that the property would vest in his bankrupt estate even in the absence of fraud. In that case, however, the debtor was not bankrupt, and so the doctrine of reputed ownership did not apply. The first reported decision directly on point appears to be *Stephens v Sole* (1736),[30] where Lord Talbot LC ruled that a mortgage of three boats ('hoys') by B to A, of which B was to retain possession, was contrary to the reputed ownership doctrine. The interrogatories and court order show that counsel's argument in that case focused on whether B appeared to remain owner of the boats,[31] while the court order also shows that Lord Talbot justified his decision on the basis that B 'appeared to all intents the visible owner, and persons lent him money upon the credit of his being the owner'[32] of the boats.

The decision was doubted by Lord Hardwicke LC in *Bourne v Dodson* (1740)[33] and *Browne v Heathcote* (1746).[34] Lord Hardwicke accepted that the doctrine did not require *actual fraud*, but he took the view that it could never apply to mortgages. The statute after all required the *true owner* of goods to consent to their being in a bankrupt's possession. Imagine a case where A lent money to B, took a mortgage over B's goods, but allowed B to retain possession of them. Were B to become bankrupt, the doctrine of reputed ownership would only apply if B had had possession of the goods with the consent of the 'true owner'. Given that A only had a mortgage over the goods—and would have had to retransfer title to the goods if B had paid off the debt—how could he have been the 'true owner'? If A were not the 'true owner', how could the reputed ownership doctrine apply?

The point was determined finally by the House of Lords in *Ryall v Rolle* (1750).[35] The court unanimously ruled that the doctrine of reputed ownership did not

[29] *Bucknal v Roiston* (1709) Prec in Ch 285–88, 14 ER 136 (Ch).

[30] Cited in *Bourne v Dodson* at 1 Atk 157 (Ch), 26 ER 100; C 33/366, 500r–501r (court order).

[31] C 11/948/1 (interrogatories, Counsel for B's estate asked witnesses whether B had 'retained possession of the said Hoys', whether he did 'appear to be the Visible Owner thereof', and whether he was believed to be 'Owner of them' having used them after the mortgage was given); C 33/366, 500v (court order, B's counsel ultimately argued that B had retained 'actual possession' of the hoys, and had thereby 'obtained great credit' through use of them, and so that the mortgage was 'fraudulent & void (at least as to the hoys) against the creditors of [B] … by virtue of the statute 21st of King James the 1st', and so B's bankrupt estate had the 'right to dispose thereof for the benefit of [B's] creditors').

[32] C 33/366, 500v.

[33] Barnard Ch 200, 27 ER 612 (Ch).

[34] 1 Atk 160, 26 ER 103 (Ch).

[35] 1 Ves Sen 348, 27 ER 1074; 1 Atk 165, 26 ER 107; 1 Wils KB 260, 95 ER 607 (HL).

depend on actual dishonesty or fraud, and further that the doctrine would apply to non-possessory mortgages of goods. Sir William Lee CJKB and Burnet JKB justified the ruling as follows. If B were indebted to A, and B gave a mortgage over goods to A, this involved the transfer of B's title to those goods to A. A therefore was 'true owner' of the goods within the meaning of the statute, despite the fact that A would have to retransfer title to B were B to repay the debt.

Lord Parker LCB and Lord Hardwicke reached the same conclusion, but on a narrower basis. They ruled that the term 'true owner' in the statute simply meant another person with title to the property who was not the 'reputed owner'—and so the fact A held title to mortgaged goods only as security did not prevent A from being the 'true owner' within the statute's meaning. As in the early nineteenth-century ostensible authority cases, the key point was that A had allowed B to appear to have unencumbered title to the property, potentially misleading third parties. Lord Hardwicke had therefore changed his mind on the ambit of the reputed ownership doctrine, but he stated reservations about having done so:

> It has been said, that great mischief might arise to trade and credit from such a determination as this, as tending to prevent making use of that credit persons have to support themselves in trade, as they cannot make a security without exposing their circumstances to the world; and on the other hand it is contended, that the other construction would in fact repeal the act of parliament, and let in a mischief: some inconvenience might perhaps arise from a determination of this case on either, side; but I agree with *Lee*, Chief Justice, that, as this is a law, we must adhere to it; and while it is a law be bound by it; and if any inconvenience results from it, that is for the consideration of the legislature.[36]

In other words, Hardwicke had not fully shaken the concerns expressed previously about the potentially negative effect on trade of the doctrine of reputed ownership. However, in the next paragraph of his judgment he suggested the doctrine might play a useful role in restraining what he saw as the rising tide of reckless trading and borrowing:

> But this I will say, that as some inconvenience may be to particular persons on one hand, great inconvenience may be on the other, by creating that appearance, as having the substance of which they remain in possession, though they have not at all the real property: and that this was the intent of the legislature, I am clear: and I may go so far as to say, that the simplicity of those times did not let in these large and airy notions of credit as of late; which, from the number of bankruptcies we have had of late years, is rather an evidence, that the departing from

[36] 1 Ves Sen 374, 27 ER 1089–90.

the rule this law has laid down, and giving way to these notions, has been rather a mischief.[37]

In other words, Hardwicke thought that in the mid-eighteenth century credit was given too freely, and that the doctrine of reputed ownership might help solve the problem. It would prevent traders borrowing money against the security of their stock in trade, and so reduce the level of borrowing. As above, bankruptcy rates did increase in the eighteenth century,[38] and there were a number of financial crises in the first half of the century,[39] though the sharpest increase in rates post-dated the decision in *Ryall*.[40] It would be after 1750 when a mixture of inflation, increased commercial risk-taking, and finance through gratuitously drawn bills of exchange[41] would prompt the real rise in 'airy notions of credit' and a rise in bankruptcy rates.[42] In this respect, Lord Hardwicke's judgment was a prescient one, and his desire to limit risky lending explains why he had come to accept that the doctrine of reputed ownership could be applied to non-possessory mortgages of personalty. That being said, the decision was limited in that it only applied to goods *capable of delivery*, and so did not prevent the continued practice of mortgaging book debts by bill of sale, or goods which were still at sea by bill of lading.

2. Trusts and the Doctrine of Reputed Ownership

During the Regency era it was decided in a series of rather opaque judgments that trusts were unaffected by the doctrine of reputed ownership: if a trustee went bankrupt, the trust assets would not vest in his bankrupt estate under the doctrine of reputed ownership, because the trustee did not 'take upon them the Sale Alteration or Disposition' of trust assets 'as Owners'. Not even his bare legal title would pass to his assignee in bankruptcy.[43]

The reason for this development is again not completely clear. In the seventeenth century Lord Nottingham—'in flat contradiction of the year-book cases on uses'—ruled that 'the beneficial interest in equity would be protected by equity against judgment creditors of the trustee'.[44] In the early eighteenth century there

[37] ibid 374, 1090.
[38] Text to (n 27).
[39] Ashton (n 18) 5.
[40] Hoppit, *Risk and Failure in English Business 1700–1800* (n 13) 46.
[41] Discussed below at Section 3.1.
[42] Hoppit, *Risk and Failure in English Business 1700–1800* (n 13) 52–55, 162–68. Note that inflation was significant, because a debtor could only be declared bankrupt where he owed a debt of at least £100 to one creditor or partners, £150 to two individual creditors, or £200 to three or more, 5 Geo II c 30, s 23 (1732). In real terms, the financial threshold for suing out a commission of bankruptcy fell.
[43] T Lewin, *The Law of Trusts* (1st edn, A Maxwell 1837) 254. See also (n 67).
[44] DEC Yale, *Lord Nottingham's Chancery Cases*, vol II (79 Selden Soc) (Bernard Quaritch 1961) 93. See *Medley v Martin* (1673), R. t. Finch 63, 23 ER 33, affirmed in *Finch v Earl of Winchelsea* (1715) P Wms 277.

were a number of decisions—where reputed ownership does not appear to have been considered—to the effect that the trustee's bankruptcy likewise would not affect the trust estate.[45] Indeed, rulings to the effect that a principals' property would not vest in his bankrupt factor's estate were justified on the basis that the factor was a trustee.[46] The argument that the doctrine of reputed ownership applied to trusts seems to have first been made in *Copeman v Gallant* (1716),[47] where A gave his property to B to hold on trust for the purpose of paying A's debts. B became a bankrupt, and it was argued for his creditors that the trust assets had vested in B's estate under the doctrine of reputed ownership: to rule otherwise would undermine the bankruptcy process by effectively allowing the creation of preferences. Lord Cowper LC rejected the argument. He ruled that because A had created the trust with the 'honest intent' of paying his debts, the doctrine of reputed ownership was inapplicable.

The 1716 decision in *Copeman* was premised on the seventeenth-century view of the reputed ownership clause as relating to actual fraud; for that reason Lord Hardwicke and Lord Parker in *Ryall v Rolle* disapproved of Lord Cowper's reasoning. As it became established that the reputed ownership doctrine did *not* depend on actual fraud, the question arose as to whether or not the doctrine applied to trusts. Counsel argued the point in *Ex p Marsh* (1744).[48] A trader held a bond and silver plate on trust for his wife's children, and then became bankrupt. The plate had been received from his wife's first husband, who had died intestate. After his bankruptcy, the children sought to enforce the trust, and one of the arguments raised by the husband's bankrupt estate was that the trust assets vested in it under the doctrine of reputed ownership. The argument was given short shrift by Lord Hardwicke, who seems to have taken it for granted that the doctrine would not apply. Although they are not cited in the report, presumably he treated the early eighteenth-century authorities providing that trust assets did not vest in a bankrupt trustee's estate as binding. This was despite the fact that reputed ownership was not argued in those early eighteenth-century cases, which were decided *before* reputed ownership was treated as not requiring actual fraud. Lord Hardwicke therefore allowed the children's claim, and justified his rejection of the reputed ownership argument as follows:

[45] *Burdett v Willett* (1708) 2 Vern 638, 23 ER 1017 (Ch); *Ex p Chion* (1721) cited in the report to *Godfrey v Furzo* (1733) 3 P Wms 185, 24 ER 1022 (Ch); *Jacob v Shephard* (1725) cited in the report to *Bourne v Dodson* (1740) Barnard Ch 200, 27 ER 612 (Ch).

[46] *Burdett* (n 45); *Scott v Surman* (1742–43) Willes 400, 125 ER 1235 (CP). Note that in *Wiseman v Vandeput* (1690) 2 Vern 203, 23 ER 732 (Ch) the same decision was reached without reported reasons, while in *Godfrey* (n 45) 187; 1023, Lord King LC ruled on the point having 'discoursed with merchants about the matter' and having learnt that 'this was the practice amongst them'.

[47] 1 P Wms 314, 24 ER 404 (Ch).

[48] 1 Atk 158, 26 ER 102 (BC). The entry in the Bankruptcy order books is at B 1/18, pp 202–05, but no mention is made of the reputed ownership point.

> If this was the plate of the first husband, and came into the possession of the administratrix, or into the hands of the person marrying that administratrix, this certainly is not within the meaning of the statute of the 21 *Jac.* 1 (*which says that all goods in the possession of a bankrupt, whereby he gains a general credit, shall be liable to his creditors*), because here the administratrix had them in *auter droit*, and the husband could have them in no better right, and therefore not at all liable to the debts of the second husband; for the meaning of the statute (if it is possible to put any meaning upon some clauses of this statute, which are very darkly penned) is only with regard to goods the bankrupt has *in his own right*.[49]

The reasoning here is striking. Lord Hardwicke could have allowed the children's claim in a number of ways. He might have reasoned that the property had come through the trustee's wife, had not been used in trade, and so would not have misled the husband-trustee's creditors into extending him credit. It could likewise have been argued that the statute applied only when the bankrupt himself had made dispositions of property which remained in his possession, and so was inapplicable on the facts of the case. Instead, he set out a broader rule that property held by another *in auter droit*, that is to say in a different right or capacity, could not vest in his bankrupt estate under the doctrine of reputed ownership. For this reason the law would not treat trust assets as within a trustee's powers of 'Sale Alteration or Disposition *as Owners*', as necessary to engage the reputed ownership clause. The decision was confirmed in *Ryall v Rolle* (1750),[50] where Lord Hardwicke and Lord Parker agreed with outcome of *Copeman* that the trust assets should not have vested in the bankrupt trustee's estate, if not with Lord Cowper's reasoning. However, it was in *Ex p Dumas* (1754)[51] that Lord Hardwicke would best explain his view. That case also concerned the effect of a trustee's bankruptcy on trust assets:

> It is true, the general end, intent, and view of the laws of bankruptcy is to level all creditors, and that all, which belongs to the bankrupt, may be equally divided among all without regard to superiority in point of law: but that is the bankrupt's estate, and therefore whatever is both in law and equity his, is so liable in an equitable proportion; but if the subject matter of the question is not the bankrupt's estate in point of law and equity, especially if not in equity, the consequence is, that it is not considered in the distribution as his estate, but that the person intitled either to the legal interest for his own benefit or to the equitable is intitled to have that to himself in specie: *for the assignees under the commission take the estate of the bankrupt and any legal interest in the bankrupt subject to all the same equities*

[49] 1 Atk 159, 26 ER 103. Emphasis original.
[50] (n 35).
[51] 1 Atk 232, 26 ER 149; 2 Ves Sen 582, 28 ER 372 (Ch); B 1/29, pp 199–203.

> *as it stood in the bankrupt at the time of the bankruptcy: otherwise the admission of commissions of bankruptcy would be intolerable, for it would so change the property as not to be endured.*[52]

In other words, a bankrupt's creditors could only claim the assets that the bankrupt had enjoyed beneficially before his bankruptcy. A solvent trustee could not freely use trust assets, as his authority to deal with the trust assets were limited in equity by the terms of the trust. If the trustee were declared bankrupt his creditors could be in no better position: just as the trustee could not use the trust assets for his own benefit, nor could his creditors. The point was affirmed a number of times throughout the eighteenth and early nineteenth centuries,[53] despite occasional judicial grumblings that the rule was unfair to creditors.[54]

Lord Hardwicke's ruling that trust assets were unavailable to trust creditors therefore became an axiom of the law, one which persists today. However, it is important to recognise that Lord Hardwicke himself took the rule as axiomatic: his purported reasoning in *Ex p Marsh* and *Ex p Dumas* was not so much a justification as the statement of a foregone conclusion. If the reputed ownership doctrine was designed to protect third parties from invisible interests—much like the authority and priorities doctrines examined in Part II—then there was a good argument that it should have applied to trusts. Trustees after all had legal title to trust assets and so might appear to be beneficial owners of those assets—third parties might be led to extend credit to trustees on that basis. The fact the trustee did not enjoy the assets beneficially was, strictly speaking, irrelevant to the issue of whether the trustee *appeared* to own trust assets beneficially. Likewise, to say that trust assets were not within the trustee's control 'as owner' within the meaning of the statute was again to express a conclusion, rather than to explain one. Lord Hardwicke simply took it for granted that trust assets should be wholly separate from the personal wealth of the trustee, as the purposes of the trust might fail if the trustee's creditors were able to claim the assets. He saw this aspect of the law of trusts as too well established to yield to the expanding ambit of the reputed ownership doctrine.

For that reason, trusts were not an exception carved out of reputed ownership rules: the rules governing trustees' creditors and bankruptcy were already established by the time the doctrine expanded beyond the ambit of actual fraud. Creditors were held to expect that there might be equities affecting an estate held by a debtor who might also be a trustee, and the onus lay on the creditors to find

52 2 Ves Sen 585, 28 ER 373. Emphasis added.

53 See (n 101).

54 See *Farr v Newman* (1792) 4 TR 621, 640–41;100 ER 1209, 1220 (KB), 'In my opinion, it is highly inconvenient to the public that goods should ever be so fettered or limited as not to be liable to the debts of those who have the enjoyment, and are suffered to appear as the real owners of them. Some cases have gone a great way on that subject; and, as far as they have gone, perhaps we may be bound by them' (per Buller J).

out—not for the trustees or beneficiaries to offer them notice. The fact that bona fide *purchasers* of trust estates were treated differently and more protectively was a tension the system would just have to live with.

3. Commercial Uses of Specific Purpose Trusts

Trusts were of crucial importance to traders in the Regency era because of the rule that trust assets would not vest in a bankrupt trustee's estate. Whereas the reputed ownership doctrine prevented traders from taking fully enforceable mortgages and charges over the personal property of their debtors, at least whilst also allowing their debtors to retain possession of that property, in some cases traders could use trusts to achieve the same end. In this way the law of trusts allowed traders greater ability to insulate themselves from possible insolvency of those they did business with. In this sense, it encouraged trade.

The advantages of using trusts in this way are clearest from the case law concerning 'specific purpose trusts'. Imagine that A wants to give B money or an asset for a specific purpose—for example so B can pay off another creditor or for use in a particular business venture—but is concerned that B might go bankrupt before fulfilling the purpose. In such cases, the law regarded A as retaining the 'property'[55] in the money or asset: allowing A to claim it with priority upon B's bankruptcy. B was treated as holding the asset on trust for A.[56] This appears to have been the case even when A had (and retained) legal title to the asset in question: B acquired a legal title through physical possession of the property, which was held on trust for A. The arrangement was to A's advantage: if B became bankrupt before the purpose were carried out, then A could reclaim the property advanced to B.[57] Likewise, although the tracing rules of the period were different to those of today[58]—most notably due to the uncertainties concerning tracing money[59]—the

[55] For examples of the use of the proprietary language in this area see *Godfrey* (n 45); *Dumas* (n 51); *Tooke v Hollingworth* (1793) 5 TR 215, 101 ER 121; *Ex p Sayers* (1800) 5 Ves Jun 169, 31 ER 528; *Joy v Campbell* (1804) 1 Sch & Lef 328 at 345–47; *Ex p Pease* (1812) 19 Ves Jun 25, 34 ER 428; 1 Rose 232; B 1/91, pp 180–83. Lewin described such assets as a 'trust estate or fund', Lewin (n 43) 254.

[56] On the other hand, if A intended B to have free use of the asset, then legal and beneficial title passed to B, and A retained no interest in the property. See *Joy* (n 55) 345–47.

[57] For examples of how such claims were pleaded see *Dumas* (n 51) B 1/29, pp 199–203 at 203; *Ex p Oursell* (1756) B 1/31, pp 311–12 at 312; *Ex p Cramer* (1815) B 1/133, pp 45–48 at 48; and *Ex p Ogden* (1815) B 1/133, pp 42–45 at 44–45.

[58] Although some contemporary treatises presumed that A could assert title to the substitutes, eg Lewin (n 43) 254–56, the matter received no proper judicial consideration until *Re Hallet's Estate* (1880) 13 Ch D 696, where it was stated that A would have only a charge on substitute assets where B had mixed the property with his own. The modern rule that A can claim the full value of any substitute only arose later, see *Foskett v McKeown* [2001] 1 AC 102 (HL).

[59] A number of statements to this effect can be found in contemporary cases, though it is not clear whether the point is that money as a matter of evidence could not be traced, or whether a claim to traced money would fail even when the money could be proven to be the produce of trust assets. The relevant passages are reproduced in *Ex p Dale* (1879) 11 Ch D 772, and the historical ambiguity is discussed in *Re Hallett's Estate* (n 58) 713–19.

existence of this trust allowed A to assert equitable title to the proceeds of the original property at a time when such claims were relatively uncommon compared to personal claims for breach of trust. A could simultaneously advance property to B to use for a particular purpose, whilst protecting himself from the possible effects of B's bankruptcy.

Although the doctrine of bailments to uses by way of security (discarded by the Regency era) operated in a similar way,[60] the origins of these special purpose trusts appear to have been in cases concerning factors. There are a number of early eighteenth-century cases, both at common law and in equity, in which it was ruled that property entrusted by a principal to a factor, that is for the purpose of sale, would not vest in the factor's estate upon his bankruptcy.[61] In the Regency era this rule was crucial: as discussed in Chapter 4, factors played a crucial role in allowing British firms to access overseas markets, as well as the growth of warehousing early in the nineteenth century.[62] It was important that a principal who entrusted his property to a factor did not risk losing it if the factor were declared bankrupt. Although MS Servian argues that this was simply to give effect to merchant expectations,[63] this principle was justified on the basis that 'A factor is in the nature of a trustee only for his principal',[64] as the advance made to B was 'brought under a notion of a trust',[65] and so exempt from the doctrine of reputed ownership. Servian has argued that the courts in these cases 'mistook' the relationship of agent and principal for trustee and beneficiary, on the basis that a factor did not acquire his principal's legal title, but this is inconsistent with the assertions of courts of equity *and* common law that they were vindicating equitable title in such cases.[66] The point seems to be that a factor would hold his possessory title—'special property'—to the assets on trust for the principal, until the time of sale, even where his principal had retained his legal title to those same assets. In other words, there was relativity of legal title between principal and agent, and a principal had one legal title, but was also the beneficiary of a trust of another lower priority legal title in the same property, as illustrated in Figure 6.1.

[60] See McGaw (n 3) 69, 161–75 (esp 167–69 and 174–75).

[61] Eg *L'Apostre v Le Plaistrier* (1708), cited 1 P Wms 318–19; *Whitecomb v Jacob* (1710) 1 Salk 161, 91 ER 149 (KB).

[62] Chapter 4, Section 3.

[63] MS Servian, 'Eighteenth Century Bankruptcy Law: From Crime to Process' (University of Kent 1985) 103–06. Servian roots his argument on the basis of comments in *Godfrey* (n 45) and *Dumas* (n 51), without reference to much of the reasoning in *Dumas*, and offering no further evidence that merchants generally were in favour of allowing principals' proprietary claims against factors and to trace proceeds in their hands.

[64] *Burdett* (n 45).

[65] *Scott* (n 46).

[66] Discussed at Section 3.2 below.

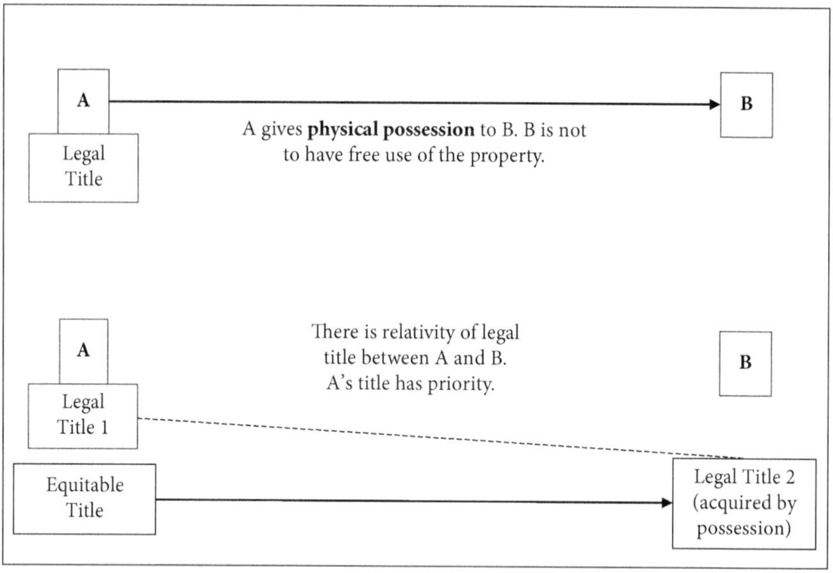

Figure 6.1 Relativity of title: factors as trustees

Early nineteenth-century treatise literature thus described factors as a species of trustee,[67] and the terms trustee and factor were sometimes used interchangeably. For instance, a trustee-bank in *Ex p Pease* (1812)[68] was stated in both the report and court record to hold the bills as an agent,[69] and even received commission for handling the petitioners' business.[70] Lord Eldon LC's reasoning, as evident from the reported case and his notebook, shows that he saw the issue of whether the bank was a trustee as identical to the issue of whether the bank was an agent.[71] He used the terms interchangeably. The point has been acknowledged by Mark McGaw, who goes so far as to assert that factors were purely trustees and were not seen as agents until the end of the eighteenth century, as the rules governing factors and agents converged,[72] though the assertion would seem to fly in the face of

[67] Henry Maddock, *In A Treatise on the Principles and Practice of the High Court of Chancery* (1st edn, J and WT Clarke 1815) 511. ('[i]f bills be sent for the purchase of *specie*, and before such commission is executed, the Agent becomes a Bankrupt, the Principal has a Lien on the Bills or produce of the same in the hands of the Assignees; for the Bankrupt was only a Trustee'); William Cooke, *The Bankrupt Laws* (8th edn, W Reed, C Hunter 1823) 382. (that '*Assignment does not pass Property in Possession of the Bankrupt as Factor, Executor,* or other Trustee', italics as in the original text, emphasis added); Lewin (n 43) 254 ('It is clear that in the case of a *bare trust*, the property . . . will not vest by the bankruptcy in the assignees, even at law. And the proposition applies not only to the case of *express trustees*, but also of *trustees virtute officii*, as executors, administrators, factors &c', italics as in the original text).

[68] 19 Ves Jun 25, 34 ER 428; 1 Rose 232 (BC).

[69] B 1/91, p 180; 19 Ves Jun 25, 49; 34 ER 436.

[70] B 1/91, p 181.

[71] Eldon Notebook 1810–1812, p 118, ('I decided in favour of all the Country Banks. Country Banks, principals. Town Banks[,] Agents'). Lord Eldon is reported however as also treating the matter as relating to trusts.

[72] McGaw (n 3) 112–18.

contemporary usage.[73] The better view seems to be that a factor was an agent—governed by the same authority doctrines as other agents[74]—and was also a trustee of possessory title to his principal's goods.[75] It was not until later in the nineteenth century that lawyers would reject the notion that a factor was a trustee—arguing that a factor's possessory title could not be held on trust—and instead treat him as a fiduciary.[76]

The rule governing factor-trustees was developed into a principle that whenever A advanced property to B for a particular purpose, B would hold that property on trust. For instance, there are reported Regency era cases where A advanced money to B for the purpose of supplying an army camp,[77] purchasing exchequer bills,[78] and purchasing gold bullion.[79] If B became bankrupt before fulfilment of the purpose, A could recover the property in priority to B's general creditors.[80] In all these cases B was found to hold the money on trust for A, effectively with a power to use the money for the specific purpose. A's intention that B *only* use the property for a specific purpose, and not use it freely, was treated as intention to declare a trust.

3.1 Specific Purpose Trusts for the Payment of Debts

Specific purpose trusts could arise for a range of reasons, but the most prominent class of examples in the reported cases and court record involve specific purpose trusts for the payment of debts.[81] The relevant cases involve money being settled on trust for the purpose of paying sums owed on a bill of exchange—a credit medium which played an important but controversial role in finance in the eighteenth and nineteenth centuries.

A bill of exchange was a piece of paper. Its creator (A), promised another party (C), that the sum stated on the bill would be paid to C by a third party (B) on a

[73] See Charles Molloy, *De Jure Maritimi et Navali* (London 1722) 465 ('A Factor is a servant'); Malachy Postlethwayt, 'Factors' in *The Universal Dictionary of Trade and Commerce, Translated from the French of the Celebrated Monsieur Savary*, vol 1 (London 1751) 760 ('A factor is a merchant's agent').

[74] Discussed in Chapter 3, Section 2 and Chapter 4.

[75] This explains the continued references to an 'agent or factor' even after the time at which McGaw suggests that the concepts became assimilated: see the Factors Act 1823 (4 Geo 4 c 83); Factors Act 1825 (6 Geo IV c 94); Larceny Act 1827 (7&8 Geo IV c 29), s 51; Agency Select Committee, 'Report from the Select Committee on the Law Relating to Merchants, Agents, or Factors' (HC 1823, 452-IV); John Russell, *The Laws Relating to Factors and Brokers* (S Sweet; V & R Stevens & GS Norton 1844) 124.

[76] See Andreas Televantos, 'Losing the Fiduciary Requirement for Equitable Tracing Claims' (2017) 133 LQR 492, 500–04.

[77] *Smith v Everett* (1792) 4 Brown 64, 29 ER 780 (Ch).

[78] *Taylor v Plumer* (1815) 3 M&S 562, 105 ER 721 (KB).

[79] *Ex p Sayers* (1800) 5 Ves Jun 169, 31 ER 528 (BC).

[80] For discussion see *Joy* (n 55) 345–47.

[81] It should be noted that these trusts were distinct from trusts where a debtor settled *all* his property on trust for the payment of his debts generally, essentially by way of compromise with his creditors, Michael Lobban, 'Bankruptcy and Insolvency' in William Cornish and others (eds), *Oxford History of the Laws of England*, vol XII (OUP 2010) 783–84. See Chapter 2, text to (n 12).

particular date. Typically, A and B would both be liable to C if B failed to pay the bill on the date it was due.[82] Bills of exchange offered a number of legal advantages, but were most significant for providing an easy way of one firm guaranteeing the debts of another (any party who signed the bill would be liable to pay it) and for creating assignable debt claims—bills of exchange (and the right to sue the parties who had signed it) could be transferred simply by delivery of the piece of paper. This was very convenient and avoided the common law rule that debts could not be assigned.[83]

These advantages made bills of exchange a common means of raising finance. Large firms (especially country banks) would create bills of exchange, payment of which was guaranteed by another large firm, and would sell the bill before it was due—an act known as 'discounting'—as a way of borrowing money. The firm would be paid for the bill which was not yet due, but would have to pay the bill with interest at the date it became due. In areas like Lancashire, where there was a shortage of currency, bills of exchange would circulate much like Bank of England notes.[84] The fact that several large firms would often be liable to pay the same bill, meant that traders would accept bills in lieu of cash: so long as one was solvent, the holder of the bill would receive payment. The willingness of large firms to create bills in this way was recognised by contemporaries, and is recognised by modern historians, as making credit easier to obtain. Martin Daunton argues that bills of exchange finance was central to early nineteenth-century Britain's ability to industrialise, because it made it easier to borrow money. This meant that British firms could raise capital relatively easily, despite the absence of a banking sector keen to provide businesses with long-term finance.[85] Contemporaries, however, emphasised more the pernicious effects of bills of exchange as a means of finance.[86] Political economists,[87] politicians,[88] essayists,[89] and lawyers[90] argued that firms

[82] This is a slight simplification: B would only have been liable on a bill created by A if B 'accepted' the bill—wrote his name upon it. Further, if B did not pay according to the bill when it was presented for payment, A would be liable as principal for the sum due on the bill, B would only have been a surety.

[83] Joseph Chitty, *A Practical Treatise on Bills of Exchange, Checks on Bankers, Promissory, Bankers' Cash Notes, Bank Notes* (5th edn, Butterworth & Son; Clarke & Son; C Hunter; T Hamilton; W Walker and G Wilson; H Butterworth 1818) ch 1.

[84] Thomas Ashton, 'Bills of Exchange and Private Banks in Lancashire 1790-1830' [1945] Economic Hist Rev 15.

[85] Daunton (n 25) 247–52.

[86] For an overview see James Rogers, *The Early History of the Law of Bills and Notes: A Study of the Origins of Anglo-American Commercial Law* (CUP 1995) 223–32.

[87] Adam Smith, *An Inquiry into the Nature and Causes of the Wealth of Nations* (RH Capmbell and AS Skinner eds, OUP 1976 (first published 1776)) Book 2, ch 2. Smith criticised 'the well-known shift of drawing and redrawing [bills of exchange]; the shift to which unfortunate traders have sometimes recourse when they are upon the brink of bankruptcy. The practice of raising money in this manner had been long known in England, and during the course of the late war, when the high profits of trade afforded a great temptation to overtrading, is said to have carried on to a very great extent.'

[88] See Chapter 3, text from (n 16) to (n 19).

[89] Gisborne (n 1) 283–321; Jun Colbert, *The Age of Paper; or An Essay on Banks and Banking; Containing the History of the Most Remarkable Paper Bubbles* (Parsons; Mason 1795).

[90] Edward Christian, *The Origin, Progress and Present Practise of Bankrupt Law, Both in England and Ireland.*, vol II (2nd edn, W Clarke & Sons 1818) 364–432; Chitty (n 83) 5–6.

(especially country banks[91]) were willing to create and guarantee bills of exchange without ensuring that they had sufficient liquidity to pay the bills. This was another example of irresponsible commercial practice blamed for contemporary economic instability. Indeed, modern historians have recognised that bills of exchange created debt contagion: if a few large firms which were liable on lots of bills defaulted on repayment, this could cause a chain reaction within the financial system.[92]

The specific purpose trust cases involved more responsible use of bills of exchange. In these cases A—typically to pay off a debt to C—would give C a bill of exchange which was payable and guaranteed by B. Whereas reckless traders created bills of exchange without making provision for their payment, in these cases A behaved responsibly by giving B property *for the specific purpose* of paying C. From the middle of the eighteenth century, until B had paid C, B would hold that property on trust for A. If B went bankrupt before C was paid, and A was forced to pay C himself, A could claim the full value of the property and its proceeds from B's estate. In this sense the device can be seen as foreshadowing the so-called modern *Quistclose* arrangements—the trust avoided the doctrine of reputed ownership just as *Quistclose*-style trusts avoid statutory registration requirements for company charges.[93] It can be seen as encouraging the creators of bills of exchange to make provision for their payment—they were encouraged to behave responsibly by the knowledge that the property given to B for the purpose of paying a bill of exchange *would* be used for that purpose, even if B were declared bankrupt.

The leading case was *Ex p Dumas* (1754),[94] which involved the same facts as the example above. A brought a petition in bankruptcy to recover the property

[91] Gisborne (n 1) 283–321; S Quinn, 'Money, Finance and Capital Markets' in Roderick Floud and Paul Johnson (eds), *Cambridge Economic History of Modern Britain* (CUP 2003) 161–67; Boyd Hilton, *Corn, Cash Commerce: The Economic Policies of Tory Government* (OUP 1978) 204, 207–08; Boyd Hilton, *A Mad, Bad, & Dangerous People? England 1783–1846* (OUP 2006) 300–04.

[92] Ian Duffy, *Bankruptcy and Insolvency in London during the Industrial Revolution* (Routledge 1985); Daunton (n 25) 247–52.

[93] See *Barclays Bank Ltd v Quistclose Investments Ltd* [1970] AC 567; *Twinsectra v Yardley* [2002] UKHL 12, 2 AC 164 (per Lord Millett); Robert Stevens, 'Insolvency' in William Swadling (ed), *The Quistclose Trust* (Hart Publishing 2004); Kelry Loi, '*Quistclose* Trusts and Romalpa Clauses: Substance and Nemo Dat in Corporate Insolvency' (2012) 128 LQR 412. Note though that there is a significant distinction between historical specific purpose trusts and most modern *Quistclose* trusts. In a typical *Quistclose* scenario, A and B have no relationship before the trust is created. A then advances B money on trust to pay a particular creditor, and once B has paid that creditor, A is left as B's creditor. A can always recover the trust money before B pays the creditor in question. A is thus protected from the effects of B's insolvency if B becomes insolvent before using the money for the agreed purpose, while B can reassure its other creditors by showing enough liquidity to meet present obligations. In the historical cases whether A was ultimately B's creditor, or vice versa, would depend on the facts—including the relative value of A's debts that B had paid and the trust assets B had been given for that purpose. In addition, in the historical cases A usually created the trust in a way which meant that C was treated as a creditor of the trust, and so able to claim the assets by way of subrogation (in modern terms) to B's right of indemnity in respect of them. This is not true for typical modern *Quistclose* trusts, though C's rights depend on the trust's terms, see Robert Chambers, 'Restrictions on the Use of Money' in William Swadling (ed), *The Quistclose Trust* (Hart Publishing 2004); Peter Birks, 'Retrieving Tied Money' in William Swadling (ed), *The Quistclose Trust* (Hart Publishing 2004).

[94] (n 51).

advanced to B for the purpose of paying C.[95] The Bankruptcy Order books make clear that A's counsel specifically alleged that B had been given the property on an '[a]ccount Separate and Distinct from any other account',[96] and that allowing B's estate to keep the property would be 'not only a Gross Fraud and Breach of Trust on the part of the said John Jullian and Son [B] but would be absolutely illegal'.[97] Lord Hardwicke granted the prayer of the petition, allowing A's claim, on the basis that 'one man's property, whether a chattel in possession or chose in action, may not be dissipated to pay another's debts'.[98] He ruled that B were 'trustees for the petitioners [A]',[99] but also inclined to the view that A had retained legal title to the property, and so could have recovered it in an action for trover, though he considered the matter a 'very extensive question'[100] and did not rule on it. It appears that Lord Hardwicke thought that B held the legal title acquired through possession of the property on trust, even if A had not parted with his legal title. There was thus relativity of title between A and B. The decision in *Dumas* was affirmed by the Bankruptcy Court and Chancery in reported and unreported cases throughout the later eighteenth century and Regency era.[101]

Specific purpose trusts of this type not only allowed A to insulate himself from the possible effects of B's bankruptcy but protected the presumptive reliance and expectations of B and C too. They protected B from A's possible bankruptcy, and C from the bankruptcy of both A *and* B—a point Lord Eldon LC explained in *Ex p Waring* (1814–15).[102] *Ex p Waring* again involved facts where A had given a bill of exchange to C (on which A and B were liable), and later given B property with which to pay the bill. The difference was that, on the facts, both A and B had become bankrupt before C was paid. C sought to claim the property directly from B's bankrupt estate, with priority over B's (and A's) general creditors.

Lord Eldon allowed the claim. In so doing, he explained the protection specific purpose trusts could give B and C.

First, because A had been declared bankrupt before C was paid, B could not have been compelled by A's estate to give up the trust assets. Otherwise B would find himself liable to pay C, but without the assets he was given for that purpose. Doctrinally, B's liability to C was treated as a debt incurred on behalf of the trust: as

95 B 1/29, p 203.
96 ibid 200–201.
97 ibid 202.
98 2 Ves Sen 582, 585; 28 ER 372, 373.
99 ibid 584; 372.
100 ibid 583; 372.
101 *Ex p Oursell* (1756) Amb 297, 27 ER 200; B 1/31, pp 123–25, 205–206, 311–1 (Lord Hardwicke); *Hassall v Smithers* (1806) 12 Ves Jun 119, 33 ER 46 (Ch); C 33/541, 321r–322r (Sir William Grant MR); *Ex p Rowton* (1810) 17 Ves Jun 426, 34 ER 165 (Ch); *Ex p Cramer* (1815) B 1/133, pp 45–48; *Ex p Rayner* (1825) B 1/171, pp 193–209, pp 205–06 (Lord Eldon); *Ex p Ogden* (1815) B 1/133, pp 42–45 (Sir Thomas Plumer V-C).
102 2 Rose 182; 2 G&J 404; 19 Ves Jun 345, 34 ER 546; B 1/138, pp 77–81 (BC). Applied and affirmed in *Ex p Parr* (1818) 1 Buck 191 (BC).

discussed in Chapter 2, a trustee has a right of indemnity and lien over trust assets in respect of such debts and so can recover the value of any expenditure he makes on behalf of the trust from the trust assets.[103] The practical effect of this was that B was protected from meeting the liability to C out of his own assets if A went bankrupt—A could not collapse the trust while the debt to C was outstanding. This would have encouraged B to agree to guarantee A's bills of exchange, so long as A had given B assets for the purpose of paying the bill.

Next, Lord Eldon explained that C could claim the trust assets where A and B both became bankrupt before the sum due on the bill of exchange was paid. Although C had no direct claim on the property, which was held on trust by B for A, C was treated as a creditor of the trust. Where the trustee went bankrupt, a trust creditor could take the benefit of any rights of indemnity and lien the trustee had over the trust assets, in respect of that creditors debt, as had been explained in *Ex p Garland* (1804).[104] Again, in *Waring* B's rights of indemnity and lien over the trust assets subsisted, because B's liability to C on the bill of exchange continued. C could claim the trust assets by taking the benefit of these rights. In modern legal terms, C could be subrogated to B's right of indemnity and lien. As Lord Eldon put it, C had 'A Right to these Bills [the trust property] in Preference to any other Creditor ... by the Effect of some Equity subsisting between *Bracken* and Co [A] and *Brickwood* and Co [B]', as opposed to a 'direct Demand attaching on any Fund in the Hands of *Brickwood* and Co [B]'.[105]

Accordingly, C's right to be paid under the bill of exchange was in effect secured by a claim on the trust assets held by B. It would not have been possible to reach this result simply using a mortgage or charge rather than a trust. The doctrine of reputed ownership would have meant that mortgaged or charged assets would have formed part of B's estate if B had been declared bankrupt. However, because trusts were unaffected by the doctrine of reputed ownership, the specific purpose trust was able to grant security for C's right for payment on the bill of exchange. This in turn would have encouraged C to receive payment from A by means of a bill of exchange, where C knew that A had given B property specifically for the purpose of paying the bill.

The specific purpose trusts therefore played an important role in allowing commercial parties to control the effects of bankruptcy in cases concerning bills of exchange—at a time when statute restricted the use of mortgages and charges of personalty. In an age when irresponsible use of bills of exchange was perceived as a serious problem, specific purpose trusts encouraged responsible practice by making sure assets earmarked for the payment of bills of exchange were dedicated to that purpose.

[103] Chapter 2, Section 3.1.
[104] 10 Ves Jun 110, 32 ER 786 (BC); B 1/105, pp 306–10
[105] 2 Rose 185.

3.2 Specific Purpose Trusts and the Common Law Courts

The reasoning in the specific purpose trusts cases, as above, was applied by the Bankruptcy Court and Chancery throughout the Regency era. More surprisingly, the common law courts were equally willing to enforce such trusts, despite the prevailing orthodoxy (discussed in Chapter 5[106]) that in the period after Lord Mansfield, common law courts would refuse to enforce equitable rights.

For instance, where A gave B money for the purpose of paying C, C could typically claim that money by bringing a claim for money had and received.[107] Further, if A had given B money to pay a bill of exchange, and B went bankrupt before doing so, A could claim the money from B's bankrupt estate—with priority over B's other creditors—at law as well as in equity. The matter was first suggested in *Scott v Surman* (1742–43),[108] which was cited in *Dumas*, where Willes CJCP suggested that A could recover the *whole* of the proceeds of the property advanced to B by bringing a claim for money had and received against his bankrupt estate.

The first case considering the issue at length was *Tooke v Hollingworth* (1793),[109] the facts of which were materially similar to *Dumas*: A had given C a bill of exchange on which both A and B were liable, and A had given B property for the sole purpose of paying C. B was declared bankrupt before C was paid. In *Tooke*, the difference was that A had brought a common law conversion claim against B's bankrupt estate, seeking to recover the property advanced for the purpose of paying C. By majority, the King's Bench allowed A's claim. The most straightforward way of doing this would have been to say that A retained legal title to the assets—as Lord Hardwicke had suggested in *Dumas*. Surprisingly though, A's claim was allowed because he would have received relief in equity. Lord Kenyon CJKB ruled:

> [t]here are indeed various cases in which the separate jurisdictions of Courts of Law and Equity must be kept distinct; it being for the interest of the public, and the forwarding of justice, in a variety of cases that might be put, that they should not be blended; but in the determination of this case there can be no difference between the rule which ought to prevail in Courts of Law and Equity; for equity will go no further than the law.[110]

Lord Kenyon, Ashurst J, and Grose J therefore allowed the conversion claim, on the basis that A had given B the property only for the purpose of paying C, and so

[106] See Chapter 5, text to (n 57) and from (n 57) to (n 80).
[107] *Williams v Everett* (1811) 14 East 582, 104 ER 725 (KB); *Grant v Austen* (1816) 3 Price 58, 146 ER 191 (Ex).
[108] (n 46).
[109] 5 TR 215, 101 ER 121 (KB).
[110] ibid 225; 127.

would have received relief in equity.[111] B had never enjoyed the property beneficially, and so nor could his creditors. The ruling flies in the face of the assertion that trusts could only be enforced in Chancery in the period.[112] Buller J dissented, though (unlike in *Farr v Newman*[113]) he agreed that the same rules should be applied in courts of equity and law, particularly in mercantile cases.[114] First, he distinguished *Dumas* on the facts: he argued that in *Tooke* A had not given the property to B for a sufficiently specific purpose, in not specifying which debts B was to pay with the trust property. Secondly, he attacked the decision in *Dumas* on the basis that A should not be able to avoid the risk of B's insolvency in specific purpose trusts cases, and so reduce the assets available for distribution to B's general creditors. Buller J saw this as unjustifiably undermining the principle of rateable distribution in bankruptcy.[115] That being said, it appears from the report of *Bent v Puller* (1794)[116] that Buller J came to accept the law as set out in *Tooke*,[117] which was affirmed by the King's Bench,[118] the Court of Common Pleas,[119] and the Exchequer[120]—just as it was by Chancery and the Bankruptcy Court[121]—throughout the Regency era.

4. Conclusions

The cases concerning trusts and insolvency examined here suggest that we must revise two widely held assumptions about the development of trusts law and equity.

First, the specific purpose trust cases show that from the mid-eighteenth century commercial parties and their lawyers did make use of trusts; there is no real split between a business world governed by property and contract on the common law side and a family or private world governed by conscience and equity. Where A handed B assets for a specific purpose, and B became bankrupt before the fulfilment of that purpose, then A's lawyers could recover the assets from B's bankrupt

[111] In this sense it resembles the controversial modern decision in *Shell v Total Oil* [2010] EWCA Civ 180, [2011] QB 86 (noted by Peter Turner, 'Consequential Economic Loss and the Trust Beneficiary' [2010] CLJ 445) to allow a negligence claim to be brought on the basis of equitable title.

[112] See Chapter 5, text from (n 64) to (n 73).

[113] 4 TR 621, 100 ER 1209 (KB).

[114] *Tooke* (n 109) 229, 128. This view echoed civil law, see Charles Donahue, 'Equity in the Courts of Merchants' (2004) 72 Tijdschrift voor Rechtsgeschiedenis 1.

[115] 5 TR 230–31, 101 ER 130 (KB).

[116] 5 TR 494, 101 ER 278 (KB).

[117] ibid 496; 279.

[118] *Bent v Puller* bid, *Parke v Eliason* (1801) 1 East 544, 102 ER 210 (KB), *Toovey v Milne* (1819) 2 B&A 683, 106 ER 514 (KB) (cited as 'the genesis of the principle' applied in *Barclays Bank* v *Quistclose* (n 93), by William Swadling, 'Orthodoxy' in William Swadling (ed), *The Quistclose Trust* (Hart Publishing 2004) 25–26); *Moore v Barthrop* (1822) 1 B&C 5, 107 ER 2 (KB).

[119] *Bolton v Puller* (1796) 1 B&P 539, 126 ER 1053 (CP)

[120] *Grant v Austen* (n 107).

[121] (n 101).

estate by pleading the matter as an equitable proprietary claim based on the parties' presumptive expectations and reliances. This facilitated trade by allowing commercial parties greater control over where risk of insolvency lay and was made possible by the exemption of the trusts from the doctrine of reputed ownership. Indeed, from the early eighteenth century it was taken as axiomatic that a trust beneficiary's right would be unaffected by the bankruptcy of the trustee. Though this rule brought about desirable results in cases concerning factors and payment of bills of exchange, this dogmatism presupposed the outcome of priority disputes, and so excluded policy arguments about the desirability of different outcomes. It was this dogmatism which also allowed commercial parties to rely on specific purpose trusts just as modern commercial parties make use of *Quistclose* arrangements. The specific purpose trust cases, together with those concerning trusts of businesses examined in Chapter 2, show that Regency era lawyers were familiar with commercial trusts.

The second revision, growing from the last points made, concerns the relationship between law and equity. While the influence of common law reasoning on Lord Eldon's trusts law has been well documented,[122] the specific purpose trusts cases show that the King's Bench was willing to enforce trusts by allowing priority claims for money had and received and trover against bankrupt estates. The most striking example of this was in *Tooke v Hollingworth*, where Lord Kenyon's King's Bench allowed a trover claim on the basis that relief would have been available in equity, despite the fact the court could have justified the same decision on the basis of legal title alone.[123] While the King's Bench could not have dealt with trusts cases requiring Chancery's accounting procedures, no such procedures were needed in these cases. Along with the King's Bench's decision to recognise executors as a species of trustee,[124] the decisions show that the property law of the Regency era was much more unified than has been hitherto supposed, and that the influence between law and equity was mutual.

[122] Gregory Alexander, 'Transformation of Trusts as a Legal Category, 1800–1914' (1987) 5 L & Hist Rev 303; Stuart Anderson, 'Trusts and Trustees' in William Cornish and others (eds), *Oxford History of the Laws of England*, vol XII (OUP 2010).

[123] Discussed above at Section 3.2.

[124] Discussed in Chapter 5, text to (n 57) and from (n 57) to (n 80).

7
Partnership Dissolution and Bankruptcy

Joint stock trading in the Regency era was a hazardous business. The absence of general incorporation and limited liability meant that the prosperity of the merchant classes was precarious, and anyone who owned a share of a joint stock firm risked *the whole* of their assets if the firm failed—such failure was far from uncommon given the regular market shocks and crashes of the period. As discussed in Chapter 2, Lord Eldon LC strongly opposed the formation of commercial corporations due to fears that the formation of very large joint stock entities would encourage fraud and market instability, and the perception was a popular one. The regular failure of traders themselves was seen as a proportionate deterrent to immoral and reckless overtrading which caused economic instability. Indeed, the knowledge that partners personally would become bankrupt if the firm failed was seen as encouraging them to trade responsibly.

This chapter looks at those cases where a partnership failed and looks at the rules governing how its assets would be distributed on the bankruptcy of its partners. This is used as a way of examining the extent to which a partnership was treated as an entity separate from the partners, given contemporary ideas about the importance of traders' personal liability for their business debts. Exactly *how* partnership law prioritised business creditors' claims over the personal creditors of a partner has to be examined in cases where the firm collapsed. Only in cases of insolvency did the issue of which assets different types of creditor could claim matter. By examining the rights of creditors upon a partnership's insolvency in this way, the extent to which the law encouraged creditors to lend money to partnerships—and so facilitated trade—will be examined.

Within this broader enquiry, this chapter has two main themes. The first concerns the notion of personal responsibility which was integral to partnership. A creditor of a partnership was seen to trust the partners individually and the personal reputation of the partners would help a firm to acquire credit.[1] At the same time, however, traders' accounts would tend to treat partnerships as if they were separate entities, and business creditors might well see the business as their debtor *as well as* the partners individually.[2]

[1] Thomas Gisborne, *An Enquiry into the Duties of Men in the Higher and Middle Classes of Society in Great Britain*, vol 2 (5th edn, J White; Cadell and Davies 1800) 237–38, 241–43; James Taylor, *Creating Capitalism: Joint Stock Enterprise in British Politics and Culture, 1800–1870* (The Boydell Press 2006) 23–32. See Chapter 1, Section 4.

[2] Isaac Cory, *A Practical Treatise on Accounts* (2nd edn, W Pickering 1837) 71. ('The Mercantile notion of a partnership is simply that it is a kind of CORPORATION. The *firm* is always regarded as a kind

Capitalism Before Corporations. Andreas Televantos, Oxford University Press (2020). © Andreas Televantos.
DOI: 10.1093/oso/9780198870340.003.0008.

This tension was reflected in the legal structure of partnership, particularly as developed by Lord Eldon. On the one hand, partners would be co-owners of the assets of the business, creditors of the firm would acquire rights against partners jointly, and upon bankruptcy the personal assets of any partners (after their personal creditors had been paid) would go to satisfy business debts. Courts were adamant that, by private agreement, partners of a firm could not rob its creditors of a claim against a partner who wished to leave the firm. On the other, a bankrupt partnership's assets would be distributed to business creditors in priority to the personal creditors of the partners, and firms which shared partners were treated for some bankruptcy purposes as separate entities. Although Lord Eldon was famous for his hostility to commercial corporations, this is not really reflected in his jurisprudence—supporting Michael Lobban's suggestion that Lord Eldon's perceptions of the separation between politics and law meant that his political views were not voiced in his judgments.[3] Lord Eldon was willing to give effect to creditors' expectations that partnerships were in some sense separate from their partners, so long as this did not interfere with their equally legitimate expectation that partners were personally responsible for the debts the firm contracted, and did not undermine the law's established doctrinal forms. As we will see, however, Lord Eldon's attempts to balance the law in this way were not always successful, in that rules which protected partnership creditors' legitimate expectations in some cases could have the opposite effect in others.

The second theme of this chapter concerns the effectiveness of those partnership rules which involved separating the personal wealth of partners from the assets of the firm. It argues that the priority claim partnership creditors had to partnership assets did encourage creditors to deal with the firm, in that they could asses its solvency without investigating the private affairs of the partners, as Hansmann, Krakmann, and Squire argue.[4] However, it will be suggested that this is only part of a more complicated story, and that Hansmann, Krakmann, and Squire overlook limitations on partnership law's ability to preserve business assets for business creditors. Business creditors might have no protected claim against business assets in cases where a partnership had continued trading after the death or retirement of a partner—a complicated area which very much vexed the courts.

Ultimately, it will be argued that Lord Eldon's attempts to create a law which protected the legitimate expectations of partnership creditors was a qualified success.

of impersonification', emphasis original). See also Joshua Getzler and Mike Macnair, 'The Firm as Entity before the Companies Acts' in Paul Brand, Kevin Costello, and WN Osborough (eds), *Adventures of the Law: Proceedings of the Sixteenth British Legal History Conference* (Four Courts 2005).

[3] Michael Lobban, 'The Politics of English Law in the Nineteenth Century' in Paul Brand and Joshua Getzler (eds), *Judges and Judging: in the History of the Common Law and Civil Law* (CUP 2012).

[4] Henry Hansmann, Reiner Kraakman, and Richard Squire, 'Law and the Rise of the Firm' (2006) 119 Harv L Rev 1333.

Although in most cases the expectations of partnership creditors would be upheld, in cases involving partnerships which dissolved and reformed, the law created hazards for the firm's creditors. In order to show this, it is necessary to look at the four main rules which governed the distribution of the personal and business assets of partners upon their bankruptcy, and so partitioned the assets and liabilities of the partnership from those of the individual partners.

1. Rule I: The 'Jingle' Rule

As described in Chapter 1, the bankruptcy of a partnership was not treated simply as the bankruptcy of the individual partners.[5] This was the effect of what has become known as the 'jingle rule', the most fundamental rule of partnership bankruptcy. It provided that where the partners of a firm were declared bankrupt, the partnership assets would be administered as a distinct estate, separately from the individual estates of the bankrupt partners. Joint creditors of the partners—that is partnership creditors—would prove their debts against the partnership estate, and the partnership assets would be divided rateably amongst them. Conversely, a separate creditor of a partner—that is a personal creditor— would instead prove his debt against the partner's separate estate, and the partner's separately owned property would be distributed rateably amongst personal creditors. Business creditors would therefore not compete with personal creditors for a share of the business assets and vice versa,[6] though in some instances partnership creditors could choose to be treated as separate rather than joint creditors,[7] and would always be treated as separate creditors where no joint assets remained and all the partners were bankrupt.[8] In this way, the law treated the assets and liabilities of the firm as distinct from those of the partners.

[5] Chapter 1, Section 2.4.

[6] Though joint creditors could prove against the separate estate for the purpose of voting on whether a bankrupt should be discharged from his debts. There are a number of examples of such petitions in the record, for representative examples see *Ex p Wender* (1805) B 1/107, pp 11–13; *Ex p Moore* (1805) B 1/106, pp 99–101; *Ex p Tate* (1815) B 1/133, pp 59–60; *Ex p Edwards* (1815) B 1/132, p 325.

[7] 'Joint and several' creditors of a partnership could elect whether to be treated as partnership or personal creditors, and so whether to prove against the partnership estate or the separate estates of the partners, *Ex p Bevan* (1804) 10 Ves Jun 107, 32 ER 784 (BC—Bankruptcy Court); *Ex p Matthews* (1805) B 1/106, pp 113–16; *Ex p Mason* (1811) 1 Rose 159 (BC). More arbitrarily, a partnership creditor who petitioned for a separate commission of bankruptcy against a partner would be treated as a separate creditor of each of the partners rather than a joint creditor, *Ex p Chandler* (1803) 9 Ves Jun 35, 32 ER 513 (BC); *Ex p Ackerman* (1808) 14 Ves Jun 604 (see 605 for Eldon's doubts), 33 ER 653 (BC); *Ex p Detastet* (1810) 1 Rose 10; 17 Ves Jun 247, 34 ER 95 (BC); *Ex p Bolton* (1816) 2 Rose 389, Buck 7 (BC).

[8] The 'Rule in Bankruptcy—Joint Creditors may take with separate creditors where there is no joint Estate and no solvent partner of the bankrupt.' Eldon Notebook 1807–1809 p 3. For no joint assets see, eg, *Ex p Clegg* (1793) 2 Cox 372, 30 ER 171 (BC); *Ex p Machell* (1813) 2 V&B 216, 35 ER 301 (BC); *Ex p Peake* (1814) 2 Rose 54 (BC); *Robson v Curtis* (1815) 1 Stark 78, 171 ER 407 (KB); *Ex p Almond* (1815) B 1/133, pp 57–59; *Ex p Wylie* (1816) 2 Rose 393 (BC); *Ex p Wilcock* (1816) 2 Rose 392 (BC); *Ex p Harris* (1816) 1 Madd 583, 56 ER 214 (BC); *Cowell v Sikes* (1827) 2 Russ 191, 38 ER 307 (Ch). For no non-bankrupt partner see *Ex p Ames* (1805) B 1/106, pp 337–38; *Ex p Sadler* (1808) 15 Ves Jun 52, 33 ER 675

The separation though was not absolute. Any surplus remaining in the separate estates of the partners after the personal creditors had been paid off would be paid to the partnership estate for distribution amongst partnership creditors. Likewise, if any surplus remained in the partnership estate after paying off the partnership creditors, this would be paid into the partners' separate estates in proportion to their shares[9] for distribution amongst their personal creditors.[10]

In this way the 'jingle rule' played two distinct functions which would have been seen by contemporaries as encouraging legitimate commerce in difference ways. First, the rule allowed partnership creditors to assess a firm's creditworthiness by looking at the solvency of the business alone, without having to make potentially costly inquiries about the debts of the individual partners. This was because partnership creditors could claim partnership assets on the firm's dissolution *with priority* over the partners' personal creditors. The jingle rule therefore encouraged third parties to extend credit to partnerships and in that sense encouraged trade.

At the same time, the fact that a partner's separate property was ultimately available to pay business debts would have encouraged creditors to deal with the partnership: not just because of the prospect of an additional asset pool against which they might claim should the business fail, but because each partner was incentivised to trade responsibly, as well as to responsibly choose and monitor the actions of his co-partners.[11] Failure to do so could lead to his own ruin and, as James Taylor has argued, that threat was seen as encouraging good governance[12]—just as government ministers and Malthusian thinkers saw the threat of bankruptcy more broadly as usefully warning against reckless trading.[13] The personal liability of partners for their firm's debts was not seen by contemporaries as problematic.[14]

2. Rule II: Partners Cannot Compete with their Creditors

After the jingle rule, the next most fundamental principle of Regency era partnership bankruptcy law was that partners could not compete with the creditors of their firm. This was very much a corollary of the principle that it was the *partners* themselves who were liable to pay the debts of the firm. If the firm should prove

(Ch); *Ex p Janson* (1818) 2 Buck 227; 3 Madd 229, 56 ER 493 (BC); *Ex p Bradshaw* (1821) 1 G&J 99 (BC); *Ex p Bur* (1821) 1 G&J 32 (BC).

[9] These would be set out in the articles of partnership, but by default partners would take in equal shares, regardless of their relative contribution to the partnership assets, Neil Gow, *A Practical Treatise on the Law of Partnership* (3rd edn, C Hunter and J Richards 1830) 8–9.

[10] In modern law and economics terms there was 'soft' entity shielding and asset partitioning, Hansmann, Kraakman, and Squire (n 4).

[11] Gisborne (n 1) 256, 264–65.

[12] Taylor (n 1) 23–32.

[13] Chapter 3, Section 1.1.

[14] Chapter 1, Section 4.

insolvent, it was for the partners to take the hit before the creditors. Imagine a case where firm ABC becomes bankrupt, and partner A had lent money to the firm. Had A's separate estate been able to prove the debt against the partnership, then it would have reduced the total sum available for the business's external creditors. For that reason, A's separate estate would not have been able to do this. The principle thus buttressed the jingle rule, by making sure that business assets were distributed to business creditors in priority to the separate creditors of the partners.

The principle that partners could not compete with their creditors was also justified by the rights of partners against one another, a point best understood through the doctrinal mechanism by which it was expressed. As discussed in Chapter 1, each partner had a right against his co-partners to force them to contribute towards the payment of partnership debts. This right was referred to as an 'indemnity'. This indemnity, however, was not purely personal, but was secured by a lien—effectively a charge—over the partnership assets. Practically, this meant that each partner could force the others to use their share of the partnership property to discharge the joint debts. For that reason, upon dissolution of a partnership no partner could claim a share of partnership property until the partnership's creditors had been paid off. In other words, partners were residual claimants of the assets of their firm, a point explained by Lord Hardwicke LC in *West v Skipp* (1749)[15]

> The partners themselves are clearly joint-tenants in the stock and all effects: not only that particular stock in being at the time of entering into the partnership; but to continue so throughout; whatever changes might be made in the course of trade. Otherwise it is impossible to carry it on: And being seised *per my & per tout*, when an account is to be taken, each is intitled to be allowed against the other every thing he has advanced or brought in as a partnership . . . and to charge the other in the account with what that other has not brought in, or has taken out more than he ought: and nothing is to be considered as his share, but his proportion of the residue on balance of the account.[16]

The ruling was affirmed a number of times both in equity and at common law.[17] This reasoning explained why a partner could not withdraw his stock from a factually insolvent firm before bankruptcy: his share of the partnership at such a time was a liability rather than an asset.[18] A natural implication of the residual nature of

[15] 1 Ves Sen 239, 27 ER 1006 (Ch); C 33/392, ff 198r, 215r.
[16] ibid 242; 1008. References omitted.
[17] *Fox v Hanbury* (1776) 2 Cowp 445, 98 ER 1179 (KB); *Smith v De Silva* (1776) 2 Cowp 469, 471; 98 ER 1191, 1193 (KB); *Taylor v Fields* (1799) 4 Ves Jun 396, 31 ER 201 (Ex); *Dutton v Morrison* (1810) 1 Rose 213; 17 Ves Jun 193, 34 ER 75 (Ch); Eldon Notebook 1807–1809 pp 174–79; Eldon Notebook 1809–1810, p 130; *Ex p Harris* (1813) 35 ER 298, 1 Rose 437, 2 Ves & B 210 (BC); *Re Wait* (1820) 1 J&W 605, 609; 37 ER 499, 500 (Ch); *Bray v Fromont* (1821) 6 Madd 5, 56 ER 990 (Ch).
[18] *Anderson v Maltby* (1793) 2 Ves Jun 244, 30 ER 616; 4 Brown CC 423, 29 ER 970 (Ch); C 33/481, ff 693r–695r.

a partner's interests in the firm's assets was that a partner could not prove against the bankrupt partnership's joint estate in competition with the joint creditors.[19] Likewise, where a separate creditor of a partner levied judgment against that partner's share of the partnership assets, he could only claim the partner's right to the residue of the partnership assets after the partnership creditors had been paid.[20]

However, there were two exceptions to the rule that a partner could not compete with his creditors. First, where the separate assets of one partner were converted to the use of the partnership, the partnership would have to account to him for the use of those assets. An example of this would be where a partner died, but his former partners carried on the business, and made use of the deceased partner's share of the capital without paying what was owed to the testamentary estate. In the early nineteenth century, the continuing partners in such a case would hold the deceased partner's assets on trust for his estate and be liable for the value of the assets as well as any profit generated from them.[21] However, instead of bringing a proprietary claim, through his personal representatives, the deceased partner's estate could choose to be treated as a creditor of the partnership.[22]

Secondly, the Bankruptcy Court would allow partners effectively to prove against their own estates in cases of 'overlapping partnerships': where one individual was partner in two partnerships, one of which was indebted to the other. If the debtor and creditor firms went bankrupt, then the rule was that the bankrupt estate of the creditor firm could prove against the debtor firm provided that their trades were distinct, and the creditor firm had made an advance to the debtor firm whilst acting in the creditor firm's separate course of business.[23] Lord Eldon explained the principle in *Ex p Sillitoe* (1824),[24] making clear that the rule was a way

[19] *Ex p Sillitoe and Hunter* (1824) 1 G&J 374 (BC); B 1/167, pp 18–22. Also see *Ex p Burrell* (1793) Cooke (8th edn) 528 (BC); and *Ex p Parker* (1793) Cooke (8th edn) 528 (BC); *Ex p Pine* (1793) Cooke (8th edn) 528 (BC); *Ex p Ellis* (1827) 2 G&J 312 (BC). The separate partner's creditors could not bring such a claim either, see *Ex p Baker* (1780), *Notes of Cases in Chancery and Exchequer 1780–1788* at 9, part of the Lord Eldon Collection, Georgetown Law Library. (A partner lent money to the firm, the partner and firm went bankrupt, and the separate creditors of the partner sought to prove against the partnership estate, Thurlow LC ruled 'I do not understand how the creditors of the Bankrupt can have a better title than the Bankrupt himself under whom he derives Title').

[20] Gow (n 9) 205.

[21] *Crawshay v Collins* (1808) 15 Ves Jun 218, 33 ER 736 (Ch); *Featherstonaugh v Fenwick* (1810) 17 Ves Jun 298, 34 ER 115 (Ch). This changed later in the century, see *Knox v Gye* (1871–72) LR 5 HL 656 codified in Partnership Act 1890, s 43.

[22] This was expressly recognised by Lord Eldon: 'To that rule [that the separate estate may not prove against the joint] there is an exception, manifestly founded in justice, and that is, where a partner becomes a creditor in respect of a fraudulent conversion of his separate estate to the use of the partnership.' See *Sillitoe* (n 19) 382.

[23] *Ex p Ring* (1796) Cooke (8th edn) 534 (BC); *Ex p St Barbe* (1805) 11 Ves Jun 413, 32 ER 1147 (BC); *Ex p Hesham* (1810) 1 Rose 146 (BC); *Sillitoe* (n 19); *Ex p Richardson* (1827) 5 LJR 129 (BC). The court made an order allowing proof by one partnership against another with common partners in the unreported case of *Ex p Moore* (1825) B 1/171, pp 247–51, but the reasoning is not apparent from the court order, though the facts suggest that the reasoning was the same as that in the cases cited above.

[24] (n 19).

of solving the 'infinite difficulty' of dealing with the 'the more complicated nature of commercial relations' in which one individual might be involved in litigation or bankruptcy 'in many distinct characters'.[25] Although, controversially, Lord Eldon was of the view that the rule only applied where one firm had provided goods or services, rather than credit, to another[26]—a distinction other judges rejected[27]—this exception nevertheless involved treating partnerships as being more than the sum of their partners, and therefore as having entity-like characteristics.

3. Rule III: Joint Creditors Can Claim against Partners who Withdraw Joint Funds without Authority

As indicated above, a partner's entitlement to his firm's assets was residual, and so he had no entitlement to withdraw his capital from the partnership where the firm was insolvent. As a corollary of this, where a firm went bankrupt, and one partner had taken sums from the joint stock of the firm without authority under the terms of the partnership agreement, the joint estate would be able to claim against the errant partner or his bankrupt estate.[28] Lord Eldon, rejecting Lord Thurlow LC's earlier position,[29] ruled that the joint estate could pursue such claims simply because the partner had withdrawn the sums without authority under the partnership agreement, no actual fraud was needed.[30] The rule therefore buttressed the protection that the jingle rule gave to partnership creditors: by making sure that assets taken out of the business by partners without authority under the partnership agreement would nevertheless be treated as part of the partnership estate.

4. Rule IV: Joint Creditors Have Rights against the Partners' Jointly, *not* a Firm

The final rule central to the distribution of partnership assets related to a partnership's lack of legal personality and provided that on dissolution of a partnership the rights of its creditors would effectively be frozen. The rule was designed to prevent partners by private agreement from depriving partnership creditors of their rights against a retiring or deceased partner. For that reason, like the rules

25 *Sillitoe* (n 19) 382–83.
26 ibid.
27 *Wilson v Wetherell* (1805) C 33/536, ff 106r–v (unreported, Sir William Grant MR); *Ex p Castell* (1826) 2 G&J 124, 126–27; 5 LJR 71–72 (BC); *Ex p Brenchley* (1826) 5 LJR 73 (BC); *Ex p Stroud* (1826) 5 LJR 72 (BC) (Sir John Leach V-C).
28 *Ex p Blake* (1735) Cooke (8th edn) 528 (BC); *Ex p Cust* (1774) Cooke (8th edn) 531 (BC).
29 *Ex p Harris* (1813) 1 Rose 437, 438–39; 2 V&B 210, 35 ER 298 (BC); *Ex p Young* (1814) 2 Rose 40; 3 V&B 31, 35 ER 391 (BC).
30 ibid.

considered above, the rule was designed to protect partnership creditors' legitimate expectations, and so encouraged third parties to deal with partnerships. However, the complexity of the rules and scenarios involved meant that the rule did not always have this effect.

The rule is more complicated than those considered above and so it is worth explaining at length. Corporations have legal personality and are capable of owning property. If a creditor lends money to a corporation, then his rights are essentially unaffected by any change in the ownership of the shares or management of the corporation. The corporation remains his debtor and the creditor can still claim the assets owned by the corporation should it default on repayment of the debt.

Partnerships do not have legal personality, and this could cause very complicated legal problems where a single business had been carried on through several changes of partners. As discussed in Chapter 1, the retirement or addition of any partner to a firm *automatically* caused the partnership to dissolve and a new partnership to form.[31] This new partnership as a matter of law would form a separate estate from the previous partnership, which meant that a single firm in fact could as a matter of law have consisted of successive different partnership estates. The courts faced a real difficulty in deciding the extent to which a firm's assets should be treated as a single independent fund despite this. More specifically, the issue was whether the joint creditors of a dissolved partnership which continued trading were to be treated as creditors of the old partners, or only those that had continued the trade. The problem was particularly felt in cases involving country banks, which would continue to deal with customer accounts through changes of partners as if nothing had happened, and many of which collapsed in the crises of 1810–11 and 1825–26.

For example, imagine that A, B, and C form a banking partnership. A depositor, X, deposits £100 in the bank. A retires, and D joins the partnership. The assets are therefore transferred to BCD. BCD become insolvent and are declared bankrupt. From who can X claim? Can X claim from A, who has retired from the concern? After all, although X might have trusted A at the time of making the deposit, A no longer had recourse to partnership assets to pay the debt.[32] On the other hand, could X seek a rateable share of BCD's estate, given that X had never advanced money to D, and so was not a creditor of BCD? X, after all, might see himself as a creditor of the bank as a *business*—only a very legally aware depositor might be aware of the effect of dissolution on any claim to partnership assets.

Problems of this type brought into sharp relief the tension creditors' beliefs that they could claim against partners personally *and* against a business. Regency era

[31] See Chapter 1, Section 3.1.

[32] Though typically, upon A's retirement, the continuing and new partners would agree to indemnify A in respect of any continuing liabilities he had in respect of the firm's business. Eg see *Ex p Harvey* (1825) B 1/171, pp 84–109; *Ex p Pyke* (1825) B 1/171, pp 257–60.

law's answer to problems of this type was to affirm that a partnership creditor was a creditor *of that partnership* and not of the firm—and so would remain a creditor of the partners *at the time the debt was contracted*, unless the creditor had accepted the new partners as his debtors in lieu of the old ones. For instance, the courts would generally find that a creditor of a dissolved partnership who took a bill or other security from the remaining partners had released any retiring partners.[33] However, such a conclusion would depend on a number of factors, such as whether the receipts or bills issued by the old partnership had been delivered up in return for the new security;[34] and whether the wording of the new instrument stated it to be further or collateral security.[35] Indeed, in the absence of such a transaction, the courts were unwilling to infer that the creditors' rights had been affected by dissolution. After all, if X had extended credit to ABC, why should the fact he had continued to deal with BC after A's retirement involve forfeiting his claim against A? Were BC not X's debtors also? Like Rules II and III, this rule was rooted in a desire to prevent the actions of partners inter se affecting creditor rights without their consent.

The difficulty was that this compromise did not properly protect creditor expectations in all cases. In some factual scenarios being a creditor of the partners of a dissolved partnership could rob business creditors of their claim against business assets, where those assets had been transferred to some combination of continuing or new partners. In others, business creditors might risk being robbed of claims against a partner whose credit they had trusted, where they were found to have surrendered their claims against a retired partner by having dealt with the business post-dissolution.

Understanding the position better requires a separate consideration of the position of partnership creditor claims vis-à-vis former partners, continuing partners, and new partners following the dissolution of a firm.

4.1 Liability of Former Partners

The issue of whether a retired partner would remain liable to partnership debts after his retirement was raised as early as *Heath v Percival* (1720).[36] Lord Macclesfield LC allowed a claim on a joint bond against the executor of a partner who had retired before his death. Upon retirement the testator had left the partnership, and it had been agreed that his partner (bankrupt at the time of litigation) was to continue

[33] Either alone or in conjunction with any new partners. *Evans v Drummond* (1801) 4 Esp 89, 170 ER 652 (KB); *Newmarch v Clay* (1811) 14 East 239, 104 ER 592 (KB).

[34] *Daniel v Cross* (1796) 3 Ves Jun 277, 30 ER 1009 (Ch); *Gough v Davies* (1817) 4 Price 200, 146 ER 439 (Ex); *Bedford v Deakin* (1818) 2 Stark 178, 171 ER 612; (1818) 2 B&A 210, 106 ER 344 (KB).

[35] *Twopenny v Young* (1824) 3 B&C 208, 107 ER 711 (KB).

[36] 1 P Wms 683, 24 ER 570; 1 Str 403, 93 ER 595 (Ch).

the concern and to discharge the partnership's joint obligations. The plaintiff had already proved the value of the bond against the bankrupt continuing partner's estate. Lord Macclesfield LC made his reasons for allowing the claim against the retired partner transparent: 'As to the agreement between … [the former partners], that was res inter alios acta, which ought not to prejudice the plaintiff, as it will do if it be of any avail, because it tends to lessen his security.'[37] A private agreement between the partners to dissolve the firm, and have one partner take up its debts, could not as a matter of principle be allowed to deprive partnership creditors of their claim against the retiring partner—who was after all their debtor. The ruling that retired and deceased partners remained liable to their firm's debts remained the prima facie legal position throughout the long eighteenth century.[38]

The effect of a partnership's dissolution on its creditors' claims against former partners was discussed at greatest length in the litigation arising out of the insolvency of the banking house Devaynes, Dawes, & Co. Devaynes, a partner in the bank, died. The accounts with the customers were continued as if nothing had happened, as was the usual practice of banks at this time.[39] During the financial crash of 1810–11, which caused a number of banks to collapse, the four remaining partners then went bankrupt, whilst Devaynes's estate was solvent. The litigation surrounding the bankruptcy centred on the extent to which creditors of the bank could claim against Devaynes's estate. Had the bank been a corporation, rather than a partnership, no such claim would have been available.

The cases concerning the liability of Devaynes's estate to the firm's creditors were *Ex p Kendal* (1811),[40] *Sleech's Case* (1816), and the more famous *Clayton's Case* (1816). The relationship between these cases is not straightforward. *Sleech's Case* and *Clayton's Case* are reported as part of the 1816 case of *Devaynes v Noble; Baring v Noble*,[41] which originated as two separate suits in 1810–11. The first was brought by Devaynes's estate against the surviving partners, while the latter was brought by the joint creditors against both Devaynes's estate and the surviving partners. In *Ex p Kendal* the joint creditors also brought a petition before Lord Eldon in his capacity as a bankruptcy judge, praying that the distribution of the bankrupt partnership's assets be delayed until Chancery had reached a determination in *Devaynes v Noble*. Although the petition was refused, Lord Eldon's judgment is of interest in that he expressed his opinion on the merits of *Devaynes v Noble*, an opinion which loomed over much of the subsequent litigation. *Devaynes v Noble* later resulted in an 1815 Master's report on the state of the bank's accounts vis-à-vis Devaynes and its creditors.[42] Merivale's report of the case consists of a record of the appeals against the

[37] 1 Str 404; 93 ER 595.
[38] *Daniel v Cross* (1796) 3 Ves Jun 277; 30 ER 1009 (Ch); *Dickenson v Lockyer* (1798) 4 Ves Jun 36, 31 ER 19 (Ch).
[39] See *Devaynes v Noble* (1816) 1 Mer 529, 535–37; 35 ER 767, 769–70 (Ch).
[40] 1 Rose 71; 17 Ves Jun 514, 34 ER 199; B 1/123, pp 132–35 (BC).
[41] (n 39).
[42] ibid.

Master's conclusions on the entitlements of different classes of creditors, as heard by Sir William Grant MR. The two appeals which concern us are *Sleech's Case* and *Clayton's Case* itself.

4.1.1 *Ex p Kendal*

As stated above, the joint creditors of the partnership had brought a petition before Lord Eldon in *Ex p Kendal* (1811).[43] The petitioners included some creditors whose debts had been contracted before dissolution, others who had contracted debts afterwards, as well as creditors who were owed debts from both periods. They had already brought a bill in Chancery for a decree that the residue of Devaynes's estate, once his personal creditors had been paid, was to be applied in satisfaction of all the firm's debts under the jingle rule.[44] At the same time they brought a petition praying that the bankruptcy proceedings be halted until the decree on the bill had been obtained, that is until a resolution of the proceedings in Chancery. More particularly, they prayed that the payment of the dividend on the partnership estate be delayed until Devaynes's estate had been made to contribute.

Lord Eldon refused to order a delay on the distribution of the bankrupt estate, but it is his remarks on the merits of that bill that are of interest for present purposes. Lord Eldon made clear that the pre-dissolution creditors prima facie would have a claim against Devaynes' estate, unless it could be shown that they had released their claim against Devaynes through their dealings with the bank after his death.[45] However, he made clear that the creditors who had advanced money to the partnership after Devaynes's death could not claim anything from his estate—Devaynes had never been their debtor.[46]

4.1.2 *Sleech's Case* (1816)

The bill referred to above in *Ex p Kendal* resulted in a reference to a Master on 2 March 1812 to take the accounts of Devaynes's estate and the firm. The Master made his report on 15 March 1815, and much of it is set out in the report of *Devaynes v Noble* (1816).[47] The litigation in *Devaynes v Noble* ultimately consisted of appeals against the Master's findings as to the entitlements of different classes of creditor.

The first such appeal heard by Chancery was *Sleech's Case*. Miss Sleech was a creditor of the partnership before Devaynes's death. After his death she had been

[43] (n 40).
[44] Discussed above at Section 1.
[45] (n 40) 520; 201.
[46] ibid 523; 203. Lord Eldon also rejected the argument that the court should force the creditors with claims against Devaynes to pursue those before claiming a share of the partnership assets in order to leave a greater share of those assets available to the creditors without claims against Devyanes.
[47] (n 39) 529; 767. Given that Masters' reports in The National Archives are not properly catalogued, it would be impossible to identify either the report itself, or the Master's accounts, without an extensive search. See Henry Horwitz, *Chancery Equity Records and Proceedings 1600–1800* (2nd edn, PRO 1998) 80–88.

paid several sums by the surviving partners. After the bankruptcy, she had also proved against the joint estate of the surviving partners, had received a dividend on the assets, and had signed their bankruptcy certificates; that is to say, she had given her consent to them being discharged from their pre-bankruptcy debts. The Master in his report concluded that Miss Sleech retained her entitlement to prove against Devaynes's estate and had done nothing to give up her right against it.

Devaynes's representatives, however, appealed against the Master's finding on point, and their counsel advanced two main arguments—to the effect that Miss Sleech was really a creditor of the business, and so should have no claim against the estate of a retired partner. The first related to 'a peculiarity in the custom of dealing between bankers and customers, which renders their case quite distinct from that of ordinary borrowers and lenders',[48] that is, that 'a banker is rather the bailee of his customer's funds than his debtor', and that it was only the surviving partners who were liable to the joint creditors.[49] In other words, it was argued that bank customers retained a proprietary interest in their bank deposits, and that this property right was the basis of a bank's liability to its customers. As the continuing partners had had control of the deposits, they alone were liable to the bank's customers—meaning that a banking partnership could be treated as an entity rather than a succession of partnerships for the purposes of dissolution.[50]

It was also argued that a ruling that a deceased partner's estate remained liable for the debts of the banking partnership would cause chaos. It would mean that, when a partner died, the depositors would immediately claim against a deceased partner's estate, forcing his executor to claim the estate's share of the partnership assets to answer those claims. Such a practice would necessarily involve liquidating the firm's assets, thereby preventing the usual practice of bankers carrying on to trade with customers despite technical legal dissolution. By implication, this would destabilise the already precarious position of many country banks.

It was also argued that by her conduct Miss Sleech had adopted the remaining partners as her debtors, discharging Devaynes by leaving her money with the surviving partners and not pursuing her claim against Devaynes's estate earlier; by continuing to deal with the surviving partners and accepting part payment from them; and by proving her debt against the bankruptcy of the surviving partners and signing the certificate of discharge.

In support of the Master's report, on behalf of Miss Sleech and the creditors of her class, three main points were made. The first was that the ruling in *Ex p Kendal* made clear that the 'custom of bankers' to carry on the accounts after a partner's death could not make a difference to Miss Sleech's case; Lord Eldon's decree in that

48 *Devaynes* (n 39) 541; 771.

49 ibid.

50 Sir Samuel Romilly had unsuccessfully advanced a similar argument in *Ex p Ruffin* (1801) 6 Ves Jun 119, 31 ER 970 (BC). Discussed below at Section 4.2.

case took notice of the fact that the partnership was a bank, yet proceeded on the presumption that Devaynes's estate was prima facie liable to the pre-dissolution creditors. Further, they argued that Miss Sleech's actions had not made the surviving partners her debtors in lieu of Devaynes. Her actions towards the surviving partners were explicable simply on the basis that they too were her debtors and did not amount to a discharge of Devaynes's estate. In addition, it was argued that there was no reason to conclude that her claim was time barred; it certainly would not have been time barred under the Statute of Limitations 1624[51] and were the court to rule that a bank customer had to withdraw his or her funds upon the death of a partner or discharge his estate, this would create a risk of bank runs.

Sir William Grant ruled as follows. First, he rejected the idea that a mere commercial custom could vary the law of partnerships as it applied to banks, stating that 'the common law, though it professes to adopt the *Lex Mercatoria*, has not adopted it throughout in what relates to partnership in trade',[52] making it clear that bankers would not on the basis of alleged custom be treated as bailees for their customers rather than debtors:

> There is a fallacy in likening the dealings of a banker to the case of a deposit, to which, in legal effect, they have no sort of resemblance. Money paid in to a banker's becomes immediately a part of his general assets; and he is merely a debtor for the amount. Therefore, when a man lodges money with a partnership of bankers, he is as much concerned to look to the solvency of each particular partner, as if he was lending the money to any other partnership. The money, in each case, equally ceases to be his the moment he has parted with it, and he has only to trust, for the return of it, to the solvency of the persons into whose hands it passes: but he has, in each case alike, the credit, and the responsibility of all the partners in the firm.[53]

In other words, partners of banking partnerships were personally liable to depositors, in the same way as partners of other types were liable to their creditors—and by implication would remain so after retiring from the concerning or dying. Sir William Grant was not willing to bend the normal rules of property and contract—which provided that a bank depositor absolutely transferred his money to the bank and had only a personal right for payment against the partners—for the sake of a new rule which treated banks as a single entity, rather than a succession of partnerships, for insolvency purposes. The fact such a rule would have mirrored the way banks did business was not sufficient justification for disapplying the normal rules of property and contract.

[51] 21 Jac I c 16.
[52] *Devaynes* (n 39) 564; 778.
[53] ibid 568–69; 780.

Further, nothing Miss Sleech had done by dealing with the continuing partners was held to discharge Devaynes's estate in the way Lord Eldon had intimated might be possible in *Kendal:*

> In that case of *Ex parte Kendal*, the *Lord Chancellor* took it to be clear, that the only question which Mr. *Devaynes's* representatives could make, was, whether these creditors had so dealt with the surviving partners as to make it inequitable in them to resort to his assets? Then, what is that sort of dealing by which this effect is to be produced? I apprehend it must be something very different from what has taken place in Miss *Sleech's* instance.[54]

Accordingly, the fact that Miss Sleech had received interest payments from the surviving partners,[55] proved against the bankrupt estates, and signed their certificates of discharge, was not held to amount to a release of Devaynes's estate.[56] After all, the continuing partners were also her debtors, and her actions were explicable on this basis. Further, the fact that the bank had kept continuous accounts with customers pre and post-dissolution (in accordance with usual contemporary practice) was treated as incapable of affecting creditor rights as a matter of principle; to hold otherwise would be to allow customers' rights to be varied by an agreement to which they were not privy.[57]

Sir William Grant also dismissed the argument that Miss Sleech had forfeited her right to prove against the deceased partner's estate by not bringing her claim at the time of the dissolution, referring to this as a 'short arbitrary limitation'.[58] He adopted counsel for Miss Sleech's argument in justifying this construction of the law as in the interest of banks:

> if creditors were told that the only way in which they could preserve their recourse against the estate of a deceased partner, is by using all possible diligence to compel an immediate payment by the surviving partners, of the whole of their balances; there are very few houses which could stand such a sudden and concurrent demand as that would necessarily bring upon them. A house might be reduced to a state of bankruptcy, which, in the ordinary course of business, would have been able to fulfil all its engagements; and a demand would be brought on the estate of a deceased partner, from which it might otherwise have wholly escaped; and, therefore, if expediency were to be taken into the consideration, I do not see what purpose of general convenience would be answered by compelling creditors to such a rigorous course as the condition upon which

[54] ibid 566; 779.
[55] ibid 570; 781.
[56] ibid 571; 781.
[57] ibid.
[58] ibid 566, 779.

> alone the hold which equity gives them on the estate of a deceased partner could be retained.[59]

In other words, if upon the dissolution of a banking partnership, creditors were forced to either give up their rights against the former partners or withdraw their money, this would create the risk of 'bank runs' upon every dissolution, potentially ruining the remaining partners.

In short then, *Sleech's Case* made clear that a partnership creditor would not be deemed to have released a former partner from liability on the basis of the creditor's general conduct alone. The decision made clear that a creditor's claim against a former partner would be enforced in the absence of strong evidence of discharge, and would come to be affirmed a number of times.[60] It made clear that the courts would not treat banks as entities simply because they continued to keep running accounts with customers despite dissolution, and that a retired partner could not escape liability for debts incurred before his retirement, simply because the creditor had dealt with the partnership after he had left it. The court rejected the argument that, as a matter of commercial reality, it should treat a succession of partnerships as a single entity. This was due to concern about causing bank runs and maintaining the integrity of established doctrines of property and contract, but also chimed with contemporary ideas about the importance of personal responsibility for debts.

4.1.3 *Clayton's Case* (1816)

We now turn to the second appeal against the Master's conclusions in *Devaynes v Noble*, *Clayton's Case*. Clayton, and other creditors of his class, had been creditors of the bank before it was dissolved by Devaynes's death. However, unlike Miss Sleech, Mr Clayton had received payment from the surviving partners which was equivalent to the full value of the debt he was owed at the time of Devaynes's death. He nevertheless remained a creditor of the bank due to subsequent dealings.

The issue was whether the payments made by the bank after Devaynes's death discharged the debt owed to Clayton *before* Devaynes died (ie by the dissolved partnership), or the debt owed to Clayton which had been contracted after Devaynes's death (by the new partnership). If the latter, then Devyanes's estate would remain liable to Clayton. Neither Clayton nor the bank had appropriated the payment to a particular debt owing.[61] The Master's report concluded that the payments made by

59 ibid 569–70; 780.

60 Eg *Gough v Davies* (1817) 4 Price 200, 146 ER 439 (Ex); *Lodge v Dicas* (1820) 3 B & A 611, 106 ER 784 (KB); and *David v Ellice* (1826) 5 B & C 196, 108 ER 73 (KB). Sir John Leach V-C appears to have reached a different result in *Campbell v Campbell* (1825) 3 LJ Ch 129 (Ch), but the decision appears anomalous, and the report contains little reasoning.

61 The debtor in the first instance could make such an election, and if he did not the creditor could, see *Peters v Anderson* (1814) 5 Taunt 596, 128 ER 823 (KB). The issue in *Clayton's Case* was how to treat the account where no such election had been made.

the new partnership had discharged the debts owed by the dissolved partnership. This was on the basis of what modern lawyers will recognise as the 'first in first out' rule: payments made by the bank discharged the debt incurred first.

Counsels' arguments on appeal to the Master of the Rolls therefore focused on the question of which debt had been discharged by the bank's payments following Devaynes's death: was it the debt contracted with Clayton before Devaynes died, or the debt contracted after his death? Counsel for Clayton argued as follows. First, they cited common law authority to the effect that where A owed two debts to B, and made payment to B, B could choose *which* debt was discharged by the payment if A had not done so. On the facts, they said the bank had made no such election when it paid Clayton, and Clayton now chose to treat the payment he received as discharging the debt incurred *after* Devaynes's death—leaving his claim against Devaynes outstanding. Further, counsel for Clayton sought to build on the ruling in *Sleech's Case* by arguing that no action by Clayton had discharged Devaynes's estate.

Counsel for Devaynes's estate, argued more subtly in support of the Master's conclusions. They said that because the surviving partners had had Devaynes's assets in their hands, they were bound first to pay off the debts on which Devaynes too had also been liable. Clayton could have appropriated the payment to a particular debt *at the time* it was made, but had not done so. In the absence of an actual appropriation, Clayton ought to be treated as having taken payment in discharge of the older debt: firstly because simply as a matter of 'common sense' the payment would naturally go to the debt for which there had 'been the longest forbearance, and against which, if remaining unsatisfied, the Statute of Limitations'[62] would 'soonest operate'[63] and; secondly, because if the court were to allow Clayton to deal with the surviving partners, and keep Devaynes's estate as a surety for all those transactions due to a privately held intention, this would be tantamount to allowing fraud. It was further argued that Clayton's dealings with the bank amounted to a discharge of Devaynes's estate within Lord Eldon's meaning in *Ex p Kendal*, implicitly suggesting that accepting payment of the full value of the debt from the post-dissolution partnership discharged the deceased partner, though *Sleech's Case* provided that part payment did not have such an effect.

In reply, counsel for Clayton made a number of additional points. They argued that the first in first out rule could not apply on the facts of the present case: the partnership before and after Devaynes's death was not a *single entity*. Surely it made more sense to treat the continuing partners as paying off the debt they *alone* were liable upon, rather than the debt they were jointly liable upon with Devaynes? Counsel also took issue with the argument that the surviving partners, because they had Devaynes' assets in their hands, were in fact obliged to pay off the

[62] (1624) 21 Jac I c 16.
[63] (n 39) 595–96; 789.

pre-dissolution debt first, on the basis that the relationship between the partners inter se could not as a matter of principle be allowed to affect Clayton's rights as a creditor.

Sir William Grant ultimately held that Clayton could not claim against Devaynes's estate, endorsing the first in first out rule on the basis of the presumed intention of the debtor, making heavy reference to Roman law:

> This state of the case has given rise to much discussion, as to the rules by which the application of indefinite payments is to be governed. Those rules we, probably, borrowed in the first instance, from the civil law. The leading rule, with regard to the option given, in the first place to the debtor, and to the creditor in the second, we have taken literally from thence. But, according to that law, the election was to be made at the time of payment, as well in the case of the creditor, as in that of the debtor, 'in re præsenti; hoc est statim atque solutum est:[64]—cæterum, postea non permittitur.'[65] (Dig. Lib. 46, tit. 3, Qu. 1, 3.) If neither applied the payment, the law made the appropriation according to certain rules of presumption, depending on the nature of the debts, or the priority in which they were incurred. *And, as it was the actual intention of the debtor that would, in the first instance, have governed; so it was his presumable intention that was first resorted to as the rule by which the application was to be determined.* In the absence, therefore, of any express declaration by either, the inquiry was, what application would be most beneficial to the debtor. The payment was, consequently, applied to the most burthensome debt,—to one that carried interest, rather than to that which carried none,—to one secured by a penalty, rather than to that which rested on a simple stipulation;—and, *if the debts were equal, then to that which had been first contracted. 'In his quæ præsenti die debentur, constat, quotiens indistincte quid solvitur, in graviorem causam videri solutum. Si autem nulla prægravet,—id est, si omnia nomina similia fuerint,—in antiquiorem.'*[66] (Dig. L. 46, t. 3, Qu. 5.)[67]

Accordingly, Sir William ruled that where a creditor was owed multiple debts by his debtor, and received payment from his debtor, he could not retrospectively appropriate such payment to a particular debt (having failed to do so at the time it was made). He distinguished the cases cited by counsel for Clayton which held that a creditor had an indefinite right to apportion payments, on the basis that:

64 '... and to decide as in the present state of affairs, that is, as soon as the payment is made', A Watson (ed), *The Digest of Justinian*, vol 4 (University of Pennsylvania Press 1985) 216, D.46.3.1.

65 'But it is not allowed later', ibid 216, D.46.3.3.

66 'Among debts presently due, it is settled that whenever it is unclear which is being paid, the payment is attributed to the more onerous and, if none is more onerous, that is, if all are similar, the longest standing.' ibid D. 46.3.5.

67 *Devaynes* (n 39) 605–06; 792. Emphasis added.

> ... this is the case of a banking account, where all the sums paid in *form one blended fund, the parts of which have no longer any distinct existence* ... In such a case, there is no room for any other appropriation than that which arises from the order in which the receipts and payments take place, and are carried into the account. Presumably, it is the sum first paid in, that is first drawn out. It is the first item on the debit side of the account, that is discharged, or reduced, by the first item on the credit side. The appropriation is made by the very act of setting the two items against each other. Upon that principle, all accounts current are settled, and particularly cash accounts. When there has been a continuation of dealings, in what way can it be ascertained whether the specific balance due on a given day has, or has not, been discharged, but by examining whether payments to the amount of that balance appear by the account to have been made?[68]

It was therefore held that in a case of a running account, a creditor would not be deemed to have made any specific allocation of payments he received, and the first in first out rule would determine which sums would go in extinguishment of which.[69] Sir William Grant seems to have been motivated by a fear that a more expansive right of election would give too much power to the creditor by allowing him unilaterally to transform the account to his advantage depending on later circumstances.[70]

Accordingly, Clayton's claim was dismissed on the basis that debts he was owed by the bank were all to be treated as part of the same fund. This meant that the payments by the new partnership discharged the oldest debts, those owed by the old partnership. Although the ruling was doubted by the King's Bench in *Simson v Ingham* (1823)[71]—where the majority ruled that a creditor could appropriate payments of debts to any account even after making payment—it was affirmed many times in the Regency era,[72] and has survived as good law today.[73]

4.1.4 Conclusions: Liability of Former Partners

The bankruptcy of Devaynes, Dawes & Co brought several thorny issues before Chancery and the Bankruptcy Court. To what extent should a trade which had legally constituted a succession of partnerships be treated as a single entity? How could the court balance contemporary creditor expectations that they had

[68] ibid 608; 793. Emphasis added.

[69] Indeed, the modern position is that the rule applies only to *running* accounts, see EP Ellinger, E Lomnicka, and CVM Hare, *Ellinger's Modern Banking* (5th edn, OUP 2011) 768–69. Also see *'The Mecca'* [1897] AC 286 (HL), 294; *Seymour v Pickett* [1905] 1 KB 715 (CA).

[70] *Devaynes* (n 39) 609–10; 793.

[71] 2 B&C 65, 107 ER 307 (KB).

[72] *Bodenham v Purchas* (1818) 2 B&A 39, 106 ER 281 (KB); *Brooke v Enderby* (1820) 2 B&B 70, 129 ER 884 (CP); *Simpson v Cooke* (1824) 1 Bing 452, 130 ER 181 (CP); *Pemberton v Oakes* (1827) 4 Russ 154, 38 ER 763 (Ch).

[73] Eg see Ellinger, Lomnicka, and Hare (n 69) 765–70; David Fox, *Property Rights in Money* (OUP 2008) para 7.62.

acquired claims both against individual partners and a business? Should rules of property, contract, and debt be moulded to recognise the typical commercial practice of country bankers? Again, had the bank been a corporation, then no claim against Devaynes's estate would have been available.

In *Ex p Kendal* and *Sleech's Case* the courts responded to these questions by emphasising personal responsibility of partners through the adherence to established doctrinal forms. If depositors had advanced money to the firm during Devaynes's life, they had trusted his credit and should be able to claim against his testamentary estate. It was entirely to be expected that they should continue to deal with the firm after Devaynes's death: the continuing partners were their debtors also, and such dealings did not prima facie deprive those depositors of a claim against Devaynes.

What appears to be the only surviving interrogatory of the case suggests that Devaynes's estate's counsel saw this issue as particularly important.[74] It contains a record of the questions put to Sir Thomas Baring[75] and Sir Frank Standish who represented 'every or any other person claiming to be a creditor of the partnership … at the time of the decease of the said William Devaynes'.[76] In particular, counsel asked the creditors (i) whether the creditors did 'know or believe … that [Devaynes's] co-partners or any and which of them were persons of responsible credit', thereby addressing the issue of whose credit the customer had trusted; (ii) 'with whom did you consider yourself to be dealing & to whom did you give credit after the death of the said William Devaynes', that is with whom had the creditor thought he was dealing; and (iii) whether advice had been sought on the effect of Devaynes's death on the partnership, and their continued use of his name in the trade.[77] This perhaps explains in part why Lord Eldon and Sir William Grant were not willing to modify rules of property and contract to deprive those partnership creditors who had advanced money to the estate during Devaynes's life of their claims—whatever the normal practice of bankers in cases of dissolution.

In contrast, commercial practice and policy played a more significant role in the decision in *Clayton's Case*—where there was no established rule on the appropriation of debts in cases involving successive partnerships. The case is not significant for Sir William Grant's adoption of the 'first in first out rule' in the payment of debts, but for how that rule applied in cases involving successive partnerships.

[74] C 31/676/13. A Chancery interrogatory was part of the pleadings, and consisted of written questions put by counsel to witnesses, see John Mitford, *A Treatise on the Pleadings in Suits in the Court of Chancery by English Bill* (J and WT Clarke 1827) 329–30; Horwitz (n 47) 75–76. This is the only interrogatory in the case which is catalogued as such. There may be others but finding them would involve an extensive search through largely uncatalogued material at the National Archives.

[75] Part of the famous banking family, he had no permanent position in the bank at the time, see John Orbell, 'Baring, Thomas' in Sir David Cannadine (ed), *The Oxford Dictionary of National Biography* (OUP 2006) <https://doi.org/10.1093/ref:odnb/1385> accessed 18 March 2020.

[76] C 31/676/13.

[77] C 31/676/13, questions 3, 6, 10 respectively.

When applying the 'first in first out rule' to cases involving payment made by a firm which had consisted of a series of partnerships, the court would treat the firm *as a single debtor*—despite the fact that each partnership had a wholly separate legal existence for other purposes, such as set-off.[78]

We can see therefore that the concession to banking practice sought in *Sleech's Case* was granted by the Master of the Rolls in a more limited form in *Clayton's Case*. The sums paid before and after Devaynes's death were treated as if part of 'one blended fund', because the partners had kept a single running account with their customers throughout the course of their transactions. The continuing fund as a resource for a series of creditors to be paid by a series of partners gave a unity to the shifting partnerships, and de facto reduced the significance of the continuing liability for a retired or deceased partner for his firm's debts.

4.2 Liability of Continuing Partners

The question of whether a business which had consisted of a series of successive partnerships could be treated as an entity also came to the fore in cases concerning 'continuing partners'. The cases are interesting because they show that while an agreement between partners alone to dissolve their firm could not deprive joint creditors of their pre-existing claims, this did not prevent private agreements between partners drastically affecting the value of those rights in the bankruptcy context.

'Continuing partners' cases are those in which a partnership creditor would be prejudiced by being a joint creditor of all the members of a dissolved partnership, rather than the creditor of a remaining partner or partners per se. Imagine a case where A and B are partners, and B wishes to retire from the concern, but A still wishes to trade. The partnership assets are transferred into A's sole name, and A becomes bankrupt: the partnership assets would be part of A's separate estate. The joint creditors of A and B in such a case might seek, as in *Devaynes v Noble*, to sue B personally as well as A, especially if B were solvent.

However, in a scenario where B was not personally wealthy, and there were substantial business assets, the partnership creditors might instead want *only* to be creditors of A or otherwise to claim the business assets. This was because of the jingle rule. Upon A's bankruptcy the property would vest in his separate estate, and be distributed to his personal creditors in priority to the joint creditors of A and B. Although a joint creditor could prove against the separate estate where he

[78] Clayton could not have defeated a debt claim by the bank for sums advanced after Devaynes's death by showing he had advanced money to the bank before Devaynes's death. The court would have treated the firm as two separate bodies and therefore disallowed set-off on the basis that the debts were not 'mutual', Basil Montagu, *Summary of the Law of Set-Off, with Appendix of Cases* (1st edn, London 1801) 23. See also discussion in Chapter 3, Section 3.

was also a several creditor, or where there were no joint assets and the remaining former partners were bankrupt,[79] this rule would be of little comfort to mere joint creditors in circumstances where there remained some trifling amount in the joint estate. Such creditors might find themselves without a priority claim to the assets of the business, which would be distributed first to A's separate creditors. Creditors of A and B jointly might therefore seek to establish a priority claim to the assets of the business on some other footing, as their joint claim against A and B would be nearly worthless.

This difficulty was discussed at length in *Ex p Ruffin* (1801).[80] A and B were partners, and B sought to retire from the firm. A gave B a bond for the value of his stock, and an indemnity in respect of their joint debts and, in return, B transferred his share of the partnership property to A. All the creditors were informed of this arrangement. However, a year and a half later A was declared bankrupt, and his commission acted as both a joint and a separate commission, keeping separate accounts for A's sole trading and A and B's joint concern. The difficulty for A and B's joint creditors was that commissioners treated the business assets as belonging to A alone—because they had been transferred to A after A's retirement.[81] Under the jingle rule, the business assets would therefore be distributed amongst A's personal creditors in priority to the creditors of the business before B's retirement—effectively leaving A and B's joint creditors without access to the assets of the business they had dealt with.[82] The joint creditors brought a petition praying that the trade assets remaining in specie be sold, and their proceeds be applied in payment of the joint creditors *in priority* to A's separate creditors.

Sir Samuel Romilly[83] was lead counsel for the petitioners. He argued that the agreement between the partners could not as a matter of principle deprive the partnership of access to the business' assets, and that the transfer of the partnership assets to A alone—without first paying off the partnership creditors—effectively amounted to a fraud upon the partnership creditors, citing *Heath v Percival* (1720)[84] in support of the proposition. More interestingly though, he made the following argument in favour of the joint creditors:

> Until the partnership accounts are taken, there is no separate property but in the surplus after paying the partnership debts: the creditors standing in the place of

[79] Text from (n 6) to (n 8) above.
[80] 6 Ves Jun 119, 31 ER 970 (BC).
[81] It is not stated in the report whether the joint estate was completely emptied or contained only a trifling amount.
[82] Although joint creditors could claim rateably with separate creditors where there was no joint estate, such a claim depended on both partners being bankrupt. On the facts, B had not been declared bankrupt, and so no such claims against A and B's separate estates would have been possible.
[83] A prominent Chancery barrister, most famous as a law reformer advocate for the abolition of the slave trade, Rose Melikan, 'Romilly, Sir Samuel' in Sir David Cannadine (ed), *The Oxford Dictionary of National Biography* (OUP2008) <https://doi.org/10.1093/ref:odnb/24050> accessed 18 March 2020.
[84] (n 36).

> the bankrupt. The joint creditors therefore have a mediate, if not a direct, lien upon the whole of the partnership effects. At law the partnership creditors have more advantage than under a commission; taking the partnership effects exclusively, and the separate effects with the separate creditors. What difference arises from the circumstance, that the partnership did not exist at the time of the bankruptcy?[85]

This argument requires a little elaboration. Romilly first set out the fact that a partner was only entitled to the surplus of partnership assets after joint creditors had been paid. On this basis he argued that A and B did not between them have the authority to agree that, on dissolution of the partnership, the joint stock was to vest in A, without first satisfying the joint creditors. The joint creditors he argued should be understood as having a 'mediate lien' over the partnership assets, or what he referred to as 'an equitable claim ... in preference to the separate creditors'. In other words, the essence of Romilly's argument was that the claims of partnership creditors would follow the partnership assets, and that the partners could not by private agreement deprive the creditors of this right: 'The position, that partners can as between themselves by any act or agreement alter the partnership stock, so as to affect the rights of third persons, cannot be maintained.'[86] Accepting such an argument would have involved recognising a business as an entity existing *beyond* the end of the partnership that had originally formed it.

Mansfield, later Sir James Mansfield CJCP,[87] and William Cooke[88] argued for the assignees (ie trustees in bankruptcy), that the assignment by B to A must be treated as complete, and that to rule otherwise would allow joint creditors' claims to appear long after the dissolution of the partnership. They contended that allowing the petition would prevent the complete assignment of partnership assets upon dissolution until the debts were completely paid off, and that this could lead to those who dealt with continuing partners after dissolution being defrauded, in that creditors who had dealt with A after dissolution might find themselves unable to claim business assets. It was denied that the joint creditors had any sort of lien over the joint stock before execution of their debt claims.

Lord Eldon ultimately dismissed the claim of the joint creditors—refusing to treat the liabilities of the business as following its assets, and therefore refusing to treat it as an entity. In his judgment he addressed Romilly's reasoning by setting out his own understanding of the nature of creditor entitlement to partnership assets:

[85] *Ruffin* (n 80) 121; 971. References omitted.
[86] ibid.
[87] Douglas Hay, 'Mansfield, Sir James' in Michael Davies (ed), *The Oxford Dictionary of National Biography* (OUP 2008) <https://doi.org/10.1093/ref:odnb/17995> accessed 18 March 2020.
[88] Author of the leading textbook on bankruptcy, William Cooke, *The Bankrupt Laws* (4th edn, London 1799).

> Under these circumstances their creditors, who had a demand upon them in respect of those debts, had clearly no lien whatsoever upon the partnership effects. They had power of suing, and by process creating a demand, that would directly attach upon the partnership effects. But they had no lien upon or interest in them in point of law or equity ... The partnership might dissolve in various ways: ... So, upon the bankruptcy of one of them there would be an equity to say, the assignees stand in the place of the bankrupt; and can take no more than he could; and consequently nothing, until the partnership debts are paid. So, upon a mere dissolution, without a special agreement, or a dissolution by effluxion of time: to wind up the accounts the debts must be paid; and the surplus be distributed in proportion to the different interests. *In all these ways the equity is not that of the joint creditors, but that of the partners with regard to each other, that operates to the payment of the partnership debts.*[89]

In the above passage, Lord Eldon does not simply deny that the joint creditors have a lien over the partnership property, but provides a different theory underlying the nature of partnership creditor claims.

As discussed, partners had rights of indemnity and lien over the joint stock in respect of the partnership debts, which partnership creditors could claim the benefit of if the partners defaulted on repayment of the debt.[90] In modern terminology, Lord Eldon's analysis of the rights of partnership creditors in bankruptcy is best described as subrogation.[91] The partnership creditors, as creditors of the partners jointly, were subrogated to the partners' rights over the partnership assets such as they were at the time of litigation. This is identical to the mechanism by which creditors of a trustee, who had provided credit for the trust's purposes, could claim trust assets.[92] It explained why partnership creditors were able to claim against the joint estate in priority to separate creditors under the jingle rule, and why partners could only take partnership assets after the joint creditors had been paid:

> The joint creditors must of necessity be paid in order to [sic] the administration of justice to the partners themselves. When the bankruptcy of both [partners] takes place, it puts an end to the partnership certainly: but still it is very possible, and it

[89] *Ruffin* (n 80) 127; 974. Emphasis added.

[90] Chapter 1, Sections 2.2 and 2.4.

[91] Note that the subrogation is unrelated to unjust enrichment. The creditors of the partnership had only contracted for personal, not proprietary, rights and so there was no need to allow subrogation for the purpose of preventing the partners or their separate creditors from being unjustly enriched at the partnership creditors' expense. For the controversy over the modern rationale for subrogation compare *Bank of Cyprus v Menelaou* [2015] UKSC 66, [2016] AC 176 with *Bofinger v Kingsway Group Limited* [2009] HCA 44.

[92] Chapter 2, Section 3.1.

> often happens in fact, that the partners may have different interests in the surplus; and out of that a necessity arises, that the partnership debts must be paid: otherwise the surplus cannot be distributed according to equity, and no distinction has been made with reference to their interests, whether in different proportions, or equally.[93]

In other words, the rights of partners to joint stock were residual, the joint creditors had to be paid off first, and any sums owed by the partners to the firm calculated. It was only then that the right of an individual partner, and thus his creditors, to the partnership assets could be ascertained. A partner's separate creditors after all could have no better right to the partnership assets than he had.

On the facts of *Ruffin*, however, the partnership creditors had no priority claim to the former partnership assets. The partners' rights of indemnity and lien over the partnership stock had been voluntarily discharged by the absolute transfer of the partnership assets to A, the continuing partner, alone. The joint creditors could not therefore claim what had been the partnership assets in priority to A's separate creditors—there being no subsisting partners' lien for them to take the benefit of. The decision that a partnership's debts did not follow its assets was affirmed throughout the Regency era.[94]

To summarise, in *Ex p Ruffin*, Lord Eldon was presented with an opportunity to treat a business as an entity—by treating its creditors as collectively holding a charge over its assets, thereby protecting the claims of the firm's creditors to business assets, even if those assets were transferred through a series of partnerships. Lord Eldon refused to do this, justifying the decision through a sophisticated doctrinal exposition of the rights of partners in orthodox equitable proprietary terms—though he would later argue that the decision in *Ruffin* did not prejudice the interests of creditors of dissolved partnerships.[95] Fundamentally, however, Lord Eldon's decision meant that creditors of a partnership always faced the risk of being left with little recourse where the partnership dissolved, but the business continued trading—in that partners could voluntarily take partnership assets out of the joint estate against which its creditors had claims, potentially making claims against that joint estate worthless.

93 *Ruffin* (n 80) 127; 974.

94 *Ex p Peele* (1802) 6 Ves Jun 602, 31 ER 1216 (BC); B 1/101, pp 41, 258; *Ex p Snow* (1802) Cooke (8th edn) 537 (BC); *Ex p Matthews* (1805) B 1/106, pp 114–17; *Ex p Fell* (1805) 10 Ves Jun 347, 32 ER 879 (BC); *Ex p Williams* (1805) 11 Ves Jun 3, 32 ER 988 (BC); B 1/106 227; *Ex p Peake* (1816) 1 Madd 346, 56 ER 128 (BC). Note that Sir John Leach V-C appears to have challenged the rule *Ex p Freeman* (1821) Buck 471 (V-C), overruled in *Ex p Freeman* (1821) B 1/155, pp 215–16 (LC); *Ex p Fry* (1821) 1 G&J 96, B 1/159, pp 199–201 (BC) (note counsel's (Basil Montagu's) statement that the V-C's judgment in *Ex p Freeman* had been overruled).

95 *Williams* (n 94) 6; 989.

4.3 Liability of New Partners to Pre-dissolution Debts

Having looked at the claims of partnership creditors against retiring and continuing partners, it is now necessary to look at the claims creditors might have against any new partner who joined the concern, thus effecting dissolution of the old partnership. The mere fact that a new partner joined a firm would not make him liable to the old partnership's creditors,[96] nor would an undertaking to his new partners to pay the old firm's debts, even if given in consideration for taking a share of the joint stock.[97] However, Chancery and the Bankruptcy Court were much more willing to find that a new partner had assumed his co-partners' debts, and would infer such an undertaking of liability from 'slight circumstances',[98] 'very little',[99] or 'a very little matter'.[100]

This willingness to find that the new partner of a firm had assumed its debts stands in sharp contrast to Chancery and the Bankruptcy Court's reluctance to find such an assumption in the cases on continuing partners assuming the debts of departing partners. This difference is perhaps best explained as follows. The cases concerning continuing partners would simply turn on whether the creditors lost a right of action against a retiring partner, gaining nothing in return. However, in new partners cases, the creditors of the old partnership were effectively gaining something, a right against a new person. Accordingly, such cases did not often concern whether a creditor was being deprived of something, but whether he gained an additional right.

5. Conclusions

By the end of Lord Eldon's time on the Bench, partnership law did by and large protect the rights of partnership creditors to claim partnership assets in the event of the firm's bankruptcy. The central plank of this was the jingle rule, which ensured partnership assets would be distributed to partnership creditors in priority to the separate creditors of each partner.[101] This rule was in turn buttressed by other rules which protected this priority for partnership creditors: in particular the rule that partners (or their separate creditors) could not compete with the partnership creditors for a share of the partnership estate,[102] and the rule allowing the partnership estate to reclaim partnership assets which had been taken by partners

[96] *Saville v Robertson* (1792) 4 Term Rep 720, 100 ER 1264 (KB); *Wilsford v Wood* (1794) 1 Esp 182, 170 ER 321 (KB).
[97] *Peele* (n 94) 6 Ves Jun 602, 604; 31 ER 1216, 1217 (Lord Eldon).
[98] ibid.
[99] *Ex p Williams* (1817) Buck 13 (BC).
[100] *Ex p Jackson* (1790) 1 Ves Jun 131, 132; 30 ER 265 (BC) (Lord Thurlow).
[101] Section 1 above.
[102] Section 2 above.

from the partnership estate without authority.[103] In the vast majority of situations, therefore, partnership creditors would be sure of having a priority claim on the business's assets, and if the business appeared creditworthy could safely lend to it without having to make inquiries about the personal solvency of each partner. At the same time, partners would ultimately be personally liable to the debts of the firm—though their separate assets would first be distributed amongst their separate creditors in the event of bankruptcy—and this was perceived as providing partners with a strong incentive to trade responsibly. In sum, by balancing the personal responsibility of partners with asset partitioning features, the law of partnership provided incentives for third parties to extend credit to partnerships.

However, the law's ability to balance partnership creditors expectations that they had both a claim against the business *and* a claim against the partners was strained in cases where a partnership had technically dissolved following the retirement or death of a partner, but the business had continued trading. In particular, Lord Eldon's decision in *Ex p Ruffin* made clear that creditors who had advanced money to a partnership before it dissolved could not necessarily claim the assets of the business once they had been transferred to some subset of the previous partners—a decision Lord Eldon was compelled to by doctrinal underpinnings of partnership law.[104] Partnership creditors could thus never be safe from partners, by private agreement, emptying the partnership estate and so rendering their claims worthless.

Conversely, as made clear by Lord Eldon and Sir William Grant in *Ex p Kendal* and *Sleech's Case* respectively, a former partner (or his estate) would by default remain liable for all the business' debts contracted before his retirement or death.[105] After all, that partner had been trusted by the partnership's creditors, and so without some overt act releasing him from liability, the claims against him would survive his retirement. The courts were not willing to modify the normal rules of property and contract to change this position—which would have involved treating a business as a single entity, like a corporation—rather than a succession of partnerships. It should be noted that the tension here was not only between creditor expectations and doctrinal forms, but between those different creditor expectations of having a claim against a business *and* a claim against partners individually. The doctrines relied on in *Ex p Kendal* and *Sleech's Case* involved giving effect to the latter over the former: a partnership creditor could not be deprived of his rights against a former partner without that creditor's consent.

However, in cases not already governed by precedent, the court was willing to develop rules which instead treated a firm as an entity rather than a succession

[103] Section 3 above.
[104] Section 4.2 above.
[105] Sections 4.1.1 and 4.1.2 above.

of partnerships—as shown most clearly by Sir William Grant's ruling in *Clayton's Case*.[106] The decision to treat payments made by the bank in that case *after* Devaynes's death as discharging the debts contracted while he was still a partner recognised the business as more than a succession of partnerships: for the purpose of the appropriation of debts, the law treated the business as a single entity. Practically, this must have drastically reduced the sums retired partners might be forced to pay following the later bankruptcy of the business, thereby limiting the hazards for retired partners posed by the decisions in *Ex p Kendal* and *Sleech's Case*.

The final issue to address might be whether the limitations on the effectiveness of the partnership rules in preserving business assets for business creditors as a matter of fact discouraged traders from advancing money to partnerships. It is tentatively suggested that they did not, for two main reasons.

First, a trader's alternative to lending money to a partnership would be to lend it to a sole trader—if that trader went bankrupt there would be *no* priority for business creditors over personal creditors. Given the turbulent economy of the time, at any rate, it would have been less risky to extend credit to a partnership—with multiple partners who could ultimately pay the firm's debts—than to a sole trader. While the rule in *Ruffin* might mean that such a debt would not be repaid at all if the firm went bankrupt, it is hard to imagine that this prevented traders extending credit to partnerships, especially given the lack of alternative modes of doing business.

Secondly, the partnership rules *limiting* its asset partitioning effects were the by-product of the link between partnerships and the personality of the partners. As above, this link *helped* partnerships to acquire credit, in that partnership was seen as the most responsible form of business. Stronger asset partitioning effects, however, would have necessarily on severed or weakened that link.

[106] Section 4.1.3. above.

Conclusion

This book has focussed on one core question: To what extent did Regency era English law facilitate trade before the advent of general incorporation and modern securities law? As part of that inquiry it has asked to what extent traders were able to use the building blocks of private law to dedicate assets to the purposes of trade and security, and so 'partition' those assets from their other dealings?

English law provided a menu of forms by which parties could dedicate assets to particular purposes. Partners, trustees, and agents all had duties to use the assets they managed for the purposes delineated by their appointment. These assets were shielded (to different degrees) from their personal creditors. This was significant: if a debtor firm went insolvent, the business creditors could be sure of taking its assets in priority to the personal creditors of the business owners. Business creditors could therefore assess a firm's creditworthiness by making enquiries of the business alone, without inquiring after the individual affairs of each of the partners. Further, where partnership, trust, or agency assets were disposed of without authority, prima facie they could be recaptured from third parties, and put to their original purpose. This last principle was subject to the important qualification that the doctrine of ostensible authority[1] and bona fide purchaser defence[2] would mean that dispositions of assets made in what appeared to be the ordinary course of business—even if beyond the purposes to which the assets were dedicated—would be efficacious. The practical effect of this was to encourage third parties to deal with partners, agents, and trustees—in that they could be sure of taking good title in circumstances which were not suspicious. The ostensible authority rules also allowed debts entered into by a partner or agent in what appeared to be the course of business to bind the partnership or principal, again encouraging third parties to extend credit through agents and partners.[3] The fact that a similar rule never evolved for trustees is explicable principally on the basis that trust deeds did not often give trustees the power to borrow money on behalf of the trust.[4] Even where trustees had such power, the doctrine of ostensible authority could protect creditors where the trustee was also an agent or a partner. In sum, the interrelated doctrines of

[1] See Chapter 3.
[2] See Chapter 5.
[3] See Chapter 3.
[4] See Chapter 5, text from (n 20).

Capitalism Before Corporations. Andreas Televantos, Oxford University Press (2020). © Andreas Televantos.
DOI: 10.1093/oso/9780198870340.003.0009.

trusts, agency, and partnership did create organisational law which traders were able to take advantage of.

However, the common law would not allow a business to be treated as *entirely* separate from its owners. Although deed of settlement companies could be created using a hybrid of partnership and trusts, such entities could not act like corporations with limited liability. First, companies which purported to grant shareholders transferable shares faced the risk of being declared illegal under the Bubble Act until its repeal in 1825, and under the common law after that. Secondly, the directors and shareholders of such companies were treated as personally liable for the debts of the firm. Thirdly, a company could not sue in its own name, rather than that of its shareholders or trustees, without an Act of Parliament—even then Chancery considered whether the shareholders needed to be added as parties to any litigation as a matter of its discretion. Trust and partnership may have provided a way of trying to emulate the characteristics of a true corporation with limited liability, but to modern eyes it looks very much like a 'second best'.[5] The common law went no further than this in recognising the associational rights of business persons: the full privileges of corporate status lay in the gift of the Crown or Parliament.

The deeper point is that the unavailability of limited liability corporations was not seen as problematic by contemporaries—who saw large joint stock companies as a medium for carrying out fraudulent schemes, inefficient, and linked to the bribery of MPs. In part, this is explicable by Martin Daunton's observation that there are few signs that a shortage of capital limited growth in the early nineteenth century, in part due to the relatively modest capital requirements of the period.[6] It is also explicable in terms of contemporary thought. Christian thinkers like Malthus, Chalmers, and Coleridge emphasised that economic growth had a natural level—and blamed the economic instability of the time on reckless and imprudent trading.[7] The prominence of similar statements in *Hansard* emphasises that such thinking had an impact beyond theologians. In the 1820s, Lord Liverpool's ministry did seek to promote free trade, but only as a means of feeding the country, getting Britain ready for war, and in the hope of allowing the economy to find its 'natural' equilibrium, thereby ending the violent cycle of boom and bust which had characterised the economy since the outbreak of the Napoleonic Wars. Promoting commerce was never pursued in and of itself. The personal responsibility of traders for their debts was crucial to controlling an economy which was at risk of overheating. Although traders tended to treat firms as economically distinct from their owners, it was seen as crucial that those owners ultimately be personally liable for the firm's debts. Likewise, reckless over-traders who were blamed for causing

[5] Chapter 2, Section 2.2.
[6] Chapter 1, Section 4.
[7] Chapter 3, Section 1.1.

the rise in bankruptcy rates should bear the loss caused by their own actions—thus discouraging irresponsible trading.[8]

What is perhaps most remarkable about the law of the time is how it balanced these different political, economic, and ethical considerations. The courts gave effect to traders' presumed expectation that partnerships and trusts had an existence separate from the partners and trustees, by shielding the partnership or trust assets from the private wealth and creditors of the partners or trustees. At the same time, the law made clear that partners and trustees took personal responsibility for debts they contracted in their own name—whether as partner, trustee, or personally. Further, the view that the reckless traders should suffer loss to deter immoral behaviour can be seen as pervading judicial treatment of different legal forms, in that all involved examining the relative fault and blameworthiness of commercial parties and allocating loss accordingly. The doctrine of ostensible authority was based on the courts' own attribution of relative fault between a partner or principal—who had 'held out' a co-partner or agent as having authority to bind them—and the purchaser or creditor who had dealt with the errant co-partner or agent acting without authority. Likewise, the bona fide purchase defence arose from Chancery's desire to prevent fraud and protect those who had given value. The rules governing the distribution of an insolvent partnership's estate too were shaped by a desire to prevent the partners by their own actions depriving their joint creditors of their rights and adherence to established doctrinal forms. These rules can be seen as encouraging commerce: third parties could confidently deal with agents, trustees, and partners because they would be protected even where an agent, trustee, or partner had exceeded his authority. In part, this perhaps explains why Lord Liverpool's government after 1821, despite consciously pursuing a policy of free trade, only tinkered with commercial law. However, these rules were not formulated principally for the purpose of encouraging trade, but to balance a blend of concerns with deeper roots in contemporary religious and political economic thought. Judges were willing to give effect to trader expectations—as for instance by treating a series of partnerships as a single entity for the purpose of appropriation of the payment of debts in *Clayton's Case* (1816)[9]—but this ranked relatively low in the hierarchy of judicial concerns. Courts were not generally willing to formulate rules which either undermined established doctrinal forms,[10] increased the workload of an already overburdened Chancery and its Masters,[11] or otherwise provided incentives to trade recklessly.[12]

The story here then is not one about a conservative legal class resisting the *zeitgeist* of commercial progress, but of creating a commercial law by giving voice in

8 Chapter 3, Section 1.2.
9 Reported in *Devaynes v Noble* (1816) 1 Mer 529, 35 ER 767 (Ch). See Chapter 7, Section 4.1.3
10 E.g. see Chapter 6, Section 4 and Chapter 7, Section 5.
11 Chapter 1, Section 3 and Chapter 2, Section 2.2.
12 Part II.

law to broader political economic concerns. Although, as with the Factors Acts, there were instances of conflict between judges and merchants,[13] the overall picture here is not one of judges pushing back against merchants riding the tide of economic progress. In particular, Lord Eldon's reputation as an extreme reactionary in the field of commerce seems unfair, as his views on corporations were very similar to those voiced by many MPs and *The Times*.[14] Unlike many modern courts, judges did not see their role as simply encouraging commercial activity. This was rooted in the wider belief that commercial activity was not per se desirable, as too much trade was causing economic instability. This was not a mindset specific to judges or lawyers.

This analysis itself raises a broader question. Given that large joint stock companies were perceived as inefficient and even immoral, why did England introduce general incorporation in 1844, and limited liability in 1855? There is a vast literature on this topic, a full examination of which is beyond the scope of this work. However, it is possible from the foregoing analysis to make some observations. First, given the courts effectively rejected jurisdiction over joint stock companies, it makes sense that general incorporation was first introduced as a response to a series of frauds by such companies in the 1840s, rather than due to a belief in the effectiveness of corporate trading.[15] The Joint Stock Companies Act 1844 forced large partnerships to acquire legal personality, as well as to publish details of their shareholders, directors, and capital.[16] In turn, this would allow shareholders and creditors to take large companies to court more easily. The company itself could be sued without adding all its members as parties to the litigation, and relief could be obtained against its members more easily in that they could now be more easily identified,[17] a reform Lord Eldon had considered proposing in the House of Lords decades earlier.[18] The long eighteenth century strategy of allowing such companies to exist on the periphery of legality was deemed to have failed—because of the market crashes and frauds company promotions seemed to encourage. This insight that general incorporation was only introduced to allow companies to be better regulated is an important one today, where the issue of whether corporate personality is a natural right of profit-making joint stock companies, or a privilege

[13] See Chapter 4.
[14] See Chapter 2, text from (n 74) to (n 79).
[15] See Select Committee on Joint Stock Companies, *First Report of the Select Committee on Joint Stock Companies* (HC 1844, 119-VII.1); James Taylor, *Creating Capitalism: Joint Stock Enterprise in British Politics and Culture, 1800–1870* (The Boydell Press 2006) 137–43; Martin Daunton, *Wealth and Welfare: An Economic and Social History of Britain 1851–1951* (OUP 2007) 105; Paul Johnson, *Making the Market: The Victorian Origins of Corporate Capitalism* (CUP 2010) 120–21.
[16] 7 & 8 Vic c 110.
[17] See Chapter 2, Section 2.2.2.
[18] See Chapter 2, text to (n 108).

granted by the state which should be qualified in the public interest, remains hotly contested.[19]

Similarly, the recognition that in the nineteenth century there was a close link between personality of traders and their ability to raise credit also explains why the introduction of limited liability in 1855[20] does not seem to have been driven by traders, but by utilitarian economists: a feature opponents of the change pointed out.[21] Although Boyd Hilton sees the change as rooted in an ideological shift—as the idea of trade having a divinely ordained 'natural level' was replaced by a belief that economic growth was per se desirable[22]— James Taylor has instead suggested that the measure was really designed to encourage better monitoring of firms by shareholders and creditors.[23] The theory was that only prudent shareholders would invest in limited liability firms—those aware of the hazards of unlimited liability—and that this better class of shareholders would monitor the firm's activity more closely. Likewise, an investor would only lend money to a limited liability corporation having carefully examined its business: aware that if the corporation became insolvent there would be, at best, limited claims against the shareholders personally. At any rate, the lack of commercial demand for general incorporation with limited liability in the mid-1850s is borne out by the data showing the slow voluntary uptake of limited liability corporate status, which did not really happen until the 1870s, 1880s, and, in the manufacturing sector, the 1890s.[24] Before then, suspicion of the form may have been a barrier to limited liability corporations raising credit. Further, as Paul Johnson has pointed out, most companies which incorporated did not have transferable shares nor a large paid-up share capital.[25] This suggests that outside of sectors like utilities and transport, where capital start-up costs were high, partnerships faced no real problems in raising capital even later into the nineteenth century,[26] though as Joshua Getzler has suggested incorporation might have been driven in part to allow firms to raise finance from banks—banks which sought floating charges over the firm's entire assets as security.[27] Partnerships could

[19] See for instance The British Academy's ongoing project, *The Future of the Corporation* <https://www.thebritishacademy.ac.uk/programmes/future-of-the-corporation> accessed 18 March 2020.

[20] Limited Liability Act 1855 (18 & 19 Vict c 133), swiftly replaced by the Joint Stock Companies Act 1856 (19 & 20 Vict c 47).

[21] Taylor (n 15) 170–71; Boyd Hilton, *Age of Atonement: The Influence of Evangelicalism on Social and Economic Thought, 1785–1865* (Clarendon Press 1997) 255–67.

[22] Hilton (n 21) 262–67.

[23] Taylor (n 15) 159–64.

[24] Johnson (n 15) 122–24. See also JB Jeffreys, 'Trends in Business Organisations in Great Britain since 1856' (University of London 1938); Daunton (n 15) 105–108.

[25] Johnson (n 15) 123–26.

[26] Daunton (n 15) 105–08.

[27] Joshua Getzler, 'The Role of Security over Future and Circulating Capital: Evidence from the British Economy circa 1850–1920' in Joshua Getzler and Jennifer Payne (eds), *Company Charges: Spectrum and Beyond* (OUP 2006) 248–50; Ron Harris, 'The Private Origins of the Private Company: Britain 1862–1907' (339) 33 OJLS 2013.

not grant floating charges, only corporations could, perhaps explaining in part the late nineteenth-century move towards incorporation.

At any rate, this book's analysis certainly supports the historiography in arguing that the recognition of limited liability corporations was not the ultimate result of some 'survival of the fittest' between different trading entities, nor was it driven principally by the demands of traders. Likewise, the argument that a conservative judicial class were exceptional in their resistance towards granting corporate privileges to private enterprise does not stand up to scrutiny.

The discussion in this book also has implications for wider debates about the law's evolution, lying beyond the core question of whether Regency era law encouraged trade. These debates are relevant not only to legal historians but occupy key positions in debates about modern law. First, it has been shown that the widespread assumption about the relationship between law and equity before Victorian reforms 'fusing' them must be revised. Although Lord Eldon's modelling of trusts law jurisprudence on common law property is well documented,[28] this book has shown a *mutual* influence between courts of law and equity. The authority doctrines governing partners were clearly the result of a unified jurisprudence across the common law courts and Lord Eldon's Bankruptcy Court,[29] while common law courts were willing to recognise an executor as a species of trustee[30] and to enforce specific purpose trusts.[31] Claims of conversion and money had and received could in some instances be used to vindicate *equitable* title under such trusts.[32] The biggest difference between Chancery and the courts of common law seems to have been the availability of a Master in Chancery to take accounts, and so to discriminate between the different capacities in which property was held by an agent, partner, trustee, or executor. On the one hand, this shows why common law courts saw the recognition of property as being held in different capacities as involving the application of 'equity', but also why they would only enforce trusts in cases where Chancery's accounting procedures were not needed—as in the specific purpose trust cases where there was a straightforward substitution and no complex mixed fund. This mutual influence undermines the premise of many modern arguments about the fusion of law and equity, which imagine a complete separateness of the courts and their jurisprudence before the Judicature Acts. It also emphasises that the availability of accounting procedures in Chancery shaped the ambit of what even today we recognise as rules of equity as opposed to rules of common law.

[28] Gregory Alexander, 'Transformation of Trusts as a Legal Category, 1800–1914' (1987) 5 L & Hist Rev 303; Stuart Anderson, 'Trusts and Trustees' in William Cornish and others (eds), *Oxford History of the Laws of England*, vol XII (OUP 2010).

[29] See Chapter 3.

[30] See Chapter 5, text to (n 57) and from (n 57) to (n 83).

[31] Chapter 6, Section 3.2.

[32] ibid.

This work has further implications for modern commercial equity lawyers and historians of trusts. In a celebrated article of 1998, Lord Millett wrote that 'equity's place in the law of commerce . . . can no longer be denied . . . Even twenty years ago there was still a widely held belief, by no means confined by common lawyers, that equity had no place in the world of commerce.'[33] This book has shown that equity played a major role in commerce from the eighteenth century at least: this is why Boyd Hilton was able to surmise that equity was the law of a merchant middle class, and was predominant in commercial matters.[34] It was equitable rules which protected partnership assets from the separate creditors of the partners and, in so protecting partnership creditors, encouraged people to extend credit to partnerships. Likewise, it was equitable priorities rules which enforced dispositions entered into by trustees and executors without authority in what seemed to be the ordinary course of business. Finally, commercial parties and their lawyers were able to make use of the law of trusts to emulate some of the benefits of incorporation,[35] to create limited liability businesses for the benefit of a testamentary estate,[36] and to avoid the risk of insolvency of those they advanced property to for a specific purpose.[37]

The trusts point is a particularly important one. It shows that commercial trusts are not a recent innovation but have a long history. The specific purpose trusts illustrate that whenever A advanced money to B for a specific purpose that B would hold the money on trust for A, subject to a power to use it for that purpose. In essence, A's intention that B use the property only for a specific purpose amounted to intention to declare a trust.[38] This proposition, recognised in *Barclays Bank Ltd v Quistclose Investments Ltd* (1970),[39] *Twinsectra v Yardley* (2002),[40] and *Bellis v Challinor* (2015),[41] is not novel or unorthodox as has been suggested,[42] but has a history stretching back to the eighteenth century.[43] This fundamentally challenges the assertion that commercial trusts of this type are a relatively recent mutation from the 'true trusts' with extensive management powers rooted in the law of family settlements,[44] and so lying on the periphery of trust institutions. On the

[33] Peter Millett, 'Equity's Place in the Law of Commerce' (1998) 114 LQR 214.
[34] Boyd Hilton, *A Mad, Bad, & Dangerous People? England 1783–1846* (OUP 2006) 122.
[35] Chapter 2, Section 2.1.
[36] Chapter 2, Section 3.
[37] Chapter 6, Section 3.
[38] Note the similarity with the modern position on when resulting trusts arise, see William Swadling, 'Explaining Resulting Trusts' (2008) 124 LQR 72.
[39] [1970] AC 567 (HL).
[40] [2002] UKHL 12, [2002] 2 AC 164.
[41] [2015] EWCA Civ 59, [2015] WLUK 163.
[42] William Swadling, 'Orthodoxy' in William Swadling (ed), *The Quistclose Trust* (Hart Publishing 2004).
[43] Chapter 6, Section 3.1.
[44] For examples of this reasoning today see *Williams v Bank of Nigeria* [2014] UKSC 10, [2014] AC 1189.

contrary, in the long eighteenth century commercial trusts were a central vehicle for business activity, and from these vehicles emerged many of the key legal elements of the trust institution, including what intention to declare a trust involves,[45] the rules governing trust creditors,[46] and tracing.[47]

45 Chapter 6, Section 3.
46 Chapter 2, Section 3.1.
47 Chapter 6, text from (n 57).

Appendix: Notes on Archival Sources

The research for this monograph involved reading not just printed materials, but archival materials, most of which had either seldom or never been used before. The purpose of this short appendix is to provide information for others interested in making use of these sources and to explain the sampling methods this author used when examining the Court orders of Chancery and the Bankruptcy Court.

1. Lord Eldon's Judicial Notebooks and other Papers

The first of these sources are eleven of the judicial notebooks of Lord Eldon, covering the period 1801 to 1821.[1] The only scholars to have made use of these materials before appear to be Joshua Getzler,[2] this author,[3] and, more recently, James Oldham with Victoria Barnes and Michelle Johnson.[4] Each of these notebooks consists of about a 180 pages (rather than folios). Most of the books are indexed by Eldon himself, though the indexes do not contain entries for every case and some volumes do not to have indexes. Lord Eldon's notes mostly consist of records of counsels' arguments, annotated with his own comments, but some entries include notes on evidence and others include Lord Eldon's decisions, with reasons, in continuous prose. Most of the cases noted were heard in Chancery, but there are some instances of judgments in the Bankruptcy Court. There are also instances of House of Lords cases in the notebooks, and the 1813 notebook exclusively contains notes of appeals to the House of Lords.

The notebooks do not purport to record all of Lord Eldon's cases: in the notebook for 1801–1802, for instance, Eldon writes that he took no notes of a number of important bankruptcy cases heard the previous term.[5]

It should be observed that a large proportion of the cases in the notebooks examined also appear in the law reports and, at least in the cases examined in this monograph, Lord Eldon's notes add little to the reports. Nonetheless, there are some cases in which the notes do cast light on Lord Eldon's reasoning process, and the notes also draw attention to unreported cases.

[1] Lord Eldon Judicial Notebooks (1801–1821), Mss, 38–48, Lord Eldon Collection, Georgetown Law Library. Now available at <https://repository.library.georgetown.edu/handle/10822/1042298> accessed 18 March 2020.

[2] See for instance Joshua Getzler, 'Morice v Bishop of Durham' in Paul Mitchell and Charles Mitchell (eds), *Landmark Cases in Equity* (Hart Publishing 2012).

[3] Andreas Televantos, 'Third Party Rights and the Priority of Claims against Commercial Funds: Partnership, Trusts, agency, and Insolvency in the Era of Lord Eldon' (PhD Thesis, University of Cambridge 2016).

[4] James Oldham and Victoria Barnes, 'Carlen v Druy (1812): The Origins of the Internal Management Debate in Corporate Law' (2017) 38 JLH 1; James Oldham and Michelle Johnson, 'Law Versus Equity—as Reflected in Lord Eldon's Manuscripts' (2018) 58 Am J Legal His 208.

[5] Eldon Notebook 1801–1802 p 198.

Other materials from Lord Eldon's library were examined too, including his collection of pamphlets (mostly unannotated);[6] eighteenth-century manuscript reports;[7] opinions given by eminent lawyers;[8] and orders made by Lords Chancellors concerning Chancery procedure.[9]

2. Chancery Order Books

The second set of records consulted is the books containing the orders of Chancery, categorised under record class C 33 in The National Archives.[10] These books, referred to as Chancery order books or Chancery entry books, were records of the orders made by Chancery.[11] They are referred to as Chancery order books throughout this book. For each year, the order books are split up into two volumes: A books and B books. The former cover suits by parties whose names begin with letters A to K, and the latter cover suits by parties whose names begin with the letters L to Z. Each volume covers the legal year beginning in the volume date, so the volume for 1794 includes orders made from Michaelmas term 1794 to Trinity 1795, though the court's business seems to have continued outside term time.

Each of the entries in the order books states an order made by the court, but otherwise the substantive content of the entries varies. A large number of the entries are essentially procedural noting, for example, that the case was adjourned, that the court confirmed the sale of a mortgaged estate or a Master's report, or ordered specific performance, or granted an injunction. The most useful references are those in which the plaintiff sought a reference to a Master to take an account, or appealed against a Master's finding. Such entries typically follow the structure of Chancery pleadings in the Regency era described by John Mitford.[12] In particular, in such entries it is possible to find the plaintiff's statement of his case (the 'stating part' of the bill); his statement of the defendant's expected defence and his response to it (the 'charging part' of the bill); and the defendant's answer, in which he would admit, deny, or deny knowledge of what was alleged, and set forth further facts in support of his defence.[13] Such entries are valuable records of the facts of cases, and of the way in which they were pleaded, and also make clear the relief sought. Some entries also contain a record of the evidence examined by the court.

Chancery order books have been used in two main ways. First, the books have been used to supplement the reports of important reported cases. In a number of cases this has proved to be a useful way of verifying case reports, ascertaining additional facts, and understanding how particular cases were pleaded.

[6] Lord Eldon's Pamphlets, 125 Volumes, Lord Eldon Collection, Georgetown Law Library.

[7] *Trial Notes of Clarke v Gopp and other Cases 1758* Ms 26; *Trial Notes* Mss 27–35, 67–68.

[8] *Collection of Opinions of Counsel Given during the Years 1671–1764*, Ms 6; *Cases and Opinions* (2 vols) MSS 49 and 50; *Trial Notes 1780–1789* Ms 36 (note these are actually opinions, not notes of cases), Lord Eldon Collection (n 6).

[9] *John Dickens Chancery Orders 1774* Ms 4; *Orders in Chancery by John Beames* Ms 23, Lord Eldon Collection (n 6).

[10] See The National Archives, 'Chancery Entry Books of Decrees and Orders' (catalogue entry) http://discovery.nationalarchives.gov.uk/details/r/C3594 accessed 18 March 2020; Henry Horwitz, *Chancery Equity Records and Proceedings 1600-1800* (2nd edn, PRO 1998) 59–60.

[11] The National Archives ibid.

[12] John Mitford, *A Treatise on the Pleadings in Suits in the Court of Chancery by English Bill* (J and WT Clarke 1827) 42–47.

[13] ibid 44.

Secondly, a sample of Chancery orders in the period was taken. This sample was compiled using Chancery orders in the A books for the periods October to December 1794[14] and April to June 1815,[15] and in the B books for the periods January to March 1805[16] and July to September 1825.[17] The samples have been split into three-month periods because, as stated above, Chancery does not seem to have kept to common law terms during the Regency era. It should be noted that the samples are not of even sizes in terms of number of orders.[18] The sample for 1805 is roughly twice as large as the 1794 sample, whilst the 1815 and 1825 samples are each about the size of the 1794 and 1805 samples added together.[19]

The aim of this sampling exercise was to assess whether the reported cases in this period, as regards the law and types of litigation represented, paint an accurate picture of the court's practice in this period, in particular the jurisdiction it exercised over partnerships, agents, and trusts in the commercial context. Consistently with Patrick Polden and Henry Horwitz's statistics, much of the work of Chancery in this period related to estates and real property, and so was not of direct relevance to this monograph but, as they state, there were a sizeable number of businesses cases.[20] By and large the record confirmed the picture of the law painted by the reported cases. However, the sample did cast light on a number of relevant unreported cases, and provided a useful insight into the types of cases heard by the court day-to-day.

3. Bankruptcy Order Books

The third main archival source used was the Bankruptcy order books, that is to say orders made by the Lord Chancellor, Master of the Rolls, and Vice-Chancellor in respect of petitions of appeal from bankruptcy commissioners. This was a separate jurisdiction from Chancery. The Bankruptcy order books are categorised under record class B 1 in The National Archives, and appear to have never before received attention from commentators.[21] Unlike the Chancery order books, the Bankruptcy order books are not split up into A and B books, and are numbered by page rather than folio. The orders contained resemble the substantive Chancery orders, each setting out an account of the petitioner's case, any defence made, and the order made by the court. It is worthy of note that a far higher proportion of the bankruptcy orders contain substantive content than do the Chancery orders, in that most of the orders in the Bankruptcy court's order books are final orders.

Due to the similarities between the two record sources, the Bankruptcy order books have been sampled in the same way as the Chancery order books, detailed above. Accordingly,

[14] C 33/485, C 33/488.

[15] C 33/612, C 33/613, C 33/614 (as entries are not in exact chronological order as catalogued, it was necessary to check a number of volumes for possible entries. C 33/611 was checked but contained no cases from the sample period).

[16] C 33/536, C 33/537, C 33/538, C 33/539.

[17] C 33/736, C 33/737 (C 33/732, C 33/733, C 33/734 were checked, but contained no cases from the sample period. C 33/735 did contain cases from the period, but none which were relevant).

[18] This is consistent with Horwitz and Polden's observation that the number of bills between 1785 and 1818–19 increased, Henry Horwitz and Patrick Polden, 'Continuity or Change in the Court of Chancery in the Seventeenth and Eighteenth Centuries?' (1996) 35 J Brit Stud 25, 30–32.

[19] This statistic is based on the number of photographic images taken of each sample: 407 for 1794, 968 for 1805, 1543 for 1815, and 1475 for 1825.

[20] Horwitz and Polden (n 18) 35.

[21] The National Archives, 'Office of the Commissioners of Bankrupts and successors: Orderbooks relating to Petitions against Declarations of Bankruptcy' (catalogue description) <http://discovery.nationalarchives.gov.uk/details/r/C2753> accessed 18 March 2020.

the Bankruptcy order sample consists of the orders from October to December 1794,[22] January to March 1805,[23] April to June 1815,[24] and July to September 1825.[25]

4. Other Archival Materials

Some use has been made of Chancery pleadings in particular cases. However, as the Chancery order books are bound, and often contain accounts of the pleadings, this proved to be a more efficient way of sampling litigation and seeing how cases were argued. The bankruptcy pleadings (ie the petitions of appeal from the decisions of the bankruptcy commissioners) are either un-catalogued or destroyed.[26] Use of other archival sources was also considered. The enrolled Chancery decrees were also read through,[27] on the basis that these might contain more detail than the Chancery order books. However, the enrolled decrees contained very few cases, suggesting that by the Regency period the practice of enrolling decrees had become rare, and no relevant cases were found. Examples of the minute books of Chancery and the Bankruptcy Court were examined, that is to say the minutes of their proceedings, but these contained relatively little continuous prose, and added nothing useful to the order books.[28]

[22] B 1/89, B 1/90.

[23] B 1/105, B 1/106, B 1/107 (B 1/108 was checked, but contains no cases in the sample period).

[24] B 1/128, B 1/132, B 1/133, B 1/134, B 1/135, B 1/137, B 1/138, B 1/139 (B 1/126, B 1/129, B 1/130, B 1/131, and B 1/136 were checked but contain no cases within the sample period).

[25] B 1/170, B 1/171 (B 1/169 and 172 were checked, but contain no cases within the sample period).

[26] The only record classes catalogued as containing petitions appear to be B 2, C 28, C 36. Records from each were examined, and no petitions of appeal in bankruptcy were found.

[27] Available at University of Houston, Anglo American Legal Tradition <http://aalt.law.uh.edu/C78_79.html> accessed 18 March 2020. For details of the records see The National Archives, 'Chancery and Supreme Court of Judicature, Chancery Division: Six Clerks Office and successors: Decree Rolls' (catalogue description) <http://discovery.nationalarchives.gov.uk/details/r/C3638> accessed 18 March 2020.

[28] Record classes C 37 and B 7 respectively. For C 37 see The National Archives, 'Chancery: Registrars' Court or Minute Books' (catalogue description) <http://discovery.nationalarchives.gov.uk/details/r/C3598> accessed 18 March 2020. For B 7 see The National Archives, 'Office of the Commissioners of Bankrupts, Courts for the Relief of Insolvent Debtors and of Review, and successors: Minute Books' (catalogue description) <http://discovery.nationalarchives.gov.uk/details/r/C2759> accessed 18 March 2020.

Glossary

Assignee in bankruptcy The contemporary term for a trustee in bankruptcy. This person would be assigned all the bankrupt's property for the purpose of distributing it amongst his creditors.

Bankruptcy (including Bankruptcy Commission) Bankruptcy was a procedure by which creditors of a trader would have a 'commission of bankruptcy' issued against him. The commission's role was to oversee the distribution of the bankrupt's estate amongst his creditors. The commissioners would decide which creditors could 'prove' against the estate, and so receive a pro rata share of the bankrupt's assets. Appeal from the commissioners lay to the Lord Chancellor, Master of the Rolls, or, from 1813, the Vice-Chancellor.

Bill of exchange A piece of paper entitling the holder to present it for payment of a certain sum on a certain day to a named party. In the Regency era, principally differentiated from a promissory note in that the creator of the bill (the 'drawer') was not the person to whom the bill was to be presented for payment in the first instance. Related terms are discussed below.

Capital lock-in mechanism A legal rule which keeps the assets of a business dedicated to its purposes, and so capable of being claimed by the business' creditors. These included rules which restricted the ability of partners to take assets out of the partnership for their own private purposes, see Chapter 1, Section 2; Chapter 7, Sections 1–3.

Charge A type of security interest. If B were under an obligation to A, B might appropriate particular rights in real or personal property to secure B's performance of the obligation. A would acquire a 'charge' over those rights. If B performed the obligation, then the charge would be extinguished. If B failed to perform, then A could typically recover what he was owed by claiming the proceeds of the real or personal property to which the charge related.

Country banks These were privately owned banks based outside of London. They were perceived as too willing to make loans to those unable to pay them back, and so were blamed for the economic instability of the early nineteenth century.

Deed of settlement or joint stock company A business which raised capital by issuing shares and/or bonds. This was distinct from a typical partnership, where the partners who managed the business provided the capital. Legally, deed of settlement companies were partnerships, but made use of some rules of trusts law in an attempt to emulate the benefits of incorporation. See Chapter 2, Section 2.

Discounting a bill of exchange Where a bill of exchange (or promissory note) entitled its holder to payment at a future date, the holder could sell the bill or note immediately for less than the sum which would become payable in the future. This was called 'discounting'.

Drawing a bill of exchange meant creating it, literally drawing it up, including determining the sum to be paid, the date, and to whom the bill holder was to present the bill to receive payment (the 'drawee').

Executing judgment See levying judgment, below.

Fixed capital Referred to the assets of a business that were not to be bought and sold, like stock in trade, but to be retained by the business: such as land, buildings, and machinery. A business' start-up costs include the cost of acquiring fixed capital.

Indorsing or accepting a bill of exchange The act of becoming liable to pay a bill of exchange by writing one's name on it. The drawer of a bill of exchange directed the payee to seek payment from a third party (the 'drawee'), and the drawee, if they wrote their name on the bill, was said to 'accept' it. Where the holder of a bill of exchange sold it on, and wrote his name upon it, he was said to 'indorse' it.

Indemnity A right to receive reimbursement in respect of expenditure, loss, or liability incurred. An agent, partner, and trustee all had rights of indemnity in respect of expenses and personal liabilities incurred whilst carrying out their duties.

Insolvency The factual state of being unable to pay debts, whether due to a lack of available liquid assets ('cash-flow insolvency') or due to total liabilities exceeding total assets ('balance sheet insolvency'). Distinct from 'bankruptcy' which refers instead to a formal procedure (discussed above).

Jingle rule A rule governing the administration of partnership assets. In the event of bankruptcy of a partnership, the partnership assets would be distributed rateably amongst the creditors of the business, whilst each partner's separate assets would be distributed amongst their separate creditors. After the partnership estate had been distributed in this way, if there were a surplus, then this would be distributed rateably amongst the separate estates of the partners, and so used to pay the separate creditors (and vice versa). See discussion at Chapter 1, Section 2.4 and Chapter 7, Section 1. The naming is usually attributed to James Barr Ames, see Chapter 1, Section 2.4, (n 50).

Joint stock company See deed of settlement company (above).

Judgment debt A sum of money owed under a court order.

Levying judgment, executing judgment The act of enforcing a judgment debt, typically by the Sherriff seizing and selling the assets of the debtor.

Lien A right to retain control over property belonging beneficially to another, until the owner discharges some obligation owed to the lien-holder. An agent, partner, and trustee would all have liens over their principal's partnership and trust assets, and so could retain control over them until their rights of indemnity (above) were satisfied.

Mortgage A type of security interest. Where B was under an obligation to A, B might transfer rights in real or personal property to A to secure B's performance of the obligation. If B performed the obligation, then A would have to retransfer the rights to B. If B failed to perform, then A could typically sell the property, and recover the sum owed from the proceeds of sale or apply to Chancery to have the transfer declared absolute. Note that some mortgages of personal property were prohibited by the reputed ownership doctrine (see below).

Negotiating a bill of exchange Transferring a bill of exchange or promissory note to a third party.

Promissory note Effectively an 'IOU'. The writer of the note promised to pay a specified sum on a specified day to the note holder. In the Regency era treated much like a bill of exchange.

Reputed ownership The doctrine whereby all personal property in a bankrupt's possession, which he appeared to own, would vest in his bankrupt estate—even property belonging to third parties where they had consented to the facts creating the impression that the property was the bankrupt's. Discussed at Chapter 6, Section 1.

Set-off The legal rules governing when a debtor can escape liability for paying a debt, in whole or in part, because his creditor is in turn indebted to him. So, if A owed B £10, and B owed A £10, then if A sued B for £10, B could plead the second debt as a defence, see Chapter 3, Section 3.

Sheriff The official who had responsibility for seizing and selling a debtor's assets following a court ruling against him.

Subrogation A legal mechanism by which one person acquires rights which mirror those of another. Where creditors of trustees and partnerships could claim trust or partnership assets, this was because they could take the benefit of the rights of indemnity and liens that trustees and partners had over trust and partnership assets respectively. Accordingly the creditors were 'subrogated' to these rights, discussed in Chapter 2, Section 3.1 and Chapter 7, Section 4.2.

Trust A legal institution, whereby one person (the 'trustee') holds assets in their name, for the benefit of another (the 'beneficiary' or '*cestui que trust*') to be administered according to the terms of the trust. The trust assets were separated from the personal wealth of the trustee and so unavailable to his creditors, and he was liable to the beneficiary if he dealt with the property in any way not authorised by the trust's terms.

Bibliography

1. Manuscripts

The Lord Eldon Collection, University of Georgetown Law Library Lord Eldon Judicial Notebooks (1801–1821) Mss 38–48, <https://repository.library.georgetown.edu/handle/10822/1042298> accessed 18 March 2020.

Trial Notes of Clarke v Gopp and other cases 1758 Ms 26
Trial Notes Mss 27–35, 67–68.
John Dickens Chancery Orders 1774 Ms 4
Orders in Chancery by John Beames Ms 23
Lord Eldon's Pamphlets, 125 Volumes

The Public Record Office, Richmond

The order books of the Bankruptcy Court (record class B 1)
Pleadings from the Court of Chancery (record classes C 12, C 13, and C 31)
The order books of the Court of Chancery (record class C 33)
The enrolled decrees of the Court of Chancery (record class C 78)

The Astron Douglas Lord Eldon Collection, Wolfson College, University of Cambridge

Lord Eldon's annotated edition of Atkins's reports of the decisions of Lord Hardwicke

2. Printed Sources

Historical Treatises

Ballow H, *A Treatise of Equity* (John Fonblanque ed, 1st edn, J and WT Clarke 1793)

Bisset A, *A Practical Treatise on the Law of Partnership* (London 1847)

Cary H, *A Practical Treatise on the Law of Partnership* (1st edn, J and WT Clarke 1827)

Chalmers T, *The Application of Christianity to the Commercial and Ordinary Affairs of Life* (5th edn, A Constable; Blackwood; W Whyte; Olivery & Boyd; W Oliphant; Fairbairn & Anderson; Manners & Miller; and James Robertson 1820)

Chitty J, *A Practical Treatise on Bills of Exchange, Checks on Bankers, Promissory, Bankers' Cash Notes, Bank Notes* (5th edn, Butterworth & Son; Clarke & Son; C Hunter; T Hamilton; W Walker and G Wilson; H Butterworth 1818)

Christian E, *The Origin, Progress and Present Practise of Bankrupt Law, Both in England and Ireland.* (1st edn, W Clarke & Sons 1812–1814)

Christian E, *The Origin, Progress and Present Practise of Bankrupt Law, Both in England and Ireland.*, vol II (2nd edn, W Clarke & Sons 1818)

Colbert J, *The Age of Paper; or An Essay on Banks and Banking; Containing the History of the Most Remarkable Paper Bubbles* (Parsons; Mason 1795)

Coleridge ST, *A Lay Sermon Addressed to the Higher and Middle Classes on the Existing Distresses and Discontents* (Gale and Fenner; JM Richardson; J Hatchard 1817)

Collyer J, *A Practical Treatise on the Law of Partnership* (London 1832)

Cooke W, *The Bankrupt Laws* (4th edn, London 1799)
Cooke W, *The Bankrupt Laws* (7th edn, W Reed, C Hunter 1817)
Cooke W, *The Bankrupt Laws* (8th edn, W Reed, C Hunter 1823)
Cory I, *A Practical Treatise on Accounts* (2nd edn, W Pickering 1837)
Fonblanque J, *Observations on a Bill Now before Parliament for the Consolidation and Amendment of the Laws Relating to Bankrupts* (Philips and Yard 1824)
Gilbert G, *Law of Uses and Trusts, with a Treatise of Dower* (Edward Sugden ed, 3rd edn, London 1811)
Gisborne T, *An Enquiry into the Duties of Men in the Higher and Middle Classes of Society in Great Britain*, vol 2 (5th edn, J White; Cadell and Davies 1800)
Gow N, *A Treatise on the Law of Principal and Agent* (J and T Clarke 1819)
Gow N, *A Practical Treatise on the Law of Partnership* (1st edn, C Hunter 1823)
Gow N, *A Practical Treatise on the Law of Partnership* (3rd edn, C Hunter and J Richards 1830)
Hampson G, *Means by Which Trustees May Perform Their Duties without Incurring Responsibility* (1st edn, A Maxwell 1825)
Hill J, *A Practical Treatise on the Law Relating to Trustees* (V & R Stevens and GS Norton 1845)
Huskisson W, *The Question Concerning the Depreciation of Our Currency, Stated and Examined* (J Murray and J Hatchard 1810)
Jeremy G, *A Treatise on the Equity Jurisdiction of the High Court of Chancery* (J and WT Clarke 1828)
Lewin T, *The Law of Trusts* (1st edn, A Maxwell 1837)
Lindley N, *A Treatise on the Law of Partnership* (W Maxwell 1860)
Maddock H, *In A Treatise on the Principles and Practice of the High Court of Chancery* (1st edn, J and WT Clarke 1815)
Malthus T, *An Essay on the Principle of Population* (1st edn, J Johnson 1798)
Malthus T, *An Essay on the Principle of Population* (2nd edn, J Johnson 1803)
Malthus T, *Principles of Political Economy*, vol 1 (John Pullen ed, CUP 1989 (1st published 1820))
Mitford J, *A Treatise on the Pleadings in Suits in the Court of Chancery by English Bill* (J and WT Clarke 1827)
Molloy C, *De Jure Maritimi et Navali* (London 1722)
Montagu B, *Summary of the Law of Set-Off, with Appendix of Cases* (1st edn, London 1801)
Montagu B, *Digest of the Law of Partnership, with Cases* (1st edn, J Butterworth 1815)
Montagu B, *Inquiries Respecting the Courts of Commissioners of Bankrupts and the Lord Chancellor's Court* (1825)
Montagu B, *Summary of the Law of Set-Off, with Appendix of Cases* (2nd edn, London 1828)
Paley W, *The Principles of Moral and Political Philosophy* (London 1785)
Paley W, *A Treatise on the Law of Principal and Agent* (J Butterworth 1812)
Paley W, *A Treatise on the Law of Principal and Agent* (J Butterworth 1819)
Paley W, *A Treatise on the Law of Principal and Agent* (Lloyd ed, Saunders and Benning 1833)
Postlethwayt M, 'Factors' in *The Universal Dictionary of Trade and Commerce, Translated from the French of the Celebrated Monsieur Savary*, vol 1 (London 1751)
Pothier R, *A Treatise on the Contract of Partnership (1765)* (Owen Tudor tr, Butterworths 1854)
Russell J, *The Laws Relating to Factors and Brokers* (S Sweet; V & R Stevens & GS Norton 1844)
Sanders F, *Essays on Uses and Trusts* (1st edn, W Walker 1791)
Sanders F, *Essays on Uses and Trusts* (2nd edn, W Walker 1799)
Sanders F, *Essays on Uses and Trusts* (3rd edn, W Walker 1813)
Sanders F, *Essays on Uses and Trusts* (4th edn, W Walker 1824)

Sanders G (ed), *Orders of the High Court of Chancery, Vol 1, Part 1* (A Maxwell and Son 1845)
Smith A, *An Inquiry into the Nature and Causes of the Wealth of Nations* (RH Campbell and AS Skinner eds, (first published 1776, OUP 1976)
Spence G, *Equitable Jurisdiction of the Court of Chancery* (Lea and Blanchard 1846)
Story J, *Commentaries on Equity Jurisprudence*, vol 1 (Hilliard, Grey & Company 1836)
Story J, *Commentaries on the Law of Agency* (CC Little and J Brown 1839)
Story J , *Commentaries on the Law of Partnership* (1st edn, Boston 1841)
Sugden E, *The Law of Vendors and Purchasers of Estates* (3rd edn, J Butterworth 1808)
Sugden E, *A Practical Treatise of the Law of Vendors and Purchasers of Estates* (2nd edn, J Butterworth 1826)
Sugden E, *The Law of Vendors and Purchasers of Estates* (14th edn, H Sweet 1862)
Sumner J, *A Treatise of the Records of Creation* (J Hatchard 1816)
Taylor M, *Substance of the Speech of Mr Michael Angelo Taylor in the House of Commons on Wednesday the 30th of May 1821 on the Delays in the High Court of Chancery of England and in the Appellant Jurisdiction of the House of Lords* (T Egerton 1821)
Theobald W, *The Law of Principal and Surety and Principal and Chiefly with Reference to Mercantile Transactions* (E Hammond ed, Gould, Banks & Co 1836)
Toller S, *The Law of Executors and Administrators* (2nd edn, J Butterworth 1806)
Tomlins T, *A Familiar Explanation of The Law of Wills* (R Baldwin, BC Collins 1801)
Twiss H, *The Life of Lord Chancellor Eldon* (2nd edn, J Murray 1844)
Watson W, *A Treatise of the Law of Partnership* (2nd edn, J Butterworth 1807)
Wentworth T, *The Office and Duty of Executors* (London 1703)
Williams EV, *The Law of Executors and Administrators* (London 1832)
Winter R, *Objections to the Proposed Alteration of the Law Relating to Principal and Factor* (R Stevens and sons 1823)
Wooddeson R, *A Systematical View of the Laws of England as Treated of in a Course of Vinerian Lectures*, vol 1 (T Payne 1792)
Wordsworth C, *The Law of Joint Stock Companies* (5th edn, W Benning & Co 1845)

b. Classical Sources

Watson A (ed), *The Digest of Justinian* (University of Pennsylvania Press 1985)

c. Committee Reports

Joint Secret Committee, 'Report to Enquire into the State of the Bank of England, with Respect to the Expediency of the Resumption of Cash Payments' (1819, HL 291-III, HC 282-III)
Agency Select Committee, 'Report from the Select Committee on the Law Relating to Merchants, Agents or Factors' (HC 1823, 452-IV) 6
Partnership Select Committee, 'Report from the Select Committee on the Law of Partnership' (HC 1837, 530-XLIV)

d. Modern Secondary Sources

i. Textbooks

Banks R, *Lindley & Banks on Partnership* (20th edn, Sweet & Maxwell 2019)
Buckland W, *A Text-Book of Roman Law* (3rd edn, CUP 1963)
Cornish W and others, *Law and Society 1750–1950* (Hart 2019)
Daunton M, *Progress and Poverty: An Economic and Social History of Britain 1700–1850* (OUP 1995)
Daunton M, *Wealth and Welfare: An Economic and Social History of Britain 1851–1951* (OUP 2007)

Derham R, *The Law of Set-Off* (4th edn, OUP 2010)
Ellinger EP, Lomnicka E, and Hare CVM, *Ellinger's Modern Banking* (5th edn, OUP 2011)
Heydon J, Leeming M, and Turner P (eds), *Meagher, Gummow & Lehane's Equity: Doctrines & Remedies* (5th edn, Lexis Nexis Australia 2014)
Holdsworth W, *A History of English Law*, vols xii and xiii (AL Goodhart and HG Hanbury eds, Methuen & Co 1952)
MacLachlan J, *Handbook of the Law of Bankruptcy* (West Publishing Corporation 1956)
McGhee J (ed), *Snell's Equity* (34th edn, Sweet & Maxwell 2019)
Watts P and Reynolds F (eds), *Bowstead & Reynolds on Agency* (21st edn, Sweet & Maxwell 2017)

ii. Monographs

Anderson S, *Lawyers and the Making of English Land Law* (OUP 1992)
Ashton TS, *The Industrial Revolution* (OUP 1964)
Ashton TS, *Economic Fluctuations in England, 1700–1800* (OUP 1969)
Atiyah P, *The Rise and Fall of Freedom of Contract* (OUP 1979)
Baloch T, *Unjust Enrichment and Contract* (Hart Publishing 2009)
Calnan R, *Proprietary Rights and Insolvency* (2nd edn, OUP 2016)
Chandler A, *The Visible Hand: The Managerial Revolution in American Business* (Harvard University Press 1977)
Charles F, *Joint-Stock Enterprise in France, 1807–1867: From Privileged Company to Modern Corporation* (University of North Carolina Press 1979)
Cheffins B, *Corporate Ownership and Control* (OUP 2008)
Cooke C, *Corporation, Trust, and Company* (Manchester University Press 1950)
Defoe D, *Remarks on the Bill to Prevent Frauds Committed by Bankrupts* (London 1706)
DuBois A, *The English Business Company after the Bubble Act 1720–1800* (The Commonwealth Fund 1938)
Duffy I, *Bankruptcy and Insolvency in London during the Industrial Revolution* (Routledge 1985)
Fox D, *Property Rights in Money* (OUP 2008)
Freeman M, Pearson R, and Taylor J, *Shareholder Democracies? Corporate Governance in Britain & Ireland before 1850* (University of Chicago Press 2012)
Gayer AD and others, *The Growth and Fluctuation of the British Economy, 1790–1850: An Historical, Statistical, and Theoretical Study of Britain's Economic Development* (2nd edn, Harvester Press 1975)
Gordon B, *Political Economy in Parliament 1819–1823* (Macmillan 1976)
Harris R, *Industrializing English Law: Entrepreneurship and Business Organization, 1720–1844* (CUP 2000)
Hilton B, *Corn, Cash Commerce: The Economic Policies of Tory Government* (OUP 1978)
Hilton B, *Age of Atonement: The Influence of Evangelicalism on Social and Economic Thought, 1785–1865* (Clarendon Press 1997)
Hilton B, *A Mad, Bad, & Dangerous People? England 1783–1846* (OUP 2006)
Holdsworth W, *Charles Dickens as a Legal Historian* (Yale University Press 1928)
Holdsworth W, *A History of English Law*, vol xii (AL Goodhart and HG Hanbury eds, Methuen & Co 1952)
Holdsworth W, *A History of English Law*, vol xiii (AL Goodhart and HG Hanbury eds, Methuen & Co 1952)
Hoppit J, *Risk and Failure in English Business 1700–1800* (CUP 1987)
Horwitz H, *Chancery Equity Records and Proceedings 1600–1800* (2nd edn, PRO 1998)

Hunt B, *Development of the Business Corporation in England, 1800–1867* (Harvard University Press 1936)
Jeffreys J, *Trends in Business Organisations in Great Britain since 1856* (University of London 1938)
Johnson P, *Making the Market: The Victorian Origins of Corporate Capitalism* (CUP 2010)
Lester M, *Victorian Insolvency* (Clarendon Press 1995)
Melikan R, *John Scott, Lord Eldon, 1751–1838: The Duty of Loyalty* (CUP 1999)
Muldrew C, *The Economy of Obligation: The Culture of Credit and Social Relations in Early Modern England* (Macmillan 1998)
Oldham J, *The Mansfield Manuscripts and the Growth of English Law in the Eighteenth Century* (University of North Carolina Press 1992)
Paul H, *The South Sea Bubble: An Economic History of Its Origins and Consequences* (Routledge 2010)
Paul T, *The Poverty of Disaster: Debt and Insecurity in Eighteenth-Century Britain* (CUP 2019)
Rogers J, *The Early History of the Law of Bills and Notes: A Study of the Origins of Anglo-American Commercial Law* (CUP 1995)
Sin KF, *The Legal Nature of the Unit Trust* (Clarendon Press 1997)
Smith L (ed), *Reimagining the Trust: Trusts in Civil Law* (CUP 2012)
Stebbings C, *The Private Trustee in Victorian England* (CUP 2002)
Swain W, *The Law of Contract 1670–1870* (CUP 2015)
Taylor J, *Creating Capitalism: Joint Stock Enterprise in British Politics and Culture, 1800–1870* (The Boydell Press 2006)
Weiss B, *The Hell of the English: Bankruptcy and the Victorian Novel* (Bucknell University Press 1986)
Wilson J and Thomson A, *The Making of Modern Management: British Management in Historical Perspective* (OUP 2006)
Winch D, *Riches and Poverty: An Intellectual History of Political Economy in Britain 1750–1834* (CUP 1996)
Xu G, *Does Law Matter for Economic Growth* (Intersentia 2014)
Yale D, *Lord Nottingham's Chancery Cases*, vol I (73 Selden Soc) (Bernard Quaritch 1954)
Yale D, *Lord Nottingham's Chancery Cases*, vol II (79 Selden Soc) (Bernard Quaritch 1961)
Ziegler P, *The Sixth Great Power: Barings, 1762–1929* (Collins 1988)

iii. Articles and Book Chapters

Alexander G, 'Transformation of Trusts as a Legal Category, 1800–1914' (1987) 5 L & Hist Rev 303
Anderson S, 'Changing the Nature of Real Property Law' in W Cornish and others (eds), *Oxford History of the Laws of England*, vol XII (OUP 2010)
Anderson S, 'Leases, Mortgages, and Servitudes' in W Cornish and others (eds), *Oxford History of the Laws of England*, vol XII (OUP 2010)
Anderson S, 'Trusts and Trustees' in W Cornish and others (eds), *Oxford History of the Laws of England*, vol XII (OUP 2010)
Arthurs H, 'Without the Law: Courts of Local and Special Jurisdiction in Nineteenth Century England' (1984) 5 JLH 130
Ashton T, 'Bills of Exchange and Private Banks in Lancashire 1790–1830' [1945] Economic His Rev 15
Baloch T, 'Law Booksellers and Printers as Agents of Unchange' [2007] CLJ 389
Barnes V and Oldham J, 'Carlen v Drury (1812): The Origins of the Internal Management Debate in Corporate Law' (2017) 38 JLH 1

Birks P, 'Retrieving Tied Money' in W Swadling (ed), *The Quistclose Trust* (Hart Publishing 2004)

Blair M, 'Locking in Capital: What Corporate Law Achieved for Business Organizers in the Nineteenth Century' (2003) 61 UCLA L Rev 387

Briggs M, 'Has English Law Coped with the Lehman Collapse?' [2013] BJIBFL 131

Broadberry S and others, 'British Economic Growth and the Business Cycle, 1700–1870' <http://www2.warwick.ac.uk/fac/soc/economics/events/seminars-schedule/conferences/venice3/programme/british_economic_growth_and_the_business_cycle_1700-1850.pdf> accessed 18 March 2020

Chambers R, 'Restrictions on the Use of Money' in W Swadling (ed), *The Quistclose Trust* (Hart Publishing 2004)

Chesterman M, 'Family Settlements on Trust: Landowners and the Rising Bourgeoisie' in Rubin and Sugarman (eds), *Law, Economy And Society, 1750-1914: Essays in the History of English Law* (Professional Books 1984)

Daunton M, 'Society and Economic Life' in C Matthew (ed), *The Nineteenth Century* (OUP 2000)

Donahue C, 'Equity in the Courts of Merchants' (2004) 72 Tijdschrift voor Rechtsgeschiedenis 1

Fama E, 'Agency Problems and the Theory of the Firm' (1980) 88 J Pol Econ 288

Fama E, and Jensen M, 'Separation of Ownership and Control' (1983) 26 J L & Econ 301

Fox D, 'Purchase for Value Without Notice' in PS Davies, S Douglas, and J Goudkamp (eds), *Defences in Equity* (Hart Publishing 2018)

Getzler J, 'The Role of Security over Future and Circulating Capital: Evidence from the British Economy circa 1850–1920' in J Getzler and J Payne (eds), *Company Charges: Spectrum and Beyond* (OUP 2006)

Getzler J, 'Morice v Bishop of Durham' in P Mitchell and C Mitchell (eds), *Landmark Cases in Equity* (Hart Publishing 2012)

Getzler J, and Macnair M, 'The Firm as Entity before the Companies Acts' in P Brand, K Costello, and WN Osborough (eds), *Adventures of the Law: Proceedings of the Sixteenth British Legal History Conference* (Four Courts 2005)

Hansmann H and Kraakman R, 'The Essential Role of Organizational Law' (2000) 110 Yale LJ 387

Hansmann H, Kraakman R, and Squire R, 'Law and the Rise of the Firm' (2006) 119 Harv L Rev 1333

Harley CK, 'Trade: Discovery, Mercantilism and Technology' in R Floud and P Johnson (eds), *Cambridge Economic History of Modern Britain* (CUP 2004)

Harris R, 'Government and the Economy, 1688–1850' in R Floud and P Johnson (eds), *Cambridge Economic History of Modern Britain* (CUP 2003)

Harris R, 'The Encounters of Economic and Legal History' (2003) 21 Law & Hist Rev 297

Harris R, 'The Private Origins of the Private Company: Britain 1862–1907' (2013) 33 OJLS 339

Hayton D, 'Unique Rules for the Unique Institution, the Trust' in S Degeling and J Edelman (eds), *Equity in Commercial Law* (Lawbook Company 2005)

Hoppit J, 'The Use and Abuse of Credit in Eighteenth-Century England' in N McKendrick and RB Outhwaite (eds), *Business Life and Public Policy* (CUP 2002)

Horwitz H and Polden P, 'Continuity or Change in the Court of Chancery in the Seventeenth and Eighteenth Centuries?' (1996) 35 J Brit Stud 25

Ireland P, 'Capitalism without the Capitalist: The Joint Stock Company Share and the Emergence of the Modern Doctrine of Separate Corporate Personality' (1996) 17 JLH 40

Ireland P, 'Company Law and the Myth of Shareholder Ownership' (1999) 62 MLR 32

Jones N, 'Wills, Trusts, and Trusting from the Statute of Uses to Lord Nottingham' (2010) 31 JLH 273
Jones W, 'The Foundations of English Bankruptcy: Statutes and Commissions in the Early Modern Period' (1979) 69 Transactions of the American Philosophical Society 1
Kadens E, 'The Last Bankrupt Hanged: Balancing Incentives in the Development of Bankruptcy Law' (2010) 59 Duke LJ 1230
Kadens E, 'The Pitkin Affair: A Study of Fraud in Early English Bankruptcy' (2010) 84 ABLJ 483
Kennedy F, 'Partnerships and Partners under the Bankruptcy Code: Claims and Distribution' (1983) 40 Washington and Lee L Rev 55
Kim SJ and Oldham J, 'Insuring Maritime Trade with the Enemy in the Napoleonic Era' (2012) 47 Tex Int'l LJ 561
La Porta R and others, 'Law and Finance' (1998) 106 J Pol Econ 1113
Langbein J, 'The Contractarian Basis of the Law of Trusts' (1995) 105 Yale LJ 625
Levine R, 'The Legal Environment, Banks, and Long-Run Economic Grow' (1998) 30 JMBC 596
Lobban M, 'Bankruptcy and Insolvency' in W Cornish and others (eds), *Oxford History of the Laws of England*, vol XII (OUP 2010)
Lobban M, 'Joint Stock Companies' in W Cornish and others (eds), *Oxford History of the Laws of England*, vol XII (OUP 2010)
Lobban M, 'Property Torts' in W Cornish and others (eds), *Oxford History of the Laws of England*, vol XII (OUP 2010)
Lobban M, 'The Politics of English Law in the Nineteenth Century' in P Brand and J Getzler (eds), *Judges and Judging: in the History of the Common Law and Civil Law* (CUP 2012)
Loi K, '*Quistclose* Trusts and Romalpa Clauses: Substance and Nemo Dat in Corporate Insolvency' (2012) 128 LQR 412
Macnair M, 'Equity and Volunteers' (1988) 8 LS 172
Macnair M, 'Arbitrary Lord Chancellors and the Problem of Predictability' in E Koops and WJ Zwalve (eds), *Law & Equity: Approaches in Roman Law and Common Law* (Brill 2014)
Maitland FW, 'Trust and Corporation' in HAL Fisher (ed), *The Collected Papers of Frederick William Maitland*, vol 3 (CUP 1911)
Maitland FW, 'Why the History of English Law Is Not Written' in HAL Fisher (ed), *The Collected Papers of Frederick William Maitland*, vol 1 (CUP 1911)
Millett P, 'Equity's Place in the Law of Commerce' (1998) 114 LQR 214
Morley J, 'The Common Law Corporation: The Power of the Trust in Anglo-American Business History' (2016) 116 Colum L Rev 2145
Nolan R, 'A Targeted Degree of Liability' [1996] LMCLQ 161
Nolan R, 'Property in a Fund' (2004) 120 LQR 108
O'Brien P, 'The Political Economy of British Taxation, 1660–1815' (1988) 41 Economic Hist Rev 1
Oldham J, 'Some Effects of War on the Law of Late-Eighteenth and Early-Nineteenth Century England' in C MacMillan and C Smith (eds), *Challenges to Authority and Recognition of Rights* (CUP 2018)
Oldham J and Barnes V, 'Carlen v Druy (1812): The Origins of the Internal Management Debate in Corporate Law' (2017) 38 JLH 1
Oldham J and Barnes V, 'The Legal Foundation of Apparent Authority' (2019) 44 J Corp L 649
Oldham J and Johnson M, 'Law Versus Equity—as Reflected in Lord Eldon's Manuscripts' (2018) 58 Am J L His 208
Ollikainen-Read A, 'Creditors' Claims against Trustees and Trust Funds' [2018] Trusts and Trustees 177

Owens A, 'Inheritance and the Life-Cycle of Family Firms in the Early Industrial Revolution' (2002) 44 Business History 21
Perram N, 'The Operations and Present Operation of the Action in Devastavit' [2012] Federal Journal Scholarship 23
Polden P, 'The Court of Chancery 1820–1875' in W Cornish and others (eds), *Oxford History of the Laws of England*, vol XI (OUP 2010)
Polden P, 'The Courts of Law' in W Cornish and others (eds), *The Oxford History of the Laws of England*, vol XI (OUP 2010)
Postan M, 'Recent Trends in Accumulation of Capital' 6 Economic Hist Rev 6
Quinn S, 'Money, Finance and Capital Markets' in R Floud and P Johnson (eds), *Cambridge Economic History of Modern Britain* (CUP 2003)
Rothschild E, 'Adam Smith and the Invisible Hand' (1994) 84 Am Econ Rev 319.
Simpson A, 'Rise and Fall of the Treatise' (1981) 48 U Chi L Rev 632
Slatter M, 'The Norwich Court of Requests—A Tradition Continued' (1984) 5 JLH 97
Smith L, 'Tracing Confusion: Equity in the Court of King's Bench' [1995] LMCLQ 240
Smith L, 'Taylor v Plumer (1815)' in *Landmark Cases in Restitution* (Hart Publishing 2006)
Smith L, 'Scottish Trusts in the Common Law' (2013) 17 Edinburgh L Rev 283
Stein P, 'Mutual Agency of Partners in the Civil Law' (1958) 33 Tul L Rev 595
Stevens R, 'Insolvency' in W Swadling (ed), *The Quistclose Trust* (Hart Publishing 2004)
Swadling W, 'Orthodoxy' in W Swadling (ed), *The Quistclose Trust* (Hart Publishing 2004)
Swadling W, 'Explaining Resulting Trusts' (2008) 124 LQR 72
Televantos A, 'Losing the Fiduciary Requirement for Equitable Tracing Claims' (2017) 133 LQR 492
Thomas S, 'The Origins of the Factors Acts 1823 and 1825' (2011) 32 JLH 151
Turner P, 'Consequential Economic Loss and the Trust Beneficiary' [2010] CLJ 445
Willems C, 'Coke, Collusion, and Conveyances: Unearthing the Roots of Twyne's Case' [2015] JLH 129
Winder W, 'The Courts of Request' (1936) 52 LQR 369

iv. Edited Books

Graziadei M, Mattei U, and Smith L (eds), *Commercial Trusts in European Private Law* (CUP 2009)
Sraffa P (ed), *Works and Correspondence of David Ricardo, Volume IX* (Liberty Fund 2005)

v. Unpublished Dissertations

McGaw M, 'A History of the Common Law of Agency with Particular Reference to the Concept of Irrevocable Authority Coupled with an Interest' (DPhil, University of Oxford 2005)
Servian M, 'Eighteenth Century Bankruptcy Law: From Crime to Process' (PhD, University of Kent 1985)
Stolker F, 'The Rise and Fall of the Reputed Ownership Clause' (MSt, University of Oxford 2016).
Televantos A, 'Third Party Rights and the Priority of Claims against Commercial Funds: Partnership, trusts, agency, and insolvency in the era of Lord Eldon 1790-1827' (PhD Thesis, University of Cambridge 2016).

vi. Biography Entries

Beattie J, 'Garrow, Sir William' in Sir David Cannadine (ed), *The Oxford Dictionary of National Biography* http://www.oxforddnb.com/view/article/10410 accessed 18 March 2020

Brown S, 'Chalmers, Thomas' in Sir David Cannadine (ed), *The Oxford Dictionary of National Biography* (2007) <https://doi.org/10.1093/ref:odnb/5033> accessed 18 March 2020

Escott M, 'Heygate, William (1872–1844)' in DR Fisher (ed), *The History of Parliament: The House of Commons* (CUP 2009) <http://www.historyofparliamentonline.org/volume/1820-1832/member/heygate-william-1782-1844#footnoteref2_0ey8i3p> accessed 18 March 2020.

Fisher D, 'Tierney, George' in Sir David Cannadine (ed), *The Oxford Dictionary of National Biography* (2008) <https://doi.org/10.1093/ref:odnb/27439> accessed 18 March 2020

Hay D, 'Kenyon, Lloyd' in Sir David Cannadine (ed), *The Oxford Dictionary of National Biography* <http://www.oxforddnb.com/view/article/15431?docPos=2> accessed 18 March 2020

Hay D, 'Mansfield, Sir James' in M Davies (ed), *The Oxford Dictionary of National Biography* (2008) <https://doi.org/10.1093/ref:odnb/17995> accessed 18 March 2020

Hole R, 'Gisborne, Thomas' in Sir David Cannadine (ed), *The Oxford Dictionary of National Biography* (2014) <https://doi.org/10.1093/ref:odnb/10782> accessed 18 March 2020

Mandler P, 'Lewis, Sir Thomas Frankland, First Baronet' in Sir David Cannadine (ed), *The Oxford Dictionary of National Biography* (2004) <https://doi.org/10.1093/ref:odnb/16605> accessed 18 March 2020

Melikan R, 'Romilly, Sir Samuel' in Sir David Cannadine (ed), *The Oxford Dictionary of National Biography* (2008) <https://doi.org/10.1093/ref:odnb/24050> accessed 18 March 2020

Oldham J, 'Buller, Sir Francis' in Sir David Cannadine (ed), *The Oxford Dictionary of National Biography* <http://www.oxforddnb.com/view/article/3914?docPos=1> accessed 18 March 2020

Orbell J, 'Baring, Thomas' in Sir David Cannadine (ed), *The Oxford Dictionary of National Biography* (2006) <https://doi.org/10.1093/ref:odnb/1385> accessed 18 March 2020

Orbell J, 'Baring, Alexander' in Sir David Cannadine (ed), *The Oxford Dictionary of National Biography* (2008) <https://doi.org/10.1093/ref:odnb/1380> accessed 18 March 2020

Peach T, 'Ricardo, David' in Sir David Cannadine (ed), *The Oxford Dictionary of National Biography* <http://www.oxforddnb.com/view/article/23471?docPos=1> accessed 18 March 2020

Prest J, 'Peel, Sir Robert' in Sir David Cannadine (ed), *The Oxford Dictionary of National Biography* (2009) <https://doi.org/10.1093/ref:odnb/21764> accessed 18 March 2020

Smith E, 'Scott, John' in Sir David Cannadine (ed), *The Oxford Dictionary of National Biography* <http://www.oxforddnb.com/view/article/24897?docPos=13> accessed 18 March 2020

Stronach G and Matthew H, 'Wallace, Thomas, Baron Wallace' in Sir David Cannadine (ed), *The Oxford Dictionary of National Biography* (2013) <https://doi.org/10.1093/ref:odnb/28543> accessed 18 March 2020

vii. Catalogue Descriptions

The National Archives, <http://discovery.nationalarchives.gov.uk/discovery> accessed 18 March 2020

Index

CPSIA information can be obtained
at www.ICGtesting.com
Printed in the USA
BVHW041721030322
630577BV00001B/2

9 780198 870340